McGraw-Hill's

U.S. Citizenship Test with DVD

DISCARD

Karen Hilgeman
Winifred Ho Roderman
Kristin Sherman
Jennifer Wilson Cooper

Nev   City

1 2 3 4 5 6 7 8 9 10 11 12 13 14 15 16 17 18 19 20   QPD/QPD   0 9

ISBN   978-0-07-160516-8   (book and DVD set)
MHID   0-07-160516-9   (book and DVD set)

ISBN   978-0-07-160517-5   (book for set)
MHID   0-07-160517-7   (book for set)

Library of Congress Control Number: 2008925282

Acknowledgments
Many thanks to our team of experts whose invaluable advice contributed immeasurably to the development of this book.
Gemma Catire, Miami-Dade County Public Schools
Kathleen Bywater, Riverside Adult School; Riverside, CA
Jennifer Gagliardi, Milpitas Adult School; Milpitas, CA
César Holguín, Los Angeles Southwest College; Los Angeles, CA
Reyna P. Lopez, Belmont ECC, Los Angeles Unified School District; Los Angeles, CA
Mechelle Perrott, San Diego Community College District; San Diego, CA
Thanks also to:
Susan Ricondo, B.A., The English Center, Miami-Dade County Public Schools District
José Montes, M.S.-Ed., The English Center, Miami-Dade County Public Schools District
Many thanks and best wishes to the subjects of the Connect to the Topic section.

Series editor: Mary P. Sutton
Developmental editor: Amy Lawler
Interior designer: Chris Kelly

The Credits section for this book begins on page xvi and is considered an extension of the copyright page.

McGraw-Hill books are available at special quantity discounts to use as premiums and sales promotions or for use in corporate training programs. To contact a representative, please visit the Contact Us pages at www.mhprofessional.com.

Contents at a Glance

Welcome to
McGraw-Hill's
U.S. Citizenship

Prepare to **pass** the new test with
Pass the New Test Interview DVD.

NEW! McGraw-Hill's U.S. Citizenship with DVD

McGraw-Hil's U.S. Citizenship is a citizenship preparation program, fully up-to-date to ensure success on the new naturalization test. With plenty of self-directed activities and an interactive DVD, it is ideal for self study.

▶ Student Text is thoroughly revised for the new test.

▶ The accompanying DVD builds student confidence and comfort level with the interview.

▶ Accompanying DVD also provides support for the Interview Skills and 100 History and Government questions.

▶ Fully-endorsed by a national team of citizenship experts!

WELCOME TO THE *PASS THE NEW TEST INTERVIEW DVD!*

An engaging self-study resource for **STUDENTS**

Ensure student success!

▶ **Unlimited Repetition**

Learners can watch the interviews as many times as they want. They can stop the interview and answer the questions themselves or practice the interview skills.

▶ **Easy Navigation**

The DVD menus allow students to view the content according to their own needs. Less proficient students can add subtitles to better understand the content.

▶ **Self-assessment**

The self-correcting quizzes enable students to take short, 10-question quizzes on different topics, approximating the History and Government Questions they will have to answer during the interview.

▶ **Confidence-building**

The Pass the New Test Interview DVD helps learners build confidence by allowing them to practice at home as often as they wish.

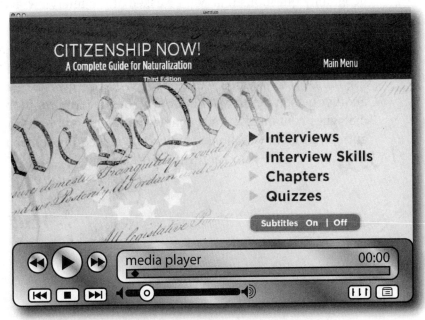

McGraw-Hill's U.S. Citizenship is a citizenship preparation program that has been developed to ensure applicants pass the new naturalization test. With plenty of self-directed activities and an interactive DVD, it is ideal for self study.

Features:

☆ **Thoroughly revised to address the NEW TEST,** the new edition offers in-depth practice for both critical-thinking and factual recall aspects of the test

☆ **Interactive DVD** featuring three complete sample interviews helps students become familiar with the format of the interview. Self-correcting quizzes provide practice with the 100 history and government questions.

☆ **Interview skills** featured in each chapter provide important interview skills which correspond to the interviews on the Interactive DVD

☆ **Enhanced vocabulary practice** familiarizes students with key test vocabulary

☆ **Clear design** enhances visuals and helps make key information more memorable

☆ **Civic Engagement** sections provide students with opportunities to work with a partner and become involved in their local communities through project-oriented activities

To the Student

Congratulations on seeking U.S. Citizenship! This program will help you prepare to succeed on every aspect of your citizenship test. It will prepare you for the day of your test by teaching you valuable interview skills. It will teach you the U.S. history, government, and geography questions that will be asked at the interview and prepare you to pass the reading and writing components of the citizenship test.

You can use this book by yourself or with a partner. If you are using it by yourself, you can check the answers to all of the activities in each chapter in the back of the book. You can use the DVD to practice your interview skills. However, it is also important to practice with another person before your interview. Be sure to have friends or family practice the interview dialogues contained in each chapter with you, and have them quiz you on the 100 history and government questions. Many are practiced in each chapter and all 100 questions with their answers are listed at the back of the book.

Where to Learn More

It is important for students to become as informed as possible about the complexities of the naturalization process. To do this, students can:

☆ Read A Legal Overview of the Naturalization Process on page 182 of this book.

☆ Become familiar with the information on the official United States Citizenship and Immigration Services Web site, www.uscis.gov

☆ Determine which local agencies provide legal or other citizenship services

Features of Each Chapter

Connect to the Topic. Each chapter starts with the true story of an immigrant to the United States, many of whom have become U.S. citizens. The people featured are from a variety of backgrounds and came to the U.S. for different reasons.

Readings. The readings focus on important topics in U.S. history and government that students must learn to pass the civics test at their interview. Each reading has visuals and pre- and post-reading activities that lead up to and follow up on the information in the reading. In addition, the first sentence of each paragraph is in boldface type to highlight the main idea. A vocabulary box, "Words to Know" containing vocabulary from the reading is also included to highlight essential vocabulary about U.S. history and government.

100 History and Government Questions. These are the actual questions from U.S. Citizenship and Immigration Services (USCIS) that might be asked at the citizenship test. The questions are divided among the first 11 chapters and are organized thematically. Comprehension activities are included to help students master the material. Additional practice is provided by the self-correcting quizzes on the DVD.

The N-400 Application. Each chapter focuses on a portion of the N-400, Application for Naturalization. Definitions and explanation of questions and vocabulary on the N-400 help students understand so that they can formulate their answers. Each application portion is preceded by a short presentation and activities that provide additional practice on the questions, vocabulary or grammar most likely to trouble students.

The USCIS Interview. This section introduces important interview skills such as asking for clarification or repetition, followed by activities that practice these strategies. Students then can watch the three interview segments on the DVD to see an applicant use those strategies in an interview. The script of one of the three interviews from the DVD as well as important interview tips are included in each chapter. The scripts for all three interviews are included at the back of the book.

Reading and Writing Test Practice. This section contains the actual vocabulary words that will be used for the reading and writing test portion of the citizenship interview. It provides practice activities to help students understand the meaning of the words and also simulates the question and answer format of the reading and writing test.

Grammar Review. The grammar practice in each chapter focuses on a language structure that is important for students to master before their citizenship test. Each grammar review utilizes examples and sentences similar to what students will need to say at their interview.

Civic Engagement. This new section features activities that allow students to experience civics in their community. Activities guide students through the process of exploring where they live, interviewing their community members, finding information about their state and local government, and locating community resources.

Table of Contents

⭐(1)⭐ Steps to Citizenship

New U.S. citizens take the oath of allegiance at a naturalization ceremony.

Connect to the Topic

ARCENE ATANGANA came to the United States from Cameroon in 2000 to be with his wife. He built a new life for himself in San Francisco, California. He started giving French lessons, and now he teaches many students and is writing a book on French grammar. Arcene became a U.S. citizen in 2006 because of all the opportunities in the United States. He is able to do things that make him happy, such as teaching and writing. He also sends money to his family in Cameroon. Next, Arcene wants to go back to school to continue learning.

Getting into the Reading

Answer the questions.

1. Where are the people in the picture above? What are they doing? How do you think they feel?

2. What are some reasons people want to be U.S. citizens? Why do you want to be a U.S. citizen?

3. Reread the *Connect to the Topic* profile above. Why did Arcene Atangana want to be a U.S. citizen?

⭐⭐⭐⭐⭐⭐⭐⭐⭐⭐⭐⭐⭐
WORDS TO KNOW

apply	oath of
eligible	allegiance
federal	permanent
fingerprints	resident
jury	truth
naturalization	USCIS
naturalization	USCIS
ceremony	interview

Why Become a U.S. Citizen?

There are many rights and responsibilities of U.S. citizens. Every year many people become naturalized, or become U.S. citizens. When you become a U.S. citizen, you will have these rights and responsibilities as well.

The most important right for U.S. citizens is the right to vote in elections. You can vote for someone who represents your opinions. In this way, you can play a part in the U.S. government. You can help shape the future of the United States.

As a U.S. citizen, you have the right to carry a U.S. passport. You can travel to many countries with your U.S. passport. You also can live outside of the United States. As a permanent resident, you can lose your legal residence status and not be allowed to return without a new visa if you leave the United States for more than one year at a time. Also, the government cannot deport a U.S. citizen.

U.S. citizens have the right to apply for a federal job. U.S. citizens can apply for jobs in many areas of the federal government, including postal workers, nurses, airport security screeners, and more.

As a U.S. citizen, you have the right to run for office. Arnold Schwarzenegger was born in Austria. He moved to the United States, became a U.S. citizen, and then became governor of California!

U.S. citizens have responsibilities as well as rights. Voting is a right, but it is also a responsibility. Your vote is very important to the democratic process. You must find out information about the people running for office before you decide who to vote for.

Another responsibility of U.S. citizens is to serve on a jury if selected. A jury is a group of people who hear a case in a courtroom. The jury helps decide what the truth is and determines punishment. If you are called to serve on a jury, it is your responsibility to listen carefully and make a good decision.

How to Become a Naturalized U.S. Citizen

Naturalization is the process by which persons who were not born in the United States become U.S. citizens. You may be eligible, or qualified, for naturalization if you have been a permanent resident for five years or if you are a permanent resident and have been married to a U.S. citizen for three years. You can apply for citizenship three months before you are eligible. See page 8 for more information on eligibility.

First, you must fill out Form N-400: Application for Naturalization. You must tell the truth on the N-400. If you do not tell the truth, or if you make a mistake, the United States Citizenship and Immigration Services (USCIS) officer may ask you difficult questions during your interview or deny your application.

Next, you should mail the application to the USCIS Service Center that serves your area of residence. Include with pictures of yourself a money order for your application and a copy of your Permanent Resident Card (or "green card"). After that, you will receive a receipt from USCIS indicating that your application was received.

Later, you will receive a fingerprint appointment to have your fingerprints taken. You can do this at a nearby Application Support Center. Next, you will receive a letter with a date for your USCIS interview.

The USCIS interview has several parts, including:

- **Questions about your N-400 application and documents.** The USCIS interviewer does this to check the information on your application and to test your speaking skills in English. If you do not understand a question, you can ask the examiner to repeat the question or say it in different words.

- **Questions about U.S. history, government, and integrated civics.** The USCIS interviewer will ask you 10 questions from the list of 100 Civics Questions about the United States. You must answer at least six of them correctly.

- **Sentences to read and write.** The USCIS interviewer will ask you to read a question aloud. Then the interviewer will dictate a sentence for you to write on a piece of paper. If you do not pass the first set of sentences, you will get two more chances.

Some people with disabilities or people who are over a certain age may not be required to take the test in English. See the Legal Overview on page 182 for more information about these exceptions.

After your USCIS interview, you will receive a letter from the USCIS with a date for the naturalization ceremony. At the ceremony, a judge or other officer will have you take an oath of allegiance, or a promise to be faithful to the United States, and give you a naturalization certificate. It is at this point that you become a U.S. citizen. Up until you take the oath, you remain a permanent resident. After the ceremony, you have the right to register to vote, obtain a U.S. passport, apply for a federal job, and run for office. You will also have the responsibility to be a good U.S. citizen and to vote and serve on a jury.

THE STATUE OF LIBERTY

The Statue of Liberty is a symbol of freedom and international friendship. It was given to the United States by France in 1886.

It is located on Liberty Island in New York Harbor. It used to be the first thing many immigrants saw when they arrived in the United States by boat. Today, the Statue of Liberty remains an important symbol and a popular place for U.S. citizens and people from other countries to visit.

Getting Information from the Reading

A. Read each sentence. Circle *True* or *False*. The first one is done for you.

1. U.S. citizens can vote in elections. (True) False

2. Permanent residents can vote in U.S. elections. True False

3. U.S. citizens have many rights, but they don't have any responsibilities. True False

4. Voting is a right and a responsibility. True False

5. People apply for U.S. citizenship with Form N-400. True False

6. You must tell the truth on your application for citizenship. True False

7. At your USCIS interview, you must correctly answer 10 questions about U.S. history, government, and integrated civics. True False

8. At your USCIS interview, you receive your certificate of naturalization. True False

9. The Statue of Liberty was given to the United States by Great Britain. True False

B. Look at the steps of the naturalization process below. Number them in the order they occur. The first one is done for you.

a. _____ Get fingerprinted.

b. _____ Apply for citizenship by sending in your N-400 Form, pictures, payment, and documents.

c. _____ Attend a naturalization ceremony, take an oath of allegiance, and become a U.S. citizen.

d. ___1___ Become a permanent resident and become eligible for U.S. citizenship.

e. _____ Attend your USCIS interview.

After you submit your N-400 Form, you will receive a notice to get fingerprinted at an authorized fingerprint site.

C. Use the words in the box to fill in each blank below. The first one is done for you.

apply	jury	oath of allegiance
federal	naturalization	~~USCIS~~
fingerprints	naturalization ceremony	

1. The United States Citizenship and Immigration Services is often called _____*USCIS*_____.

2. Many people can _____ for citizenship with the N-400 application if they have been a permanent resident for five years.

3. People born in other countries can become United States citizens through the process of _____.

4. After you send in your N-400, you will get an appointment to have your _____ taken at an Application Support Center.

5. To become a citizen, you must take an _____.

6. At the _____, you will become a U.S. citizen.

7. U.S. citizens can apply for _____ jobs and run for office.

8. U.S. citizens have the responsibility to serve on a _____ if selected.

D. Work with a partner. Take turns asking and answering these questions.

1. Which rights of citizenship are most important for you? Why?

2. Have you taken any steps to become a U.S. citizen? Which ones?

3. What worries you about the interview:

   _____ your ability to speak English?

   _____ your ability to understand the interviewer?

   _____ the reading and writing?

   _____ remembering information about U.S. history, government, and integrated civics?

4. How will you fit in the time you need to study and prepare?

5. When you become a U.S. citizen, will you register to vote and apply for a U.S. passport right away? Why or why not?

U.S. citizens can apply for a U.S. passport.

The 100 History and Government Questions

A. What are the rights of a U.S. citizen? What are the responsibilities? Check *Right, Responsibility,* **or** *Both* **next to each of the following items. The first one has been done for you.**

		Right	Responsibility	Both
1.	carry a U.S. passport	☒	☐	☐
2.	vote	☐	☐	☐
3.	run for office	☐	☐	☐
4.	apply for a federal job	☐	☐	☐
5.	serve on a jury	☐	☐	☐

B. Critical thinking. Think about your answer and then discuss it with a partner.

1. Why is voting both a right and a responsibility?

2. What would be a benefit of running for office in the United States? What might be a problem?

3. What does the Statue of Liberty mean to you? What do you think of when you see it?

C. 100 Questions Practice. These questions may be asked as part of the U.S. history and government test. Talk about the answers with a partner. There may be more than one correct answer. All 100 questions can be found on page 154. Go to the Quizzes menu of the DVD for more 100 Questions practice.

> 1. Name one right only for United States citizens.
> 2. What is <u>one</u> responsibility that is only for United States citizens?
> 3. Where is the Statue of Liberty?

Only U.S. citizens can serve on a jury.

The Pledge of Allegiance

The Pledge of Allegiance is a promise of loyalty to the United States and to the American flag. Many school children say it in the morning at school. People say it before important meetings or gatherings.

When you say the Pledge of Allegiance, you should stand up, face the flag, and put your right hand over your heart. You should also take off your hat if you are wearing one.

I pledge allegiance to the flag of the United States of America, and to the republic for which it stands, one nation under God, indivisible, with liberty and justice for all.

Saying the Pledge of Allegiance

Find two answers from the reading.

What do we show loyalty to when we say the Pledge of Allegiance?

1. _____

2. _____

The N-400 Application: Information Questions

On the N-400 Application, Part 1, the first space asks for your "current legal name." At the interview, however, the USCIS interviewer will most likely ask these items as information questions. For example, when asking your name, the interviewer could ask any of these questions:

> **What's your full name?**
> **What is your current legal name?**
> **What is your first name?**
> **What's your middle name?**
> **What is your last name?**

A. Write the answers to the questions above in the space provided. Then practice asking and answering each of these questions with a partner.

1. _____

2. _____

3. _____

4. _____

5. _____

The N-400 Application: Parts 1 and 2

Below are Parts 1 and 2 of the Application for Naturalization (N-400). Write information about yourself in the blanks.

Department of Homeland Security
U.S Citizenship and Immigration Services

OMB No. 1615-0052; Expires 10/31/08
N-400 Application for Naturalization

Print clearly or type your answers using CAPITAL letters. Failure to print clearly may delay your application. Use black ink.

Part 1. Your Name. *(The person applying for naturalization.)*

Write your USCIS "A"- number here: A

A. Your current legal name.
Family Name (Last Name)
Given Name (First Name) — Full Middle Name (If applicable)

B. Your name **exactly** as it appears on your Permanent Resident Card.
Family Name (Last Name)
Given Name (First Name) — Full Middle Name (If applicable)

C. If you have ever used other names, provide them below.
Family Name (Last Name) | Given Name (First Name) | Middle Name

D. Name change (optional)
Please read the Instructions before you decide whether to change your name.
1. Would you like to legally change your name? ☐ Yes ☐ No
2. If "Yes," print the new name you would like to use. Do not use initials or abbreviations when writing your new name.
Family Name (Last Name)
Given Name (First Name) — Full Middle Name

For USCIS Use Only
Bar Code | Date Stamp
Remarks
Action Block

Part 2. Information about your eligibility. *(Check only one.)*
I am at least 18 years old **AND**
A. ☐ I have been a Lawful Permanent Resident of the United States for at least five years.
B. ☐ I have been a Lawful Permanent Resident of the United States for at least three years, **and** I have been married to and living with the same U.S. citizen for the last three years, **and** my spouse has been a U.S. citizen for the last three years.
C. ☐ I am applying on the basis of qualifying military service.
D. ☐ Other (Please explain) _____

Form N-400 (Rev. 10/15/07) Y

▶ **EXPLANATION** *Eligibility* means how you qualify to apply for citizenship. The box on the right lists 10 basic requirements for citizenship. These are things that **must be true** for you to apply for citizenship.

For Part 2 of the N-400, you need to show which statement is true about your eligibility. For most people, either box A or B is true. For some people, there are other ways to be eligible. If your way is not on the list, then write it in under choice **D. ☐ Other**.

Are you eligible for citizenship? Here are the ten basic requirements:

1. You are a permanent resident now, and you have been a permanent resident for five years.*
2. You are 18 years or older.
3. You have made a home in the United States for at least five years and you have lived in your state for at least three months.*
4. You have lived in the United States for at least 2½ years (50 percent) of the 5-year period.*
5. You have not abandoned, or given up, your residence or left the United States for a long period of time.
6. You can speak and understand English at the USCIS interview.
7. You can pass an English reading and writing test.
8. You can pass a test on basic U.S. history, government, and integrated civics.
9. You have good moral character.
10. You will take an oath of allegiance.

*You can apply for U.S. citizenship after three years if you have been a permanent resident for three years and have been married to a U.S. citizen for those three years.

See the Legal Overview on page 182 for a more complete explanation of citizenship requirements.

The USCIS Interview

Interview Skill: Small Talk

Before your USCIS interview starts, the interviewer might ask you some simple questions to be friendly and make you feel comfortable. Asking and answering these kinds of questions is called *small talk*.

Small talk

How long did it take you to get here?   Who came with you here today?

How do you like the weather today?   How was the traffic?.

Go to the Interview Skills menu of the DVD to view examples of this skill.

A. Practice asking and answering the questions with a partner.

> **TIP: Remember your manners!** Make sure you say *please* and *thank you* to the interviewer when appropriate. You might forget when you are nervous, so plan ahead what to say.

B. Watch the DVD segments for this chapter. You can find them on the Chapters menu of the DVD.

C. Part of the interview segment with Ms. Garcia is included below. Practice it with a partner.

Interviewer:	Come in. You must be … Ms. Garcia.
Ms. Garcia:	Yes. Good to meet you.
Interviewer:	Please, have a seat.
Ms. Garcia:	Thank you.
Interviewer:	Who came with you here today?
Ms. Garcia:	My … spouse.
Interviewer:	I will be asking you some questions … You need to answer them truthfully… to tell the truth.
Ms. Garcia:	The truth. *La verdad*. Of course.
Interviewer:	Yes. Please stand and raise your right hand. Do you promise to tell the truth, the whole truth, and nothing but the truth?
Ms. Garcia:	I promise.
Interviewer:	Please sit down again. Do you understand what you promised?
Ms. Garcia:	Yes. To tell truth. All the truth.
Interviewer:	Could you show me your passport, your permanent resident card, and your photos? Your passport and permanent resident card.
Ms. Garcia:	Oh, *mi pasaporte*. Yes, here.
Interviewer:	Please tell me your name.
Ms. Garcia:	My name is Maria Elena Garcia.
Interviewer:	How long have you been a permanent resident of the U.S.?
Ms. Garcia:	Resident … I don't understand.
Interviewer:	You are a resident of the United States, yes?
Ms. Garcia:	Resident? Yes.

Ms. Garcia

D. With a partner, practice the interview with correct information about yourself.

Reading and Writing Test Practice

A. Complete the sentences with a word from the box.

> jury   U.S.
> President   vote
> right

1. _____ citizens can _____ in elections.

2. The most important _____ is the right to vote.

3. U.S. citizens can serve on a _____.

4. U.S. citizens can vote for the _____.

> **TIP:** At your USCIS interview, the sentence that you read and the sentence that you write do not have to be perfect. You can still pass even if you make some small errors. However, when practicing for the test, you should try to read and write the sentences as correctly as possible. Pay attention to spelling and capitalization.

B. With a partner, take turns reading the questions below to each other and writing the answers. The answers can be found on page 141.

Example:

For the reading test, the interviewer asks you to read a question like this one:
Who can vote in U.S. elections?

For the writing test, the interviewer reads a sentence like this one and asks you to write it:
U.S. citizens can vote in U.S. elections.

1. What do people in the United States want to be? _____

2. What country is south of the United States? _____

3. What country is north of the United States? _____

VOCABULARY

The following vocabulary will be on the reading and writing test. For a complete list, see pages 206–207.

Reading
country
do
in
what

Writing
Canada
free
Mexico

Reading and Writing

be	south
is	the
north	to
of	United States
people	want

Grammar Review: Question Words

How?   What?   When?   Where?   Who?   Why?

Many questions in English start with the question words listed above. These questions ask for information. You cannot answer these questions by saying just *yes* or *no*.

A. Match each question word with a correct answer. Write the letter on the line. The first one is done for you.

_____e_____ 1. What is your full name?

_____ 2. Where did you live before you moved to the United States?

_____ 3. When did you move here?

_____ 4. How do you spell your last name?

_____ 5. Why did you move here?

_____ 6. Who came with you here today?

a. My friend

b. Five years ago

c. Because I want to become a citizen

d. In Japan

e. Naoki Sato

f. My last name is spelled S-A-T-O.

B. Practice answering the questions starting with the question words. Work with a partner.

1. What is your full name? _____

2. How do you spell your family name? _____

3. Why do you want to become a U.S. citizen? _____

4. When did you become a permanent resident? _____

5. Where were you born? _____

6. Who is your husband/wife? _____

C. Now write the correct question word in each blank. Read the answer carefully before choosing the question word. The first one is done for you.

1. ___What___ is your address? (**My address is 435 W. Oak Street.**)

2. _____ were you born? (**I was born on October 3, 1980.**)

3. _____ were you born? (**I was born in Sao Paulo, Brazil.**)

4. _____ did you come to the United States? (**because my brother lives here**)

5. _____ do you live with? (**my son and my wife**)

6. _____ did you become a permanent resident? (**because I want to become a citizen some day**)

7. _____ did you become a permanent resident? (**through marriage to a U.S. citizen**)

Civic Engagement:
INTERVIEW WITH A CITIZEN

A. Find someone who has become a U.S. citizen. If you don't know anyone who has, ask friends and family if they do. Ask the person these questions and write down the answers.

Name of person you talked to: _____ Date: _____

1. When did you become a U.S. citizen? _____

2. Why did you want to be a U.S. citizen?

   _____

3. Where did you live before coming to the United States?

   _____

4. Where did you go to get fingerprinted?

   _____

5. How did you prepare for your citizenship interview?

   _____

6. What was your USCIS interview like? What was the most difficult part?

   _____

7. Who went with you to your USCIS interview?

   _____

8. How has your life changed after becoming a U.S. citizen?

   _____

2 The New World

CANADA
NORTH
AMERICA
UNITED STATES

ENGLAND — EUROPE
SPAIN —

ASIA

CHINA — JAPAN

Mississippi
River   MEXICO

ATLANTIC
OCEAN

INDIA

PACIFIC
OCEAN

Caribbean Sea

AFRICA

PACIFIC
OCEAN

SOUTH
AMERICA

INDIAN
OCEAN

AUSTRALIA

People from all over the world
come to the United States to
start a new life. What country
did you come from?

N
W   E   **THE WORLD**
S

ANTARCTICA

Connect to the Topic

JUAN CARLOS HERNANDEZ lived in Durango,
Mexico. He wanted a better life and a better job.
So, in 1979, he came to the United States. He is now
a citizen. He says that his life has improved. "I'm
married with two great kids. I have a good-paying
job that I like in a sheet metal workshop. And I'm
getting a good education at a community college."
He is taking ESL classes to improve his English. He
says he wanted to become a U.S. citizen because
"I like the freedom the United States has offered me."

Getting into the Reading

Answer the questions.

1. What did you learn about Christopher Columbus in your native country?
2. Can you find the following places on the world map?

Caribbean Sea	England	Mexico
Canada	India	Spain
China	Japan	United States

3. Why did explorers want to come to the New World? Why did other Europeans come to America?
4. Reread the *Connect to the Topic* profile above. Why did Juan Carlos Hernandez come to the
United States?

Discovering a New World

In September 1492, Christopher Columbus set sail from Spain for the Indies. The Indies was the name for Asia. Europeans made long and difficult trips to Asia for silk, spices, and other rich goods. To get to Asia they had to travel east over land. Columbus thought that sailing across the Atlantic Ocean would take less time.

On October 12, 1492, Columbus reached an island in the Caribbean Sea, not far from the coast of North America. He thought he had landed in the Indies, so he called the native people living here *Indians*. Columbus had actually landed in a part of the world that Europeans did not know about—the Americas. Europeans called it *the New World*.

American Indians were living in the New World long before Europeans arrived. American Indians are also known as Native Americans. Some American Indian tribes are the Navajo, Cherokee, Sioux, Chippewa, Pueblo, Apache, Iroquois, Creek, Blackfeet, Seminole, Cheyenne, Arawak, Shawnee, Mohegan, Huron, Lakota, Crow, and Inuit.

★ ★ ★ ★ ★ ★ ★ ★
WORDS TO KNOW
claimed
economic
immigrants
native
opportunity
original
persecution
political
settlement
tolerate
tribe

Christopher Columbus landed in North America on October 12, 1492. Americans celebrate that day with a holiday called Columbus Day.

Colonies in the New World

Explorers from Europe soon came to the New World looking for gold and wealth. The explorers discovered that the New World was two continents: North America and South America. They claimed these lands for their countries and started colonies. Spain, France, and England claimed the largest areas of the New World.

People left Europe to live in the colonies. Colonies were settlements that were under the control of European countries. Spain's colonies were in the south, west, and southwest areas of North America. France's colonies were along the Mississippi River and in Canada. England's colonies were on the east coast.

The English Colonies

In 1620, a group of people called the Pilgrims sailed to America. They were not free to practice their religion in England. They came to America to live and worship as they wished. The Pilgrims began a colony in what is now Plymouth, Massachusetts.

The Pilgrims invited Native Americans to a thanksgiving feast in 1621. Americans remember that first thanksgiving with the holiday Thanksgiving in November.

America was the land of opportunity and freedom. Other English colonies were begun, and people left Europe to live in them. People came to America to have these freedoms:

- **Political freedom:** If people in Europe disagreed with the king or nobility about the government, they could go to jail.

- **Religious freedom:** People in Europe had to have the same religion as their king. People wanted to be free to choose their own religion.

- **Economic opportunity:** Many people in Europe were poor because they could not work or own land or go to school. In America, they could find work and start their own businesses; they could own land and start their own farms; they could go to school and become more educated.

- **Freedom from persecution:** Men and women in Europe who were different than most people because of their religion, political party, nationality, or race could be put in jail or killed.

By 1700, there were 13 English colonies along the east coast of America. These colonies would become the 13 original states. The New England colonies were: New Hampshire, Massachusetts, Rhode Island, and Connecticut.

The middle colonies were: New York, New Jersey, Pennsylvania, and Delaware.

The southern colonies were: Maryland, Virginia, North Carolina, South Carolina, and Georgia.

Getting Information from the Reading

A. Use the words in the box to fill in each blank below. The first one is done for you.

American Indians	England	Pacific
Atlantic	~~Europeans~~	Pilgrims
colonies		

1. _____*Europeans*_____ came to the New World and settled in _____.

2. _____ were the first people to live in America.

3. People from _____ settled on the east coast of America.

4. The _____ came to New England for religious freedom.

5. The _____ Ocean is on the east coast of the United States.

6. The _____ Ocean is on the west coast of the United States.

B. Circle the correct answers.

1. Two New England colonies were _____ and _____.
   a. Virginia   b. Massachusetts   c. New Hampshire   d. Delaware

2. Two middle colonies were _____ and _____.
   a. New York   b. Rhode Island   c. North Carolina   d. Pennsylvania

3. Two southern colonies were _____ and _____.
   a. New Jersey   b. Maryland   c. Connecticut   d. Georgia

C. What do you think these phrases mean? With a partner, discuss their meanings and give examples.

1. freedom of religion

2. freedom from persecution

3. political freedom

4. economic opportunity

D. Think about the reading.

1. Why do immigrants come to the United States today? Discuss the different reasons with a partner.

2. Why did you come to the United States? Write your answer or share it with a group.

_____

Students studying for their citizenship test

The 100 History and Government Questions

 A. Answer the questions. Look back at the readings on pages 14–15 to find the answers. Work with a partner if possible.

1. What are four Native American tribes?

   _____   _____

   _____   _____

2. What are four reasons colonists came to America?

   _____   _____

   _____   _____

3. What colonies became the 13 original states?

   _____   _____   _____

   _____   _____   _____

   _____   _____   _____

   _____   _____

B. 100 Questions Practice. These questions may be asked as part of the U.S. history and government test. Talk about the answers with a partner. There may be more than one answer. All 100 questions can be found on page 154. Go to the Quizzes menu of the DVD for more 100 Questions practice.

> 1. What is one reason colonists came to America?
> 2. Who lived in America before the Europeans arrived?
> 3. There were 13 original states. Name three.
> 4. What ocean is on the east coast of the United States?
> 5. Name one American Indian tribe in the United States.

Members of the Inuit tribe in a classroom

The N-400 Application: Dates and Vocabulary

A. Writing Dates. You must write dates in different places on the N-400 application. Write dates in this order: month/day/year.

First write two digits for the month of the year.
Include a zero for months 1-9. January is written
this way:

    0 1 / _ _ / _ _ _ _
• Next write two digits for the day.
    0 1 / 0 6 / _ _ _ _
• Then write four digits for the year.
    0 1 / 0 6 / 2 0 0 9

01	January
02	February
03	March
04	April
05	May
06	June
07	July
08	August
09	September
10	October
11	November
12	December

Practice with Dates. Write these dates.

1. December 10, 1998   _ _ / _ _ / _ _ _ _

2. July 4, 2001   _ _ / _ _ / _ _ _ _

3. February 15, 1998   _ _ / _ _ / _ _ _ _

4. October 5, 1982   _ _ / _ _ / _ _ _ _

B. Marital Status. These words and phrases are on Part 3 of the N-400 application. Look at their meanings. Then answer the question.

Words/Phrases	Meaning
current	now
marital status	married or not married
single	never married
divorced	marriage ended by a court
widowed	husband or wife died
annulled	marriage legally declared to never have happened

What is your current marital status? _____

C. Requesting an Accommodation. These words are on the last section of Part 3 of the N-400 application. Look at their meanings. Then answer the questions.

Words	Meaning
requesting	asking for
waiver	be excused
disability	a condition that makes you unable to do things
impairment	a physical condition that makes you unable to do things
accommodation	special help or aid such as a wheelchair or a sign language interpreter

1. Do you have a disability or impairment?   ☐ Yes   ☐ No

2. Do you need an accommodation?   ☐ Yes   ☐ No

The N-400 Application: Part 3

Part 3 asks questions about your background. It is important that you answer these questions honestly. Print your answers and be sure to answer all the questions.

Part 3. Information about you.	Write your USCIS "A"- number here: A

A. U.S. Social Security Number   **B.** Date of Birth *(mm/dd/yyyy)*   **C.** Date You Became a Permanent Resident *(mm/dd/yyyy)*

D. Country of Birth   **E.** Country of Nationality

F. Are either of your parents U.S. citizens? *(If yes, see instructions.)*   ☐ Yes   ☐ No

G. What is your current marital status?   ☐ Single, Never Married   ☐ Married   ☐ Divorced   ☐ Widowed

☐ Marriage Annulled or Other *(Explain)* _____

▶ **EXPLANATION** Follow these directions to answer each item marked A–G.

A. Print your social security number. If you don't have a number, write N/A.

B. Write the date of your birth.

C. Write the date shown on your Permanent Resident Card.

D. Write the name of the country you were born in even if it no longer exists or the name has changed.

E. Write the name of the country where you are a citizen. If you are stateless, write the name of the country where you were a citizen. If you are a citizen or resident of more than one country, write the country that issued your most recent passport.

F. Mark "Yes" if at least one of your parents is a U.S. citizen. Mark "No" if both your parents are not U.S. citizens.

G. If you were married and your marriage was ended but it was not annulled or you were not divorced, you must explain what happened. For example: your husband or wife deserted you.

H. Are you requesting a waiver of the English and/or U.S. History and Government requirements based on a disability or impairment and attaching a Form N-648 with your application?   ☐ Yes   ☐ No

---

▶ **EXPLANATION** If you cannot learn English or study for the citizenship tests because you have a medical disability, you can ask to be excused from taking the tests. A doctor must complete Form N-648 to explain your condition. By marking "Yes" you are informing the USCIS that you will be asking for a waiver. If you are not asking for a waiver, mark "No."

Part 3 continues on the next page.

The N-400 Application: Part 3 (continued)

I. Are you requesting an accommodation to the naturalization process because of a disability or impairment? *(See Instructions for some examples of accommodations.)* ☐ Yes ☐ No

If you answered "Yes," check the box below that applies:

☐ I am deaf or hearing impaired and need a sign language interpreter who uses the following language: _____

☐ I use a wheelchair.

☐ I am blind or sight impaired.

☐ I will need another type of accommodation. Please explain: _____

_____

_____

▶ **EXPLANATION** The USCIS will provide aid if you are physically disabled or impaired. Mark "No" if you don't need aid. If you do need aid, mark "Yes" and explain what you need.

The N-400 Application: Part 4

Part 4 asks for information that the USCIS will use to contact you. Make sure you give up-to-date information.

Part 4. Addresses and telephone numbers.

A. Home Address - Street Number and Name *(Do **not** write a P.O. Box in this space.)* | Apartment Number

| City | County | State | ZIP Code | Country |

B. Care of | Mailing Address - Street Number and Name *(If different from home address)* | Apartment Number

| City | State | ZIP Code | Country |

C. Daytime Phone Number *(If any)* ( )   Evening Phone Number *(If any)* ( )   E-mail Address *(If any)*

▶ **EXPLANATION** Give correct information about your addresses and telephone numbers. Fill in all the boxes. Write N/A for those things that don't apply to you or that you don't have. If you do not know the name of your county, ask someone, like your teacher. If you are hearing impaired and use TTY, write "TTY" after the telephone number. Be sure to include an area code for all telephone numbers.

The USCIS Interview

Interview Skill: Using Good Body Language

Use good body language during your USCIS interview. This will show the interviewer that you are serious about getting your citizenship.

Interview Do's and Don'ts

1. Do make eye contact. Look into the eyes of your interviewer.
2. Do sit up straight.
3. Do answer questions orally.
4. Do keep a pleasant face.

1. Don't stare down at your hands, out the window, etc.
2. Don't slump in your chair.
3. Don't shrug your shoulders for an answer.
4. Don't frown or look angry.

 Go to the Interview Skills menu of the DVD to view examples of this skill.

A. Think of other dos and don'ts. Discuss your ideas with a partner.

 B. Watch the DVD segments for this chapter. You can find them on the Chapters menu of the DVD.

C. The interview segment with Ms. Garcia is included below. Practice it with a partner.

How is Ms. Garcia using good body language?

Interviewer:	Six years. And what country are you from? What nationality?
Ms. Garcia:	Nationality. El Salvador.
Interviewer:	Were you born in El Salvador?
Ms. Garcia:	I was born in San Miguel.
Interviewer:	San Miguel, El Salvador? Are you married?
Ms. Garcia:	Married? *Casada,* yes.
Interviewer:	Do you see this line that says "home address"?
Ms. Garcia:	Yes.
Narrator:	Your body language is important. You don't need to be nervous, so don't <u>look</u> nervous. Just relax, sit up straight, but comfortably. And keep good eye contact.
Interviewer:	And your phone number is 415-555-6776?
Ms. Garcia:	*Sí.* Yes, it is.

D. Now, with a partner, practice the interview with correct information about yourself. Use good body language.

Reading and Writing Test Practice

A. Read the sentences. Then read the questions. Write the sentence that answers each question.

    a. American Indians lived in our country first.

    b. Columbus Day is in October, and Thanksgiving is in November.

    c. Many people come to the United States to be free.

1. Why do many people come to the United States?

_____

2. Name the first people to be in America.

_____

3. When is Columbus Day? When is Thanksgiving?

_____

 B. With a partner, take turns reading the questions below to each other and writing the answers. The answers can be found on page 142.

Example:

For the reading test, the interviewer asks you to read a question like this one:

Who were the first people to be in America?

For the writing test, the interviewer reads a sentence like this one and asks you to write it:

American Indians lived in our country first.

1. Who lived here first? _____

2. When is Columbus Day? _____

3. When is Thanksgiving? _____

4. Why do people come to America? _____

★★★★★★★★★★★★★

VOCABULARY

The following vocabulary will be on the reading and writing test. For a complete list, see page 206–207.

Reading	
America	Who
do	Why
When	

Writing	
American Indians	in
be	November
free	October

Reading and Writing	
Columbus Day	lived
come	people
first	Thanksgiving
here	to
is	

Grammar Review: The Verb *Be*

The verb *be* is a very important verb in English. We use it in a lot of sentences. *Be* can also be a difficult verb. It is often irregular or different from other verbs.

Present Tense of *Be*

We use the present tense of *be* (*am*, *are*, or *is*) when we are talking about things that happen or are in present time. For example:

> I **am** a U.S. citizen.   She **is** smart.
> Many people **are** citizens.   The world **is**

The Present Tense Forms of *Be*

I **am**	I **am not**	We **are**	We **are not (aren't)**
You **are**	You **are not (aren't)**	They **are**	They **are not (aren't)**
He/She/It **is**	He/She/It **is not (isn't)**		

In a small group, practice forming sentences using all the present tense forms of *be*.

A. Write the correct form of the present tense of *be*.

1. New York _____*is*_____ a state.

2. Spain and England _____ in Europe.

3. The Pacific Ocean _____ on the west coast of the United States.

4. I _____ a student. I _____ in a citizenship class.

Past Tense of *Be*

We use the past tense of *be* (*was* or *were*) when we are talking about things that happened or were true in a past time. For example:

> My mother **was** a Mexican citizen.   Many U.S. citizens **were** immigrants.

The Past Tense Forms of *Be*

I **was**	I **was not (wasn't)**	We **were**	We **were not (weren't)**
You **were**	You **were not (weren't)**	They **were**	They **were not (weren't)**
He/She/It **was**	He/She/It **was not (wasn't)**		

In a small group, practice forming sentences using all the past tense forms of *be*.

B. Write the correct form of the past tense of *be*.

1. Christopher Columbus _____*was*_____ an explorer.

2. American Indians _____ the first people to live in America.

3. Plymouth _____ a British colony.

4. Freedom and political liberty _____ two reasons the colonists came to America.

Civic Engagement:
WHERE TO FIND HELP

A. Many professionals specialize in immigration and naturalization issues. If you have trouble applying for citizenship, they can help you. With a partner, think of ways to find those people in your community. Write those ideas below.

_____

_____

B. Find the name of an immigration lawyer or consultant in your town or city. Write that person's name and telephone number here.

Name: _____

Telephone Number: _____

C. Some community organizations have counselors who help immigrants. How can you find community organizations that help immigrants in your city or town?

_____

_____

D. Write the name, address, and telephone number of one community organization that helps immigrants.

Name: _____

Address: _____

_____

_____

Telephone Number: _____

You can find a lot of helpful information in your local phone book.

3 A New Nation is Born

THE 13 ORIGINAL COLONIES

The 13 colonies of the United States declared their independence from England in 1776.

Connect to the Topic

ABDERRAHIM KARRADI is from Oudzem, Morocco. He came to the United States to make a better life for himself. He now lives in Boston, Massachusetts. His job can be demanding and the weather sometimes is not as warm as it is in Morocco, but he likes living in the United States. He is learning English and plans to enroll in a college that can prepare him for a career as a personal trainer.

Abderrahim wants to become a U.S. citizen. He likes having the right to make many choices and to improve his life. He met his future wife here and is very happy.

Getting into the Reading

Answer the questions.

1. Was your native country ever a colony? If so, which country ruled it?

2. What countries today were formerly colonies?

3. What countries have fought for their independence?

4. What rights did those countries fight for?

5. Reread the *Connect to the Topic* profile above. Which rights do you think are important to Abderrahim Karradi?

Revolution and Independence

The English colonies were ruled by Great Britain, but they governed themselves. Each colony had a government, and colonists elected representatives to make their laws.

In 1763, Great Britain passed laws to make the colonies pay high taxes. The colonists did not have any representatives in the British government, so the laws were passed without their consent. The colonists were angry about the high taxes and said the laws were "taxation without representation."

The British also forced the colonists to feed and house British soldiers. The colonists had to let British soldiers live in their houses and provide food for them.

Great Britain then passed a law that colonists could buy certain things only from England. The colonists didn't like this law and refused to unload British ships. In Boston, a group of men dressed as Native Americans boarded ships in the harbor. They smashed tea chests and threw all the tea into the water to protest this law. This event is known as the Boston Tea Party.

Angry British leaders ended self-government in the colonies. They passed laws to punish Boston and set an example for the other colonies. The laws closed Boston Harbor, shut down the Massachusetts government, closed the courts, and ended town meetings. The colonists called the British laws the "Intolerable Acts," meaning that they would not tolerate, or accept, the laws.

In 1774, the colonists formed the First Continental Congress in Philadelphia, Pennsylvania. Leaders from the colonies met to discuss the Intolerable Acts. They told colonists to be ready to fight for their rights.

In 1775, a battle broke out between colonists and British soldiers in Lexington, Massachusetts. The colonists were now at war with Britain. The war is known as the American Revolutionary War or the American War for Independence.

★ ★ ★ ★ ★ ★ ★
WORDS TO KNOW
adopted
anthem
consent
declaration
declare
delegate
founding father
intolerable
pursuit
representation
representatives
self-government
town meeting

Thomas Jefferson wrote the Declaration of Independence.

A picture of George Washington is on every U.S. dollar bill.

Colonial leaders met again in Philadelphia and formed the Second Continental Congress. They chose George Washington to organize and lead an army to fight the British. In 1776, they decided to declare that America was independent from Great Britain. They asked Thomas Jefferson to write the Declaration of Independence.

The Declaration of Independence is one of America's most important documents. It says that

The Declaration of Independence declares that the United States is free from Great Britain.

1. all people are born equal;

2. all people have these basic rights that cannot be taken away: the right to life, the right to liberty, and the right to the pursuit of happiness;

3. if a government does not protect those rights, the people can change the government;

4. because Britain did not protect the people's rights, the people declared the United States to be free from Britain.

The delegates adopted the Declaration of Independence on July 4, 1776. Americans celebrate their freedom every year on that day. July 4 is known as Independence Day.

The War for Independence lasted for eight years and ended in 1783. Americans now had to decide how to run the government of their new nation. In 1787, delegates, or representatives, from each state came to Philadelphia for a meeting called the Constitutional Convention. Benjamin Franklin was the oldest delegate.

The Constitution of the United States was written at the Constitutional Convention. Then Americans elected George Washington as the first President. He is now called the "Father of Our Country." The flag has 13 stripes that stand for the 13 original colonies. "The Star-Spangled Banner" is the national anthem, or song, of our country.

Benjamin Franklin is an important founding father. He was the oldest member of the Constitutional Convention. He is famous for being a U.S. diplomat, the first postmaster general, and for starting the first public library. He wrote the *Poor Richard's Almanac* books that have many sayings we use today.

Getting Information from the Reading

A. Use the words in the box to fill in each blank below. The first one is done for you.

> Declaration of Independence   Revolutionary War   self-government
>
> "The Star-Spangled Banner"   ~~tax~~

1. Great Britain passed laws to _____ *tax* _____ the colonies.

2. Great Britain ended _____ in the colonies.

3. The colonies fought Great Britain in the _____.

4. The _____ said America was free.

5. _____ is our national anthem.

B. Circle the correct answer.

1. Thomas Jefferson wrote
   a. "The Star-Spangled Banner."
   b. the Constitution.
   c. the Declaration of Independence.

2. The Declaration of Independence was adopted on
   a. July 4, 1787.   b. July 4, 1776.   c. July 4, 1763.

3. The first President of the United States was
   a. Thomas Jefferson.   b. George Washington.   c. Benjamin Franklin.

C. How do you celebrate Independence Day in the United States? Discuss with a partner.

_____

_____

D. What do you think these rights mean? Discuss their meanings with a partner or in a small group. Give examples.

1. the right to life

2. the right to liberty

3. the right to the pursuit of happiness

The 100 History and Government Questions

A. These questions have more than one answer. Circle the ones that are correct. If you need help, look at the page numbers given after the questions.

1. Why did the colonists fight the British? (page 26)
   a. taxation without representation   b. high taxes

   c. no longer had self-government   d. British army stayed in their houses

2. What rights are in the Declaration of Independence? (page 27)
   a. freedom of speech   b. liberty

   c. life   d. pursuit of happiness

3. What is Benjamin Franklin famous for? (page 27)
   a. was a general in the colonial army   b. wrote *Poor Richard's Almanac*

   c. was a U.S. diplomat   d. was the oldest member of the Constitutional Convention

   e. was President of the United States   f. was the first postmaster general of the United States

   g. started a public library   h. wrote the Declaration of Independence

4. There were 13 original colonies. Circle the ones you see below. (page 25)
   a. Massachusetts   b. Ohio

   c. Connecticut   d. Vermont

   e. Georgia   f. Florida

   g. Texas   h. Pennsylvania

 B. 100 Questions Practice. These questions may be asked as part of the U.S. history and government test. Talk about the answers with a partner. There may be more than one answer. All 100 questions can be found on page 154. Go to the Quizzes menu of the DVD for more 100 Questions practice.

1. Why did the colonists fight the British?
2. There were 13 original states. Name three.
3. Who wrote the Declaration of Independence?
4. When was the Declaration of Independence adopted?
5. When do we celebrate Independence Day?
6. What did the Declaration of Independence do?
7. What are two rights in the Declaration of Independence?
8. What is one thing Benjamin Franklin is famous for?
9. Who is the "Father of Our Country"?
10. Who was the first President?
11. What is the name of the national anthem?

"The Star-Spangled Banner"

"The Star-Spangled Banner" is the name of the national anthem for the United States. The name refers to the American flag, which has 50 stars and 13 stripes. Each star stands for a state, and each stripe stands for one of original 13 colonies. The anthem is played and sung at official government, military, and sporting events; at important gatherings of Americans; and at worldwide events where the United States is represented, such as the Olympic games.

The N-400 Application: Your Background; More Dates

A. Race or Ethnic Group. On the next part of the N-400, you must say what your *race* is. Your *race* is the *ethnic group* you belong to. Put a check mark in the box that describes you. You may check more than one box.

You are	if your
❏ White	ethnic group was originally from Europe, the Middle East, or North Africa.
❏ Asian	ethnic group was originally from East Asia, South Asia, or Southeast Asia, for example, Bangladesh, Cambodia, China, Pakistan, India, Indonesia, Japan, Korea, Malaysia, the Philippines, Taiwan, Thailand, and Vietnam.
❏ Black or African American	ethnic group was originally from any of the black communities in Africa.
❏ American Indian or Alaskan Native	ethnic group was from any of the original peoples of North America, Mexico, Central America, and South America.
❏ Native Hawaiian or Other Pacific Islander	ethnic group was originally from Hawaii, Samoa, Guam, Tonga, and other islands in the Pacific.

B. Dates Practice. On the N-400 you must write dates that show how long you had a job or went to school. Under *from* write the date the job or school started. Under *to* write the date it ended. Complete the activity.

Example:

You began a job on January 15, 2001. You quit on November 5, 2006.

From	**To**
01/15/2001	11/05/2006

1. Started school January 3, 2001. Stopped going to school November 15, 2003.

   From ＿＿/＿＿/＿＿＿＿   **To** ＿＿/＿＿/＿＿＿＿

2. Job began October 4, 1998. Job ended December 1, 2004.

   From ＿＿/＿＿/＿＿＿＿   **To** ＿＿/＿＿/＿＿＿＿

3. Started working April 15, 1992. Retired May 11, 2005.

   From ＿＿/＿＿/＿＿＿＿   **To** ＿＿/＿＿/＿＿＿＿

The N-400 Application: Part 5

Part 5 asks for information that the Federal Bureau of Investigation (FBI) will use to find out about your background. Every person who applies for naturalization must be checked to make sure he or she is eligible for citizenship. Be sure to answer every question.

Part 5. Information for criminal records search.	Write your USCIS "A"- number here: A

NOTE: The categories below are those required by the FBI. See Instructions for more information.

A. Gender

☐ Male ☐ Female

B. Height

Feet	Inches

C. Weight

Pounds

D. Are you Hispanic or Latino? ☐ Yes ☐ No

E. Race *(Select one or more.)*

☐ White ☐ Asian ☐ Black or African American ☐ American Indian or Alaskan Native ☐ Native Hawaiian or Other Pacific Islander

F. Hair color

☐ Black ☐ Brown ☐ Blonde ☐ Gray ☐ White ☐ Red ☐ Sandy ☐ Bald (No Hair)

G. Eye color

☐ Brown ☐ Blue ☐ Green ☐ Hazel ☐ Gray ☐ Black ☐ Pink ☐ Maroon ☐ Other

---

▶ **EXPLANATION** Follow these directions to answer each item above marked A–G.

A. Check the box that tells whether you are a man (male) or a woman (female).

B. Write how tall you are in feet and inches.

C. Write how heavy you are in pounds.

D. If you come from Mexico or any Latin American country in Central or South America, check "Yes." If you do not, check "No."

E. This question asks you to choose your race. If you have a mixed background, you can check more than one box.

F. Check the color of your hair. If you have no hair, check "Bald."

G. Check the color of your eyes. If none of the choices fits you, check "Other."

The N-400 Application: Part 6

Part 6 asks you to list where you lived and worked for the past five years.

Part 6. Information about your residence and employment.

A. Where have you lived during the last five years? Begin with where you live now and then list every place you lived for the last five years. If you need more space, use a separate sheet(s) of paper.

Street Number and Name, Apartment Number, City, State, Zip Code and Country	Dates (mm/dd/yyyy)	
	From	To
Current Home Address - Same as Part 4.A		Present

▶ **EXPLANATION** Write every address where you lived for the last five years. If you lived in another country, write those addresses too. Begin with where you live now.

B. Where have you worked (or, if you were a student, what schools did you attend) during the last five years? Include military service. Begin with your current or latest employer and then list every place you have worked or studied for the last five years. If you need more space, use a separate sheet of paper.

Employer or School Name	Employer or School Address (Street, City and State)	Dates (mm/dd/yyyy)		Your Occupation
		From	To	

▶ **EXPLANATION** List the places where you worked and the schools you attended over the past five years. Include military service. If you worked for yourself, write "self-employed." Begin with your most recent job or school. Write the dates when you worked or studied in each place. Under "Your Occupation" write the name of your job. If you were in school, write "student."

The USCIS Interview

Interview Skill: Answering *Yes/No* Questions

The interviewer will ask you questions that can be answered *yes* or *no*. Listen carefully to the question. Use the correct tense of the verb that the interviewer used.

Question	Answer
"**Are** you asking for a waiver?"	"Yes, I **am**." or "No, I **am not**."
"**Is** this your correct address?"	"Yes it **is**." or "No, it **is not (isn't)**."
"**Were** you employed?"	"Yes I **was**." or "No, I **was not (wasn't)**."
"**Have** you had other names?"	"Yes I **have**." or "No, I **have not (haven't)**."
"**Do** you have a job?"	"Yes I **do**." or "No, I **do not (don't)**."
"**Can** you write in English?"	"Yes I **can**." or "No, I **cannot (can't)**."

Go to the Interview Skills menu of the DVD to view examples of this skill.

A. Write the letter of the correct answer in front of each question. The first is done for you.

_____C_____ 1. **Are** you still living in the city?

_____ 2. **Do** you have your card with you?

_____ 3. **Have** you answered everything?

_____ 4. **Did** you complete the application?

_____ 5. **Were** you a student?

_____ 6. **Can** you tell me the answer?

a. Yes, I **did.** or No, I **didn't.**

b. Yes, I **have.** or No, I **haven't.**

~~c. Yes, I am. or No, I am not.~~

d. Yes, I **do.** or No, I **don't.**

e. Yes, I **can.** or No, I **can't.**

f. Yes, I **was.** or No, I **wasn't.**

B. Watch the DVD segments for this chapter. You can find them on the Chapters menu of the DVD.

C. The interview segment with Ms. Garcia is included below. Practice it with a partner.

Interviewer: Are you Hispanic or Latino?

Ms. Garcia: Yes, I am Latina.

Interviewer: Is your hair black?

Ms. Garcia: Yes, it is.

Interviewer: Is your height five feet, two inches?

Ms. Garcia: It is.

Interviewer: It says here that you live here.

Ms. Garcia: Yes.

Interviewer: And you have lived there for five years. Is this true?

Ms. Garcia: Yes, it is.

Interviewer: And do you work at Portola Fashions?

Ms. Garcia: Yes, I do.

Interviewer: What do you do there? What is your job?

Ms. Garcia: Ah … garment worker. … I am a garment worker.

Narrator: Sometimes, if you aren't sure of a word in English, you can use body language to express the idea.

Ms. Garcia listens carefully to the interviewer's questions.

D. Now, with a partner, practice the interview with correct information about yourself. Use *yes* or *no* answers. Use the correct verb.

Reading and Writing Test Practice

A. Read the questions. Then use the words in the vocabulary box to answer the questions. Write complete sentences. The first one is done for you.

1. Who was George Washington?

   George Washington was the first President of the United States.

2. What are the colors of the American flag?

   _____

   _____

3. When is Independence Day?

   _____

4. Who is the "Father of Our Country"?

   _____

   _____

 B. With a partner, take turns reading the questions below to each other and writing the answers. The answers can be found on page 144.

Example:

For the reading test, the interviewer asks you to read a question like this one:

How many states are in the United States?

For the writing test, the interviewer reads a sentence like this one and asks you to write it:

There are 50 states in the United States.

1. Who was the first President of the United States?

   _____

2. When is Independence Day?

   _____

3. Who is on the dollar bill?

   _____

★★★★★★★★★★★★★★★★

VOCABULARY

The following vocabulary will be on the reading and writing test. For a complete list, see pages 206–207.

Reading
Who
When

Writing

are	red
blue	Washington
in	white
July	

Reading and Writing

dollar bill	of
Father of our Country	on
first	President
Independence Day	the
	United States
is	was

Grammar Review: *Yes/No* Questions and Short Answers

Yes/no questions are questions that can be answered *yes* or *no*. For example:

Are you married?	Yes, **I am.**
	No, **I am not.** (No, **I'm not.**)

The answers can be short. Some questions and answers will use the verb *be*.

A. Answer the questions with both *yes* and *no* answers. Use short answers. The first one is done for you.

1. Are you married? *Yes, I am. / No, I am not.* _____

2. Is this your application? _____

3. Is your wife/husband a U.S. citizen? _____

4. Are you still living in Miami? _____

5. Were you born in Vietnam? _____

Yes/No Questions with *Do* and *Can*

Some questions and answers will use other verbs, such as *do* or *can*. If you listen carefully to the question, you will know which verb to use. For example:

Do you want to become a U.S. citizen?	
Yes, I **do.**	No, I **do not.** (No, I **don't.**)
Can you sign here?	
Yes, I **can.**	No, I **cannot.** (No, I **can't.**)

B. Answer the questions with both *yes* and *no* answers. Use short answers. The first one is done for you.

1. Do you work for ABC Industries now? *Yes, I do. / No, I do not.* _____

2. Can you read this paper? _____

3. Do you swear to tell the whole truth? _____

4. Do your children live with you? _____

5. Do you have a Social Security number? _____

C. Take turns with a partner. Ask the questions. Answer with short *yes* or *no* answers. Use the correct form of the verb *be*.

1. Is your family name Smith?

2. Was your father an immigrant?

3. Were you born in 1962?

4. Are you a permanent resident?

5. Were the history test questions hard to answer?

6. Are you currently employed?

7. Is your address the same?

8. Are you ready to take the citizenship test?

Civic Engagement:
GETTING ORGANIZED FOR CITIZENSHIP

A. You must send these documents to the USCIS with your N-400 Application:

- photocopies of the front and back of your Permanent Resident Card

- two photographs of yourself that meet USCIS requirements

1. Where can you make photocopies or have them made for you?

_____

2. Places that take passport photos also take photos for the N-400.

What place can you go to for your photos? _____

B. The USCIS will tell you where to go for fingerprinting. It may be a police station or an FBI office.

1. Where is your local police station?

_____

2. Where is your local FBI office?

_____

C. You will need to show valid identification with your photo on it when you get fingerprinted, have your USCIS interview, and take the tests.

1. Check the valid identification that you have.

❏ passport   ❏ state driver's license
❏ state identification card   ❏ no valid identification

2. If you don't have valid identification, go to the Department of Motor Vehicles (DMV) and get a state identification card.

Where is your local DMV? _____

 # Civil War and Expansion

Without immigrants, there would be no United States of America. Most immigrants were happy to come here for new opportunities. Some, such as slaves, did not choose to come here.

Connect to the Topic

CAROLINA MONICO and her family left El Salvador in 1987 to escape the problems caused by a civil war in her country. She was just 12 when she moved to the United States. It wasn't easy for her family. At first they were homeless. Eventually, the family made a life for themselves in San Francisco, California. Carolina completed college and went to medical school. Then Carolina and other students started a medical clinic that provides free basic health care to people who need it. Today, Carolina has started her medical residency and continues to help people.

Getting into the Reading

Answer the questions.

1. What are some reasons that immigrants come to the United States today?

2. What were the reasons immigrants came to the United States in the past?

3. What is a civil war?

4. The United States *expanded* in the 1800s. What does this mean?

5. Reread the *Connect to the Topic* profile above. Why did Carolina Monico come to the United States?

Abraham Lincoln and the Civil War

Africans came to the United States during the same period of time as the first colonists did. The colonists came as free people. People from Africa came as slaves. They were captured from their homes in Africa and were brought in crowded ships. Many Africans died before they reached America.

Slaves had to work long hours with no hope of freedom or of going home. They were the property of their owners. They could be bought and sold. Many slaves worked on plantations, or large farms, to produce cotton and tobacco.

WORDS TO KNOW

agriculture	industry
assassinated	plantation
border	prohibit
captured	separate
crowded	slave
economy	territory
expanded	treaty
federal	

Southern states allowed slavery; Northern states did not. The Southern states wanted to continue slavery, but many people in the North wanted to end it. The Southern states thought that states should have the right to decide whether to allow slavery.

The economy of the South was based on agriculture, and the North's was based on industry. The South thought the federal government's policies helped the Northern economy but hurt the Southern economy. The South decided to separate from the United States. The North did not want the South to separate.

The Civil War was fought between the Northern states and the Southern states, so it was also called the War Between the States. The Northern states were called the Union, and the Southern states were called the Confederacy. The Civil War lasted from 1861 to 1865.

President Abraham Lincoln was President during the Civil War. He was against slavery. In 1863, Lincoln signed a document called the Emancipation Proclamation. It freed the slaves in the Southern states. Lincoln was assassinated soon after the Civil War ended.

The North won the war in 1865, and the North and the South became one country again. More than half a million Americans died in the Civil War. After the Civil War, the Thirteenth Amendment was added to the Constitution to prohibit slavery.

Abraham Lincoln

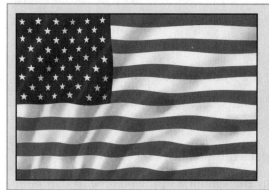

THE U.S. FLAG

The flag of the United States has 13 red and white stripes. They represent the original 13 colonies. It has 50 white stars. The stars represent the current 50 states; there is one star for each state. Because of its design, the flag is often called the "Stars and Stripes."

Moving West

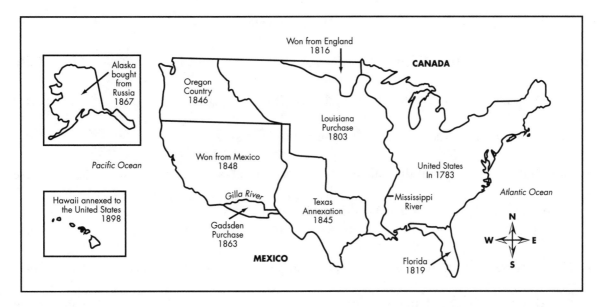

When George Washington became the first President, the United States was much smaller than it is today. The western border of the United States was the Mississippi River.

In the 1800s, the United States expanded to the Pacific Ocean. The government bought the Louisiana Territory from France in 1803 and got Florida from Spain in 1819. After the Mexican-American War, the Southwest (including California) became part of the United States. So did Texas. The United States signed a treaty with England for the Oregon Country in the Northwest. The United States bought Alaska from Russia. The United States had a war with Spain in 1898 called the Spanish-American War. In 1898, the United States also took control of Hawaii. Today, there are 50 states in our union.

Timeline

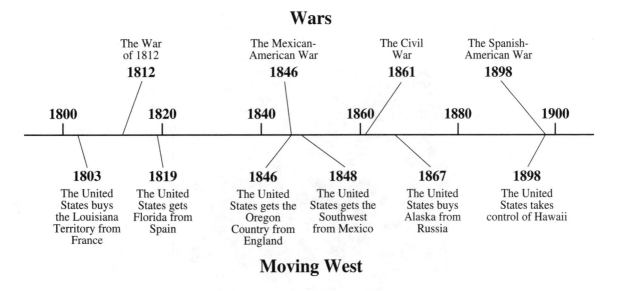

Getting Information from the Reading

A. Read each sentence. Circle *True* or *False*. The first one is done for you.

1. The Civil War was fought between the Union and the Confederacy. (True) False

2. The North, or the Union, won the Civil War. True False

3. Abraham Lincoln was President during the Revolutionary War. True False

4. The Emancipation Proclamation freed the Southern slaves. True False

5. The United States bought the Louisiana Territory from Spain. True False

6. When George Washington was President, the United States included all of the land between the Atlantic Ocean and the Pacific Ocean. True False

7. There are 50 stars on the U.S. flag because each star represents a state. True False

8. The U.S. flag has 12 red and white stripes. True False

B. Look at the definitions below. Write a word from the box in front of its definition. The first one is done for you.

assassinated	captured	expand	federal	~~slave~~	territory

1. ___slave___ a person who is made to work for no pay

2. _____ to grow bigger

3. _____ to be taken by force

4. _____ to be killed, usually for political reasons

5. _____ an area of land

6. _____ national

The Civil War was fought between the Union and the Confederacy. This photo shows Union soldiers.

C. Look at the events below. Number them in the order they occur. The first one is done for you.

a. _____ The United States buys Alaska from Russia.

b. _____ The United States buys the Louisiana Territory from France.

c. _____ The Civil War ends and Lincoln is assassinated.

d. _____ Abraham Lincoln becomes President and the Civil War begins.

e. _____ The United States fights Spain in the Spanish-American War.

f. __*1*__ George Washington is the first President of the United States.

g. _____ Lincoln signs the Emancipation Proclamation, freeing the slaves.

h. _____ The United States gets the Southwest from Mexico.

D. Answer these questions with a partner. Use short answers.

1. What were some of the problems that led to the Civil War?

   _____

2. Was there slavery in your native country? If so, what do you know about it? How did it end?

   _____

3. Why did you come to the United States?

   _____

4. Why did other immigrants you have met in the United States come here?

   _____

5. What do you think of when you see the U.S. flag? Where have you seen the U.S. flag displayed?

A U.S. flag always flies over The White House.

The 100 History and Government Questions

A. Look at the clues below. Write the letter on the line.

1. _____ land bought by the United States from France in 1803

2. _____ a war fought by the United States in the early 1800s

3. _____ one problem that led to the Civil War

4. _____ declaration that freed the slaves

5. _____ a war within the United States between the North and the South

6. _____ a group of people brought to the United States and sold as slaves

7. _____ one important thing that Abraham Lincoln did

a. slavery

b. The Emancipation Proclamation

c. The Louisiana Territory

d. Africans

e. freed the slaves

f. The War of 1812

g. The Civil War

B. The Stars and Stripes. Answer the questions about the U.S. flag.

1. How many stars are there?
   _____

2. Why? _____
   _____
   _____

3. How many stripes are there?
   _____

4. Why? _____
   _____
   _____

C. 100 Questions Practice. These questions may be asked as part of the U.S. history and government test. Talk about the answers with a partner. There may be more than one correct answer. All 100 questions can be found on page 154. Go to the Quizzes menu of the DVD for more 100 Questions practice.

1. What group of people was taken to America and sold as slaves?
2. What territory did the United States buy from France in 1803?
3. Name one war fought by the United States in the 1800s.
4. Name the U.S. war between the North and the South.
5. Name one problem that led to the Civil War.
6. What was one important thing that Abraham Lincoln did?
7. What did the Emancipation Proclamation do?
8. Why does the flag have 13 stripes?
9. Why does the flag have 50 stars?

The N-400 Application: Talking About Your Past Travel and Marital History

Many questions on the N-400 ask about your past. For your answers, use the past tense form of the verb. It is not necessary for you to have perfect grammar at your USCIS interview, but you should try to speak as correctly as possible so that the interviewer will understand whether you are talking about the present or the past.

A. Talking About Traveling. Read the chart below with a partner. Then answer the questions together.

Present	Past	Past Tense Example
spend	spent	I **spent** 27 days outside of the United States during the past five years.
take	took	I **took** three trips outside of the United States during the past five years.
leave	left	I **left** on January 22, 2008.
come back	came back	I **came back** on February 5, 2008.
go	went	I **went** to England and Poland.

1. How many days did you spend outside of the United States during the past five years?

2. How many trips have you taken outside of the United States during the past five years?

3. Think about your last trip outside the United States. When did you leave? When did you come back? Where did you go?

B. Talking About Marriages. Read the chart with a partner and answer the questions.

Present	Past	Past Tense Example
get married	got married	I **got married** in August 1998.
get divorced	got divorced	I **got divorced** in November 2003.

1. Have you ever been married? If so, when did you get married?

2. Have you ever been divorced? If so, when did you get divorced?

The N-400 Application: Parts 7 and 8A and B

Below are Parts 7 and 8A and B of the Application for Naturalization (N-400). Write information about yourself in the blanks.

Part 7. Time outside the United States. *(Including Trips to Canada, Mexico and the Caribbean Islands)*	Write your USCIS "A"- number here: A

A. How many total days did you spend outside of the United States during the past five years? ☐ days

B. How many trips of 24 hours or more have you taken outside of the United States during the past five years? ☐ trips

C. List below all the trips of 24 hours or more that you have taken outside of the United States since becoming a Lawful Permanent Resident. Begin with your most recent trip. If you need more space, use a separate sheet(s) of paper.

Date You Left the United States *(mm/dd/yyyy)*	Date You Returned to the United States *(mm/dd/yyyy)*	Did Trip Last Six Months or More?	Countries to Which You Traveled	Total Days Out of the United States
		☐ Yes ☐ No		
		☐ Yes ☐ No		
		☐ Yes ☐ No		
		☐ Yes ☐ No		
		☐ Yes ☐ No		
		☐ Yes ☐ No		
		☐ Yes ☐ No		
		☐ Yes ☐ No		
		☐ Yes ☐ No		
		☐ Yes ☐ No		

TIP: If you have a trip that lasted for six months or more, or if your total days outside of the country add up to 30 months, you need to talk to a lawyer or legal representative right away.

Part 8. Information about your marital history.

A. How many times have you been married (including annulled marriages)? ☐ If you have **never** been married, go to Part 9.

B. If you are now married, give the following information about your spouse:

1. Spouse's Family Name *(Last Name)*   Given Name *(First Name)*   Full Middle Name *(If applicable)*

2. Date of Birth *(mm/dd/yyyy)*   **3.** Date of Marriage *(mm/dd/yyyy)*   **4.** Spouse's U.S. Social Security #

5. Home Address - Street Number and Name   Apartment Number

City   State   Zip Code

▶ **EXPLANATION** *Spouse* means husband or wife.

The USCIS Interview

Interview Skill: Talking about the Past

Read and practice saying these sentences in the past tense. If you can, supply the missing information about yourself.

I **spent** _____ days outside of the United States during the past five years.

I **took** _____ trips outside of the United States during the past five years.

I **didn't take** any trips outside of the United States during the past five years.

I **left** on _____. (*give the date*)

I **came back** on _____. (*give the date*)

I **went** to _____. (*name the countries*)

 Go to the Interview Skills menu of the DVD to view examples of this skill.

TIP: Try to remember the exact day you left, but if you can't remember, just give the month. Instead of saying "I left **on** July 10th, 2006" say "I left **in** July 2006."

A. Practice. Circle the correct word.

1. I got (marryed/married) in June 1992.

2. I got (divorced/divorci) on May 8, 1998.

3. I (go/went) back to my country in December 2004.

4. I (left/leaved) the United States on February 9, 2006.

5. I (camed/came) back in March 2006.

B. Watch the DVD segments for this chapter. You can find them on the Chapters menu of the DVD.

C. Part of the interview segment with Ms. Garcia is included below. Practice it with a partner.

Interviewer: And in the last five years, how many trips outside the U.S. did you take?
Ms. Garcia: *No entiendo*. I don't understand.
Interviewer: You traveled … outside … the United States?
Ms. Garcia: Yes. I travel.
Interviewer: Traveled. Before now.
Ms. Garcia: Yes. I … traveled.
Interviewer: How many times?
Ms. Garcia: One time. Two week … weeks.
Interviewer: You went to El Salvador?
Ms. Garcia: Yes. El Salvador. I went to El Salvador.

El Salvador. I went to El Salvador.

Interviewer: Okay … how many times … have you been married?
Ms. Garcia: Married? *Casada*. One … one time.
Interviewer: When did you get married? What year?
Ms. Garcia: I … I … I can't say in English.

D. Now, with a partner, practice the interview with correct information about yourself. Remember to use the correct verb form to talk about things you've done in the past.

Reading and Writing Test Practice

A. Use the words in the box to fill in each blank below. You will use some words more than once. The first one is done for you.

Abraham Lincoln   ~~red~~
blue   white
fifty/50

1. The stripes on the U.S. flag are _____*red*_____
   and _____.

2. The U.S. flag is _____, _____,
   and _____.

3. _____ was President during the Civil
   War.

4. The United States has _____ states.

 B. With a partner, take turns reading the questions below to each other and writing the answers. The answers can be found on page 145.

Example:

For the reading part, the Interviewer asks you to read a question like this one:
Who was President during the Civil War?

For the writing part, the Interviewer says a sentence like this one and asks you to write it:
Lincoln was President during the Civil War.

1. Who was Abraham Lincoln? _____

2. What are the colors of the American flag? _____

3. How many states does the United States have? _____

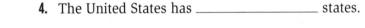

★ ★ ★ ★ ★ ★ ★ ★ ★ ★ ★ ★ ★ ★

VOCABULARY
The following vocabulary will be on the reading and writing test. For a complete list, see pages 206–207.

Reading

Abraham Lincoln	have
American flag	How
are	many
colors	of
does	Who
	What

Writing

and	has
blue	is
Civil War	Lincoln
during	President
flag	red
fifty/50	white

Reading and Writing

| the | United States |
| states | was |

Grammar Review: Past Tense

When we talk about something that we do every day, or something that is always true, we use the present tense. For example:

> You **work** very hard. New immigrants **arrive** every day.

When we talk about something that happened in the past, we use the past tense. For example:

> Slaves **worked** very hard. You **arrived** three years ago.

Past Tense of Regular Verbs

The past tense of regular verbs is formed by adding *–ed* or *–d* to a verb.

A. Write the past tense of the verb in parentheses. The first one is done for you.

1. Many slaves died before they (reach) _____ *reached* _____ America.

2. The Southern states (call) _____ themselves the Confederacy.

3. The Southern states (want) _____ to continue slavery.

4. The Civil War (end) _____ slavery in the United States.

Spelling of Past Tense Verbs

Sometimes the spelling of a verb is different when you add *–ed* for the past tense. There are three rules to remember:

• If a word ends in an **e**, just add **-d**	**arrive + d = arrived**
• If a word ends in **y**, change the **y** to **i** and add **-ed**	**study + ed = studied**
• If a verb has one syllable and ends in a vowel (a, e, i, o, u) followed by one consonant, double the final consonant and add **-ed**	**stop + p + ed = stopped**

B. Write the past tense of these verbs. Be careful of your spelling.

1. Lincoln (stop) _____ slavery in the United States.

2. Lincoln (save) _____ the Union.

3. The borders of the United States (expand) _____ in the 1800s.

4. The North (worry) _____ that slavery was not right.

5. Lincoln (sign) _____ the Emancipation Proclamation.

Civic Engagement:
YOUR STATE

A. What state do you live in?

_____

B. Find answers to the following questions.

1. What year was your state added to the United States?

   _____

2. What number state was it? _____

3. Was your state a state during the Civil War? _____

4. Did people in your state take part in the Civil War? _____ If so, for what side?

   _____

5. Have you ever lived in any other states? _____ If so, what part of the country

   are those states in? _____

5 Recent U.S. History

American soldiers land in Normandy, France, during the D-Day invasion in June 1944.

Connect to the Topic

UYEN TOC LAM was born in Saigon, Vietnam. She lived in Vietnam during the Vietnam War. Uyen didn't feel she had security in her native country. She moved to the United States on June 8, 2002. She came here to find freedom. Now she lives in San Francisco, California. She is studying to be an American citizen. She wants to bring her two sons from Vietnam, so they can have freedom and security too.

Getting into the Reading

Answer the questions.

1. How do you think the soldiers in the picture feel?

2. What is a world war?

3. How many world wars have there been? Why did people fight these wars?

4. What do you know about the Vietnam War? The Korean War?

5. Reread the *Connect to the Topic* profile above. What war did Uyen Toc Lam experience? Why did she come to the United States?

U.S. Wars and Conflicts

World War I and II

World War I began in 1914 and ended in 1918. Thirty countries fought in World War I. The Allies won after the United States joined the war in 1917. Woodrow Wilson was President during World War I.

The Great Depression began in 1929 when the stock market crashed. Many people in the United States lost a lot of money. Many were poor and didn't have jobs. Franklin Delano Roosevelt (FDR) was elected President in 1932. He helped the country recover. He was President until he died in 1945.

World War II began in 1939 when Germany invaded Poland. The leader of Germany was Adolf Hitler. Japan and Italy joined the fight on the side of Germany. This group was called the Axis countries.

The United States entered the war after Japanese planes bombed Pearl Harbor in Hawaii in 1941. More than 2,000 Americans died there. The United States joined the Allied countries, which included the United Kingdom, France, Canada, Australia, New Zealand, the Soviet Union, China, and many more. The Allied countries fought the Axis countries of Germany, Japan, and Italy.

The Allies defeated Germany in the famous D-Day invasion in Normandy, France, in 1944. The Allies won the war in Europe almost a year later. Japan surrendered after the United States dropped two atomic bombs on Hiroshima and Nagasaki in August 1945. This ended World War II. The United States and the Soviet Union became the two major world powers, or superpowers, after World War II.

The Cold War

The United States and the Soviet Union were enemies during a period called the Cold War. The Soviet Union was a communist country made up of many states, including Russia, Ukraine, and Belarus. The Cold War began after World War II and was at its peak during the 1950s, when Dwight Eisenhower, who was a general in World War II, was President. During the Cold War, the two countries did not fight each other with weapons. It was a war of ideas. The major concern of the United States was communism. The United States didn't want communism to spread to other countries. The Cold War ended in the late 1980s. The Soviet Union collapsed in 1991 breaking up into many different countries.

Soviet President Mikhail Gorbachev (left), and U.S. President Ronald Reagan helped end the Cold War.

WORDS TO KNOW

airliner
Allies
atomic bomb
Axis
coalition
Cold War
communism
concern
crash
enemy
general
The Great Depression
Pentagon
terrorist
World Trade Center

Wars in Asia

From 1950 to 1953, the United States fought to protect noncommunist South Korea from communist North Korea in the Korean War. At the end of the war, Korea remained divided.

The United States tried to defeat communism in Vietnam too. From 1964 to 1973, U.S. troops supported South Vietnam against North Vietnam in the Vietnam War. North Vietnam won the war and united the country under its leadership.

After Iraq invaded Kuwait in 1990, The United States and a coalition, or group, of more than 30 other countries fought to expel Iraq from Kuwait. This is known as the Gulf War, or the Persian Gulf War. The coalition was successful and the Iraq armies left Kuwait.

9/11

On September 11, 2001, the United States was attacked by terrorists. Nineteen men took over four planes. They flew two of the planes into the twin towers of the World Trade Center in New York City. The towers were destroyed. The terrorists crashed one plane into the Pentagon, the military headquarters near Washington, D.C. The fourth plane crashed in a field in Pennsylvania. About 3,000 people were killed on 9/11. The terrorists had been trained in Afghanistan. As a result of these attacks, President George W. Bush declared a war on terror and invaded Afghanistan. The government of Afghanistan was overturned and a president was elected.

The Iraq War

In 2003, the United States and its allies invaded Iraq. They thought Iraq had weapons of mass destruction. Saddam Hussein, the ruler of Iraq, was removed from power.

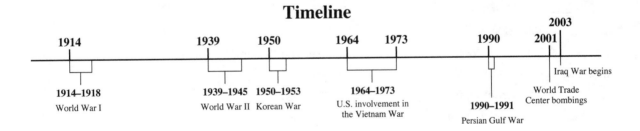

Timeline

Getting Information from the Reading

A. Use the words in the box to fill in each blank below. The first one is done for you.

Cold War	Japan	The Great Depression
general	Pentagon	~~Woodrow Wilson~~
Italy	terrorists	World Trade Center

1. The President during World War I was _____Woodrow Wilson_____.

2. The United States fought Germany, _____, and _____ in World War II.

3. Roosevelt was President during _____ and World War II.

4. Eisenhower was a _____ in World War II before he became President.

5. During the _____, communism was the major concern of the United States.

6. On September 11, 2001, _____ flew airliners into the _____ and the _____.

B. Match the event to the time period. Write the letter on the line. The first one is done for you.

____C____ 1. World War II   a. 1914–1918

_____ 2. The Gulf War   b. 1930s

_____ 3. World War I   c. 1939–1945

_____ 4. The Cold War   d. after the Second World War

_____ 5. The Vietnam War   e. 1950–1953

_____ 6. The Great Depression   f. 1964–1973

_____ 7. The Korean War   g. 1990–1991

52 • CHAPTER 5

The 100 History and Government Questions

A. Check all the answers that are correct.

1. Check the war or wars fought by the United States in the 1900s.
   - ☐ The Civil War
   - ☐ World War I
   - ☐ World War II
   - ☐ September 11
   - ☐ The Vietnam War
   - ☐ The Korean War
   - ☐ The Gulf War

2. Who was the U.S. President during World War I?
   - ☐ Woodrow Wilson
   - ☐ Franklin Delano Roosevelt
   - ☐ Dwight Eisenhower
   - ☐ George W. Bush

3. Who was President during the Great Depression and World War II?
   - ☐ Woodrow Wilson
   - ☐ Franklin Delano Roosevelt
   - ☐ Dwight Eisenhower
   - ☐ George W. Bush

4. Who did the United States fight in World War II?
   - ☐ England
   - ☐ Germany
   - ☐ Japan
   - ☐ Italy

5. Dwight Eisenhower was a general before he was President. What war was he a part of?
   - ☐ The Civil War
   - ☐ World War I
   - ☐ World War II
   - ☐ September 11
   - ☐ The Vietnam War
   - ☐ The Korean War
   - ☐ The Gulf War

6. During the Cold War, what was the main concern of the United States?
   - ☐ terrorism
   - ☐ communism
   - ☐ Iraq
   - ☐ The Great Depression

7. What major event happened on September 11, 2001, in the United States?
   - ☐ The stock market crashed.
   - ☐ Iraq invaded Kuwait.
   - ☐ Terrorists attacked the United States.
   - ☐ The Japanese bombed Pearl Harbor.

B. 100 Questions Practice. These questions may be asked as part of the U.S. history and government test. Talk about the answers. There may be more than one correct answer. All 100 questions can be found on page 154. Go to the Quizzes menu on the DVD for more 100 Questions practice.

1. Name one war fought by the United States in the 1900s.
2. Who was President during World War I?
3. Who was President during the Great Depression and World War II?
4. Who did the United States fight in World War II?
5. Before he was President, Eisenhower was a general. What war was he in?
6. During the Cold War, what was the main concern of the United States?
7. What major event happened on September 11, 2001, in the United States?

The N-400 Application: Adjectives and Other Vocabulary

The N-400 application has some difficult vocabulary. Many of the difficult words are adjectives. Some of the adjectives look like verbs, but they are not. Read the definitions of the following adjectives. The adjectives appear in Part 8 of the N-400 form on the next page.

---

annulled: no longer good; not in effect anymore
I was married when I was 15. The marriage was <u>annulled</u>.

applicable: it applies to you; it is a question you can answer
You forgot to fill out Part 9 on your N-400 when you applied for citizenship.
No, I didn't forget. That section is not <u>applicable</u> to me because I don't have any children.

given: a name your parents gave you; your first name
My name is John Smith. John is my <u>given</u>, or first, name. Smith is my family, or last, name.

lawful: legal; not against the law
Stealing is not <u>lawful</u>—it is against the law.

previous: the one before
I was a teacher in my <u>previous</u> job. Now I am a cook.

prior: the one before
My <u>prior</u> teacher was Ms. White. Now Mr. Harper is my teacher.

A. Vocabulary practice. Write the correct word from the list on the lines to complete the sentences. There may be more than one correct answer.

annulled	given	previous
applicable	lawful	prior

1. Part 8, Section F asks for my prior spouse's middle name. That question is not

    _____ because she doesn't have a middle name.

2. A _____ Permanent Resident is a person who is allowed to live permanently in the United States legally.

3. My first marriage wasn't legal because I was too young. That marriage was

    _____—it wasn't in effect anymore.

4. I know your last name is Kennedy. What is your _____ name?

5. My _____ marriage ended in 1998. I got married again in 2002.

6. _____ and _____ have the same meaning.

The N-400 Application: Parts 8C, D, E, F, and G

Part 8 asks about present and past marriages. Only answer the questions that apply to you. It is all right to leave blank the questions that don't apply to you.

Part 8. Information about your marital history. *(Continued.)*	Write your USCIS "A"- number here: A

C. Is your spouse a U.S. citizen? ☐ Yes ☐ No

D. If your spouse is a U.S. citizen, give the following information:

   1. When did your spouse become a U.S. citizen? ☐ At Birth ☐ Other

   If "Other," give the following information:

   2. Date your spouse became a U.S. citizen

   3. Place your spouse became a U.S. citizen *(Please see Instructions.)*

   City and State

E. If your spouse is **not** a U.S. citizen, give the following information :

   1. Spouse's Country of Citizenship

   2. Spouse's USCIS "A"- Number *(If applicable)*
   A

   3. Spouse's Immigration Status

   ☐ Lawful Permanent Resident   ☐ Other

F. If you were married before, provide the following information about your prior spouse. If you have more than one previous marriage, use a separate sheet(s) of paper to provide the information requested in Questions 1-5 below.

   1. Prior Spouse's Family Name *(Last Name)*   Given Name *(First Name)*   Full Middle Name *(If applicable)*

   2. Prior Spouse's Immigration Status

   ☐ U.S. Citizen

   ☐ Lawful Permanent Resident

   ☐ Other

   3. Date of Marriage *(mm/dd/yyyy)*

   4. Date Marriage Ended *(mm/dd/yyyy)*

   5. How Marriage Ended

   ☐ Divorce   ☐ Spouse Died   ☐ Other

G. How many times has your current spouse been married (including annulled marriages)?

   If your spouse has **ever** been married before, give the following information about **your spouse's** prior marriage.
   If your spouse has more than one previous marriage, use a separate sheet(s) of paper to provide the information requested in Questions 1 - 5 below.

   1. Prior Spouse's Family Name *(Last Name)*   Given Name *(First Name)*   Full Middle Name *(If applicable)*

   2. Prior Spouse's Immigration Status

   ☐ U.S. Citizen

   ☐ Lawful Permanent Resident

   ☐ Other

   3. Date of Marriage *(mm/dd/yyyy)*

   4. Date Marriage Ended *(mm/dd/yyyy)*

   5. How Marriage Ended

   ☐ Divorce   ☐ Spouse Died   ☐ Other

Form N-400 (Rev. 10/15/07) Y Page 5

The N-400 Application: Part 9

Part 9 asks for information about your childern. If you need more space to write the information, you can use one or more separate sheet(s) of paper.

| Part 9. Information about your children. | | | | Write your USCIS "A"- number here:
A |

A. How many sons and daughters have you had? For more information on which sons and daughters you should include and how to complete this section, see the Instructions.

B. Provide the following information about all of your sons and daughters. If you need more space, use a separate sheet(s) of paper.

Full Name of Son or Daughter	Date of Birth *(mm/dd/yyyy)*	USCIS "A"- number *(if child has one)*	Country of Birth	Current Address *(Street, City, State and Country)*
		A		
		A		
		A		
		A		
		A		
		A		
		A		
		A		

| Add Children | | | Go to continuation page |

The USCIS Interview

Interview Skill: Requesting Repetition

If you are not sure what the interviewer has asked you, be sure to ask for clarification. You can ask him or her to repeat the question. Here are some ways to ask:

I'm sorry. Could you repeat that, please?
I didn't understand what you said. Could you say it again?
I'm sorry, I'm nervous. Could you say that more slowly?

 Go to the Interview Skills menu of the DVD to view examples of this skill.

A. Complete the conversations below. Write the phrases from the box on the lines below.

1. **A:** Please tell me, is your wife an American citizen?

    B: _____

2. **A:** What is your spouse's country of origin?

    B: _____

3. **A:** What are the names of your children?

    B: _____

TIP: When you ask the interviewer to repeat something, he or she might repeat the question in a different way. The interviewer might rephrase it using words that are easier for you to understand.

B. Watch the DVD segments for this chapter. You can find them on the Chapters menu of the DVD.

C. The interview segment with Mr. Huang is included below. Practice it with a partner.

Interviewer: Okay. Now, please tell me, is your wife a U.S. citizen?
Mr. Huang: No, she is Chinese.
Interviewer: And what's her immigration status?
Mr. Huang: Sorry. I don't understand. Say it again, please.
Interviewer: Yes. I asked about her immigration status. Is she a lawful, permanent U.S. resident?
Mr. Huang: Yes, she have her green card.
Interviewer: Okay. And how many times has your wife been married, including annulled marriages?
Mr. Huang: What kind of marriage? Could you repeat that, please?

Could you repeat that, please?

Interviewer: Yes. Annulled marriages are marriages that have been declared void or invalid. Do you understand?
Mr. Huang: Yes. I understand. My wife has been only married to me.
Interviewer: I see one child listed on your form. Ming Mei, is she your only child?
Mr. Huang: Yes, she is.
Interviewer: That's a very pretty name!
Mr. Huang: I think so, too.

D. With a partner, practice the interview with correct information about yourself. Tell the interviewer in different ways that you don't understand the question.

Reading and Writing Test Practice

A. Look at the calendar. Write the letter on the line. The first one is done for you.

January	February	March	April
	Presidents' Day		
May	**June**	**July**	**August**
Memorial Day	Flag Day	Independence Day	
September	**October**	**November**	**December**
Labor Day	Columbus Day	Thanksgiving	

★ ★ ★ ★ ★ ★ ★ ★ ★ ★

VOCABULARY

The vocabulary in the box will be on the reading and writing test. For a complete list, see pages 206–207.

Reading
When

Writing
February
May
June
July
September
October
November

Reading and Writing
Presidents' Day
Memorial Day
Flag Day
Independence Day
Labor Day
is

_____*d*_____ 1. Presidents' Day   a. October

_____ 2. Memorial Day   b. May

_____ 3. Flag Day   c. September

_____ 4. Independence Day   ~~d. February~~

_____ 5. Labor Day   e. November

_____ 6. Columbus Day   f. July 4

_____ 7. Thanksgiving   g. June 14

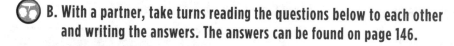 **B. With a partner, take turns reading the questions below to each other and writing the answers. The answers can be found on page 146.**

Example:

The interviewer asks you to read this question:

When is Presidents' Day?

The interviewer says this sentence and asks you to write it:

Presidents' Day is in February.

1. When is Memorial Day? _____

2. When is Flag Day? _____

3. When is Labor Day? _____

Grammar Review: Past Tense Questions and Short Answers

We often answer questions with short answers. The verbs in the answers are usually the same as those in the questions. For example:

> **Is** he Mexican? Yes, he **is.**
> **Were** they born in 1956? No, they **weren't.**
> **Do** you speak English? Yes, I **do.**

In the past tense, questions are often made with the past tense of **do,** which is **did.** When we answer these questions, we also use the word **did.** For example:

> **Did** you study history? Yes, I **did.**
> **Did** your children come with you to the United States? No, they **didn't.**

Answer these questions using *yes* or *no* and a short answer. If your answer is *no*, also write the correct information. The first one is done for you.

1. Were you married before? _Yes, I was._

2. Was your mother or father an American citizen? _____

3. Did you ever get divorced? _____

4. Was your current husband or wife married in the past? _____

5. Did you ever leave the country for more than six months? _____

6. Did you ever commit any crime? _____

7. Did you ever believe in the Communist Party? _____

8. Do you plan to live in the U.S. permanently? _____

9. Were you ever arrested? _____

10. Were you born with a title of nobility? _____

11. Did you ever get deported? _____

12. Were you born in China? _____

Civic Engagement:
HOLIDAYS

A. Memorial Day. Memorial Day is a day in May when people in the United States remember those who died in a war. A *memorial* honors an important person.

1. Look at the famous memorials in the photos below. What do they help people remember?

_____

2. Look at the list and write the event on the line next to the picture that goes best with it.

World War II	Korean War
Vietnam War	September 11 attack on World Trade Center

a. _____

b. _____

c. _____

d. _____

3. What memorials are in your city or your state? What do they help people remember?

_____

B. Holidays in your city. U.S. cities often celebrate a holiday with a parade. Some cities have named parks or statues in honor of a person or event. Work with a partner. Find out how these holidays are celebrated in your city.

Holiday	How is this holiday celebrated in your city?
Presidents' Day	
Memorial Day	
Independence Day	
Labor Day	
Columbus Day	
Thanksgiving	

The Constitution:
Supreme Law of the Land

Interview Focus:
Repeating for Confirmation

> *We the People* of the United
> insure domestic Tranquility, provide for the common defence, promote th
> and our Posterity, Do ordain and establish this Constitution for the Unite
>
> *Article. I.*
> Section. 1. All legislative Powers herein granted shall be vested in a Congress of the United States, which shall consist of a Senate and House of Representatives.
> Section. 2. The House of Representatives shall be composed of Members chosen every second Year by the People of the several States...

> The United States Constitution is on display at the National Archives in Washington, D.C.

Connect to the Topic

ARGJIRA AND DUKAGJIN RIZVANOLLI are ethnic Albanians and Muslims who used to live in Kosovo. When Kosovo was part of Yugoslavia, the Rizvanollis lived peacefully with their neighbors of all religious and ethnic backgrounds. When Yugoslavia broke up, there was fighting between people of different backgrounds and religions. The Rizvanollis moved to the United States, and after a few years they became citizens. Although they miss their native land and their families, they are happy to live in a place where they can practice their religion peacefully.

Getting into the Reading

Answer the questions.

1. What is a law? Can you give some examples of laws in the United States?

2. What is a constitution? Does your native country have a constitution?

3. What do you know about the U.S. Constitution?

4. The U.S. Constitution says that people have certain rights. What is a right? Can you give some examples of rights that people have in the United States? Which right do you think is most important to the Rizvanollis, the subjects of the *Connect to the Topic* profile above?

The U.S. Constitution

The Constitution is the highest law of the United States. All people and all laws must follow the Constitution. It is the supreme law of the land. The Constitution sets up the government of the United States, defines it, and protects the rights of Americans.

The Constitution was written in 1787. Men from 12 of the 13 states met in Philadelphia, Pennsylvania, and wrote it. The meeting was called the Constitutional Convention. Then, every state needed to approve, or ratify, the Constitution. To help states decide to ratify the Constitution, three men wrote an important document called the Federalist Papers to support passage of the Constitution. Those men were James Madison, Alexander Hamilton, and John Jay. They used the name Publius when they wrote it.

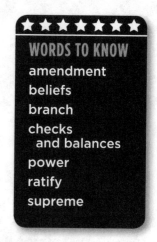

WORDS TO KNOW

amendment
beliefs
branch
checks
  and balances
power
ratify
supreme

The first part of the Constitution is called the Preamble. The Preamble is the introduction to the Constitution. It tells the purpose and basic beliefs of our government—a government by the people. The first three words of the Preamble are "We the People" to show that the United States is self-governed, that is, governed (run) by the people who live here.

The second part of the Constitution, the seven articles, includes a description of the three branches of our government. The men who wrote the Constitution didn't want any part of the government to become too powerful. So, they created a separation of powers. They divided the power of the government into three parts, or branches:

- **Legislative Branch**—includes the U.S. Congress
- **Executive Branch**—includes the President, Vice President, and Cabinet
- **Judicial Branch**—includes the Supreme Court and lower federal courts

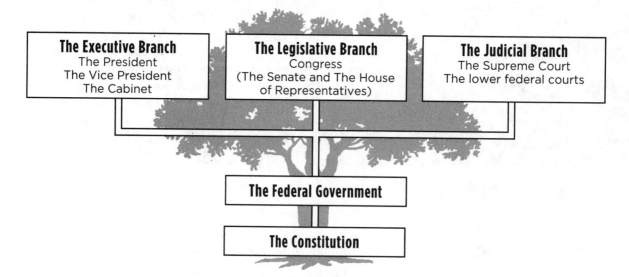

The Executive Branch
The President
The Vice President
The Cabinet

The Legislative Branch
Congress
(The Senate and The House
of Representatives)

The Judicial Branch
The Supreme Court
The lower federal courts

The Federal Government

The Constitution

The Constitution keeps the separation of powers through a system called checks and balances. For example, the Supreme Court (judicial branch) can overturn, or "check," the power of Congress (legislative branch); Congress can overturn, or "check," the power of the President (executive branch), and so on, to keep a balance of power among all three branches.

The last part of the Constitution is the amendments. Amendments are the changes made since the Constitution was written. The government must vote to add an amendment. The first ten amendments are called the Bill of Rights. There are a total of 27 amendments. The newest one was added in 1992.

Rule of law. The rule of law is based on the Constitution. It is the idea that *everyone* must follow the law—including leaders and the government. No one is above the law.

Getting Information from the Reading

A. Use the words in the box to fill in each blank below.

amendment	~~branch~~	power	supreme
beliefs	checks and balances	ratified	

1. The courts are part of the judicial _____ *branch* _____ of government.

2. The Preamble to the Constitution introduces the basic _____ of the U.S. government.

3. In the United States, the Constitution is the _____ law of the land.

4. The Constitution was _____ in 1789.

5. The system of _____ guarantees that no branch of government has more power than any other branch.

6. A change to the Constitution is called a(n) _____.

7. The legislative branch can overturn or check the _____ of the executive branch.

B. Circle the correct answer. Then practice asking and answering the questions with a partner.

1. What is the supreme law of the land?
   a. the Constitution   b. the Bill of Rights   c. the Declaration of Independence

2. What does the Constitution do?
   a. describes state laws   b. sets up the government   c. lists all laws

3. When was the Constitution written?
   a. 1776   b. 1997   c. 1787

4. What are the first three words of the Constitution?
   a. In the beginning   b. We hold these truths   c. We the people

5. What is an amendment?
   a. a law   b. a change to the Constitution   c. a branch of government

6. What stops one branch of government from becoming too powerful?
   a. checks and balances   b. judicial   c. Bill of Rights

Getting into the Reading

 Look at the pictures. Discuss with a partner.

1. What individual rights are most important to you?

2. What is happening in the photos?

★ ★ ★ ★ ★ ★ ★ ★
WORDS TO KNOW
broadcast
charged with
fine
force
guaranteed
jury
print
punishment
request
search
testify
trial
tried
warrant

The Bill of Rights

The Bill of Rights is the first ten amendments, or changes, to the Constitution. It was added to the Constitution in 1791. These rights and freedoms are guaranteed to all people in the United States.

1st Amendment:

Freedom of Speech: People can say what they want.

Freedom of the Press: People can print or broadcast what they want.

Freedom of Religion: People can practice any religion they want or not practice a religion.

Freedom of Peaceable Assembly: People can gather together peacefully to request changes in government.

Freedom to Petition the Government: People can apply for change when they think the government does something wrong.

2nd Amendment: People can own guns, with some limits on their use.

3rd Amendment: The government cannot force people to keep soldiers in their homes when there is no war.

4th Amendment: The government cannot search or take a person's property without a warrant, or order, from a court.

5th Amendment: A person cannot be tried for the same crime twice. A person cannot be forced to testify against herself or himself. People accused of crimes have the right to fair legal treatment.

6th Amendment: A person charged with a crime has the right to a trial by jury and to have a lawyer.

7th Amendment: People in civil lawsuits have the right to a fair trial, by jury in most cases.

8th Amendment: People will not have to post very high bonds, pay very high fines, or be given cruel treatment by the government.

9th Amendment: People have other rights in addition to those in the Constitution.

10th Amendment: Any power that does not belong to the federal government belongs to the states or to the people.

> ## The Right to Vote
> The most important right given to citizens of the United States is the right to vote. There are four amendments related to the right to vote:
>
> **15th Amendment:** Gave male citizens of all races the right to vote (1870)
>
> **19th Amendment:** Gave female citizens the right to vote (1920)
>
> **24th Amendment:** Stated that citizens don't have to pay to vote (1964)
>
> **26th Amendment:** Stated that citizens 18 or older can vote (1971)
>
> ## Other recent amendments:
> **25th Amendment:** Provided procedures for filling the post of vice president and procedures for when a president is unable to perform his or her duties (1967)
>
> **27th Amendment:** Limited changes to the salaries of members of Congress (1992)

Getting Information from the Reading

A. Write the number of the amendment after the statement.

1. It guarantees the right of people to gather together. _____

2. A person charged with a crime has a right to a lawyer. _____

3. You need a search warrant to go through someone's home. _____

4. People can own guns (bear arms). _____

5. The government cannot make people give evidence in court against themselves. _____

6. People can practice any religion they want. _____

7. If you are charged with a crime, you have a right to a trial with a jury. _____

8. The states have powers too. _____

9. If you are charged with a crime, you don't have to talk. _____

10. People have rights that aren't listed in the Constitution. _____

11. You don't have to pay to vote. _____

12. Women can vote. _____

B. Write answers to the questions.

1. What do we call the first ten amendments to the Constitution?

2. What is one right or freedom from the First Amendment? _____

3. How many amendments does the Constitution have? _____

4. What is the freedom of religion? _____

5. What are two rights of everyone living in the United States?

_____

The 100 History and Government Questions

A. Circle the correct answer.

1. The _____ is the supreme law of the land.

   a. Bill of Rights   b. Federalist Papers   c. Constitution

2. The Constitution sets up the government and protects people's _____.

   a. rights   b. citizen   c. voting

3. The words "We the people" express the idea of _____.

   a. speech   b. self-government   c. freedom

4. A change to the Constitution is called a(n) _____.

   a. amendment   b. right   c. bill

5. The first ten amendments are called the _____.

   a. Constitution   b. Federalist Papers   c. Bill of Rights

6. The _____ Amendment protects the freedoms of speech, press, religion, peaceful assembly, and the right to petition the government.

   a. First   b. Second   c. Sixteenth

7. There are _____ amendments.

   a. 20   b. 27   c. 10

 B. 100 Questions Practice. These questions may be asked as part of the U.S. history and government test. Talk about the answers with a partner. There may be more than one correct answer. All 100 questions can be found on page 154. Go to the Quizzes menu of the DVD for more 100 Questions practice.

1. What is the supreme law of the land?
2. What does the Constitution do?
3. The idea of self-government is in the first three words of the Constitution. What are these words?
4. What is an amendment?
5. What do we call the first ten amendments to the Constitution?
6. What is <u>one</u> right or freedom from the First Amendment?
7. How many amendments does the Constitution have?
8. What is freedom of religion?
9. What stops one branch of government from becoming too powerful?
10. There are four amendments to the Constitution about who can vote. Describe <u>one</u> of them.
11. What happened at the Constitutional Convention?
12. When was the Constitution written?
13. The Federalist Papers supported the passage of the U.S. Constitution. Name <u>one</u> of the writers.
14. What is the "rule of law"?

Martin Luther King, Jr.

Martin Luther King, Jr., was an African American minister who worked to end discrimination against minorities in the 1960s. In 1964, he won the Nobel Peace Prize. King was assassinated in Memphis, Tennessee, in 1968.

Because of his work, laws were passed that helped protect the rights of all people. For example, the Twenty-fourth Amendment to the Constitution says no one has to pay tax in order to vote. All adult citizens, rich or poor, can vote.

The N-400 Application: *Have you ever . . . ?*

Many questions on the N-400 application ask *"Have you ever _____?"* *Ever* means any time in your entire life. It means when you were a child, when you were in your country, and while you have been in the United States. If you have done something at any time in your life, you must answer "yes" to a *"Have you ever _____?"* question. Notice that we use the past participle form of the main verb in questions with *"Have you ever."*

Have you ever lived in Philadelphia?

Have you ever registered to vote in any Federal, state, or local election in the United States?

Have you ever voted in a U.S. election?

Have you ever failed to file a required Federal, state, or local tax return since becoming a Lawful Permanent Resident?

A. Answer the questions. You can use the short answers *"Yes, I have"* or *"No, I haven't"* to answer *Have you ever . . . ?* questions. The first one is done for you.

1. Have you ever claimed to be a U.S. citizen? _____*No, I haven't.*_____

2. Have you ever used a different name? _____

3. Have you ever voted in a U.S. election? _____

4. Have you ever been married before? _____

5. Have you ever failed to file your income taxes? _____

B. Your turn. Write three *Have you ever . . . ?* questions. Then ask a partner the questions.

1. _____

2. _____

3. _____

The N-400 Application: Part 10A (Questions 1-7)

Below are Questions 1–7 from Part 10A and some simple explanations that might help you answer them. It is important that you answer these questions honestly. The USCIS can check your information to see if you are being honest. If you answer "yes" to any of these questions, you should get legal advice.

Part 10. Additional questions.

Please answer Questions 1 through 14. If you answer "Yes" to any of these questions, include a written explanation with this form. Your written explanation should (1) explain why your answer was "Yes" and (2) provide any additional information that helps to explain your answer.

A. General Questions.

1. Have you **ever** claimed to be a U.S. citizen *(in writing or any other way)*? ☐ Yes ☐ No
2. Have you **ever** registered to vote in any Federal, state or local election in the United States? ☐ Yes ☐ No
3. Have you **ever** voted in any Federal, state or local election in the United States? ☐ Yes ☐ No

---

▶ **EXPLANATION** *Claim* is a very difficult word. It means to pretend or to lie. If you ever told someone you were a U.S. citizen or wrote that you were, you should see a lawyer. Stating you were a U.S. citizen in order to vote, to get public benefits, or for some other reason, is a deportable offense. If you ever registered to vote or voted in Federal, state, or local elections, you should also see a lawyer. School board elections are not a problem.

---

4. Since becoming a Lawful Permanent Resident, have you **ever** failed to file a required Federal state or local tax return? ☐ Yes ☐ No
5. Do you owe any Federal, state or local taxes that are overdue? ☐ Yes ☐ No

---

▶ **EXPLANATION** *Failed to file* is also difficult. *Fail* means to NOT do something. Question 4 is asking "Have you ever NOT filed your tax returns?" If you pay your taxes every year, answer "no." If you owe some money on your taxes, answer "yes." If you didn't file a tax return but were required to, the USCIS may deny your citizenship. It's best to pay up all the taxes you owe before applying. It's not a problem if you didn't file because your income was too low, but be prepared to explain your situation to the USCIS officer. If you can't pay all of your back taxes, try to negotiate a payment plan and bring the documents to your interview. You can also include an explanation with your N-400.

---

6. Do you have any title of nobility in any foreign country? ☐ Yes ☐ No

---

▶ **EXPLANATION** Are you a king, queen, duke, earl, or other kind of royalty in your country?

---

7. Have you ever been declared legally incompetent or been confined to a mental institution within the last five years? ☐ Yes ☐ No

---

▶ **EXPLANATION** *Declared legally incompetent* means that a judge or court ruled that a person is mentally disabled. The USCIS wants to know if you have mental problems that could prevent you from taking the oath. Note that in this *"Have you ever ____?"* question, USCIS asks just about the last five years.

The USCIS Interview

Interview Skill: Repeating for Confirmation

You may not understand every question the USCIS interviewer asks you. If you want to check or confirm what you heard, repeat the question. Use *I* instead of *you*. Then the interviewer will repeat the question or say, "Yes, that's right."

Interviewer: Have you ever registered to vote in a U.S. election?
You: Have I ever registered to vote in a U.S. election?

 Go to the Interview Skills menu of the DVD to view examples of this skill.

TIP: Even if you don't hear the entire question, repeat what you did hear, so the interviewer knows what you did and did not understand.

A. Read the questions below and then write them as questions that use the words *I* and *my*.

1. Interviewer: _What is your spouse's country of origin?_

   You: _____

2. Interviewer: _Where were you born?_

   You: _____

3. Interviewer: _What is your country of birth?_

   You: _____

4. Interviewer: _Where did your marriage take place?_

   You: _____

 B. Watch the DVD segments for this chapter. You can find them on the Chapters menu of the DVD.

 C. Part of the interview segment with Mr. Huang is included below. Practice it with a partner.

Interviewer: And have you ever registered to vote in any election in the U.S.?

Mr. Huang: Have I ever registered to vote here in the U.S.? No. I have never registered.

Interviewer: And since getting your permanent resident card—your green card—have you ever failed to file a required Federal, state, or local tax return?

Mr. Huang: Have I ever failed to file a tax return?

Interviewer: Yes, have you ever *not* filed a tax return?

Mr. Huang: No. I always pay my taxes.

Interviewer: Good. And do you owe any overdue taxes?

Mr. Huang: I no owe … I do not owe any money.

Have I ever *failed* to file a tax return?

D. Now, with a partner, practice the interview with correct information about yourself. Tell the interviewer in different ways that you don't understand the question.

Reading and Writing Test Practice

A. Complete the sentences with a word from the box.

> citizens   freedom of speech
> country   people
> free   vote

1. _____ have the right to _____.

2. Many _____ come to our _____

   to be _____.

3. One freedom in the Bill of Rights is the _____.

 B. With a partner, take turns reading the questions below to each other and writing the answers. The answers can be found on page 147.

Example:

For the reading test, the interviewer asks you to read a question like this one:

What is one right citizens have?

For the writing test, the interviewer reads a sentence like this one and asks you to write it:

One right citizens have is the right to vote.

1. Who can vote in the United States?

   _____

   _____

2. What right do people in the United States have?

   _____

   _____

3. Name one right in the Bill of Rights.

   _____

   _____

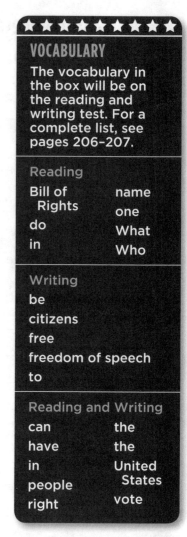

Congress meets in the Capitol building in Washington, D.C.

VOCABULARY

The vocabulary in the box will be on the reading and writing test. For a complete list, see pages 206–207.

Reading

Bill of Rights	name
	one
do	What
in	Who

Writing

be
citizens
free
freedom of speech
to

Reading and Writing

can	the
have	the
in	United States
people	
right	vote

Grammar Review: Tag Questions

Sometimes, when we think we know the answer but are not sure, we ask a question with a tag on the end. These kinds of questions seem more polite or less embarrassing than more direct information questions. When the USCIS interviewer asks you questions about your application, he or she might use some of these tag questions. The information is on the application, but the interviewer wants to make sure the information is true. For example:

> You are a Mexican citizen, **aren't you**?
>
> You have six children living with you, **don't you**?

The first part and the last part of tag questions do not seem to agree. One part is positive (+), and the other part is negative (−). For example:

> You **have been** married twice, **haven't you**?
>   (+)   (−)
>
> You **didn't leave** the country for more than six months, **did you**?
>   (−)   (+)

When you answer a tag question, listen to the first part of the question. That is what the person thinks is true. Your answer will tell the person if that part is true or not. If the information in the first part of the question is not correct, you should give the correct information. For example:

> You've been married two times, **haven't you**?
> **Yes, I have. / No, I haven't**. I've been married once.
>
> You aren't married, **are you**?
> **Yes, I am**. I got married last month. / **No, I'm not**.

Practice answering these questions.

1. You're applying to be a naturalized citizen, aren't you? _____

2. Your port of entry was New York, wasn't it? _____

3. You've filed a tax return every year, haven't you? _____

4. You haven't been arrested, have you? _____

5. You were born in Korea, weren't you? _____

6. You moved to the United States in 1995, didn't you? _____

7. You're single, aren't you? _____

8. You have four children, don't you? _____

9. You don't owe any taxes, do you? _____

10. You haven't voted in an election in the United States, have you? _____

Civic Engagement:
PLACES OF FREEDOM

A. Look at the pictures of places below. Write the name of the right or freedom each one represents.
Find a place in your city or town where this right occurs.

PLACE IN COMMUNITY	FREEDOM OR RIGHT IT REPRESENTS	NAME/LOCATION IN YOUR CITY OR TOWN WHERE IT OCCURS

7 The Executive Branch of Government

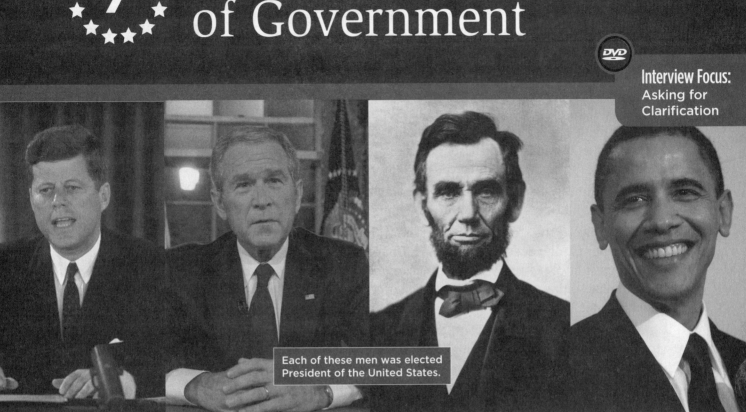

Interview Focus:
Asking for Clarification

Each of these men was elected President of the United States.

Connect to the Topic

BOPHANY HUOT came to the United States in 1981 when she was 10 years old. Before that, she lived in refugee camps in Thailand for over a year. She and her family had escaped Cambodia, which at the time, was ruled by a Communist regime. Bophany says, "I felt as though someone had either taped or sewn my lips tight. I could never express myself truthfully." Her family wanted a different life, one that included the ability to live freely, to vote, and to participate in a democracy. Bophany was happy to find those things in the United States. She was impressed when she saw the President of the United States on television, speaking to the American people.

Getting into the Reading

Answer the questions.

1. How many of the men in the pictures above do you recognize? What are their names?
2. Who are the current President and Vice President of the United States?
3. Who is the current leader of your native country? Is the leader called a *President* or something else?
4. Bophany Huot, the subject of the *Connect to the Topic* profile, was impressed when she first saw the President of the United States on television. How did you feel the first time you saw the President of the United States speak on television?

The Executive Branch

The executive branch of the federal government includes the President, the Vice President, the cabinet, and the departments led by cabinet members. The executive branch enforces, or makes people obey, laws and puts new laws into effect.

The President is in charge of the executive branch. The President signs bills, or ideas for new laws, and makes them laws. The President can veto, or turn down, a bill if he or she does not agree with it. The President is also the commander in chief of the United States Army, Navy, Air Force, and Marines (the armed forces).

The White House is the President's official home. It is located at 1600 Pennsylvania Avenue, N.W., in Washington, D.C.

According to the Constitution, a person must meet certain requirements, or necessary things, to become President. The person must be at least 35 years old, must be born a U.S. citizen (not a naturalized citizen), and must have lived in the United States for at least 14 years.

Every four years, the United States elects a President for a four-year term of office. He or she can serve no more than two full terms (eight years).

The President is elected on the first Tuesday in November and is inaugurated, or put into office, in January. The people do not elect the President; they elect the Electoral College representatives for each candidate. The candidate, or person who wants to be elected, with the most votes in a state gets all of the electoral votes for that state. Then the Electoral College elects the President.

★ ★ ★ ★ ★ ★ ★
WORDS TO KNOW
advise
appointed
bill
cabinet
campaign
candidate
Democratic
elects
enforce
inaugurated
nominate
Republican
requirement
responsibilities
term of office
veto

President Obama giving a speech about a new bill to help the economy.

The Vice President has special responsibilities, or duties, which are listed in the Constitution. He or she becomes President if the President can no longer serve. The Vice President must meet the same requirements for office as the President.

The cabinet is appointed by the President. The executive branch of government has 15 departments. The leaders of these departments are appointed by the President and, with the Vice President, form the President's cabinet. The 16 cabinet members meet with and advise the President, helping to run the important areas of government. Most cabinet members are called secretaries. For example, there is a secretary of defense and a secretary of state.

Political Parties

People who agree on how the government should be run form a group called a political party. In the United States, the two main political parties are the Democratic Party and the Republican Party. These two parties have different ideas about government and how it should work.

Before a presidential election, both of these parties have their own national conventions. Party members make a list, called a platform, of the political ideas they think are important for the next four years. They decide who, from the leaders in their party, they want to be President. Then the parties choose, or nominate, one Democratic and one Republican candidate for President. Both candidates campaign in every state. They try to convince people to vote for them, and they make promises about what they will do as President.

Democrats	Republicans
Many Democrats believe that the government has a responsibility to help people. They want to do this through such social and economic programs as unemployment insurance, national health care, literacy programs, and programs that protect the rights of women and minorities.	Many Republicans believe that people should help themselves. They think the government should do only the things that individuals cannot do for themselves, such as have military forces to protect the United States. Republicans also believe in less government involvement in business and state activities.
Recent Democratic Presidents: Bill Clinton Jimmy Carter Lyndon Johnson John F. Kennedy	*Recent Republican Presidents:* George W. Bush Ronald Reagan George H. W. Bush Gerald Ford

The donkey is the symbol of the Democratic Party.

The elephant is the symbol of the Republican Party.

Presidents' Day

George Washington was born on February 22. Abraham Lincoln was born on February 12. Americans honor them and all Presidents by celebrating Presidents' Day on the third Monday in February.

Getting Information from the Reading

A. Use the words in the box to fill in each blank below. The first one is done for you.

advise	Democratic	Republican	responsibilities
bill	~~elects~~	requirements	the White House

1. In November, the United States _____*elects*_____ a President for a four-year term of office.

2. _____ is the President's official home.

3. The President can sign a _____ to become law.

4. The cabinet members _____ the President about his or her _____ to the country.

5. In a U.S. presidential election, there is always one _____ candidate and one _____ candidate.

6. Being a U.S.-born citizen and being 35 years old are two _____ for a person who wants to become President.

B. Circle the correct answer.

1. Who is in charge of the executive branch?
   a. the Vice President   b. the secretary of defense   c. the President

2. Secretary of defense and secretary of state are _____-level positions.
   a. Electoral College   b. Democratic   c. cabinet

3. Who is the commander in chief of the military?
   a. the secretary of defense b. the President   c. the Vice President

4. Who appoints the cabinet?
   a. the President   b. the Vice President   c. the secretary of defense

5. Who elects the President of the United States?
   a. the citizens of the United States   b. the Electoral College   c. the Vice President

Now practice asking and answering the questions with a partner.

The 100 History and Government Questions

A. Look at the clues below. Write the letter on the line. The first one is done for you.

1. __c__ One part of the government

2. ____ They help the President run the government.

3. ____ The month the new President is inaugurated

4. ____ This person becomes President if the President can no longer serve.

5. ____ This person can veto a bill if he or she doesn't agree with it.

> a. the President
> b. the Vice President
> c. the executive branch
> d. January
> e. the cabinet

 **B. 100 Questions Practice.** These questions may be asked as part of the U.S. history and government ___ons with a partner. Talk about the answers. There may be more than ___stions can be found on page 154. Go to the Quizzes menu of the DVD

of the government.
ecutive branch?
resident of the United States now?
/ice President of the United States now?
ow many years?
e for President?
nger serve, who becomes President?
chief of the military?
olitical parties in the United States today?
e laws?

y of the President now?
el positions?
s cabinet do?
to be to vote for President?

President Obama and Vice President Biden

The N-400 Application: *Be associated with*

Many questions on the N-400 application ask "Have you ever been associated with _____?" As you learned in the last chapter (on page 67), *ever* means "at any time in your entire life." *Be associated with* means "be a part of something," such as a group, a club, or a political party. It can also mean "be close friends or business partners with" a specific person or group of people. For example:

Example	Explanation
Carol **is associated with** the National Organization for Women.	Carol is a member of the organization, or group, called the National Organization for Women.
Ben **is associated with** the United Farm Workers of America.	Ben is a member of the workers' union called the United Farm Workers of America.
Dan **has never been associated** with criminals.	Dan has never had a close friend or a business partner who was a criminal.

These questions follow the form:

Have + [subject] + *ever* + past participle of *be* + *associated with* + [person or organization].

A. Answer the questions. Use the chart above. The first one is done for you.

1. Have you ever been associated with a political party, or group?
   Yes. I was a member of the Communist Party for five years. It was required by law in my country.

2. Have you ever been associated with a workers' union or organization?
   _____

   _____

3. Have you ever been associated with people who have committed crimes?
   _____

4. Have you ever been associated with a group or organization that is NOT political?
   _____

   _____

B. Your turn. Write three *"Have you ever been associated with . . . ?"* questions. Then ask a partner the questions.

1. _____

2. _____

3. _____

The N-400 Application: Part 10B (Questions 8–12) and Part C

Below are the questions from Parts 10B and C of the N-400 application and some simple explanations that might help. It is important that you answer these questions honestly. The USCIS can check your information to see if you are being honest. If you answer "Yes" to any of these questions, you should get legal advice.

B. Affiliations.

8. a Have you **ever** been a member of or associated with any organization, association, fund foundation, party, club, society or similar group in the United States or in any other place? ☐ Yes ☐ No

   b. If you answered "Yes," list the name of each group below. If you need more space, attach the names of the other group(s) on a separate sheet(s) of paper.

▶ **EXPLANATION** The USCIS wants to know if you were involved in a group that would make you ineligible for citizenship, such as groups that fund terrorist organizations. However, this question asks for any association with any organization, group, etc., and you can use this space to list organizations that reflect well on your character. A *fund* is an amount of money gathered for investment or other purposes. A *foundation* is an organization that gets its money from donations. Foundations are formed for research and other purposes.

---

9. Have you **ever** been a member of or in any way associated *(either directly or indirectly)* with:

   a. The Communist Party? ☐ Yes ☐ No

▶ **EXPLANATION** If you were a member of the Communist Party, you may not be able to become a U.S. citizen. There are many exceptions: if you were a member more than 10 years before you applied for citizenship; if your membership was required by law; if your membership ended before you were age 16; if you did not fully understand the organization; or if your party membership was required to get a job, food, housing, or other necessities. If you qualify for an exception, write an explanation.

---

   b. Any other totalitarian party? ☐ Yes ☐ No

▶ **EXPLANATION** *Totalitarian party* means a party that runs a government that is not representative of the people, is usually the only political party in a country, is led by a dictator, and puts down any opposition by force.

---

   c. A terrorist organization? ☐ Yes ☐ No

▶ **EXPLANATION** *Terrorist organizations* are groups of two or more people that the United States government names as terrorist organizations and/or groups that: highjack or sabotage any vehicles; hold and threaten to kill or injure any person in order to force a third person or government to do something; attack government representatives; carry out assassinations; or use biological agents, chemical agents, nuclear weapons, explosives, firearms, or other weapons with the intent to endanger the safety of one or more people or to cause substantial damage to property. It does not matter if the group actually carries out these actions or plans, or only threatens to carry them out; they still fall under this definition.

The N-400 Application: Part 10B (Questions 8–12) and Part C (continued)

10. Have you **ever** advocated *(either directly or indirectly)* the overthrow of any government by force or violence?	☐ Yes	☐ No
11. Have you **ever** persecuted *(either directly or indirectly)* any person because of race, religion, national origin, membership in a particular social group or political opinion?	☐ Yes	☐ No

▶ **EXPLANATION** *Advocate* means to encourage or support. *Overthrow* means to defeat or take over. *Persecute* means bother or harass on a regular basis. It can also mean to torture or imprison someone or be involved in another way in these actions. If you answer "Yes" to this question, the USCIS may deny your application and/or seek to remove you from the United States.

12. Between March 23, 1933 and May 8, 1945, did you work for or associate in any way *(either directly or indirectly)* with:		
a. The Nazi government of Germany?	☐ Yes	☐ No
b. Any government in any area (1) occupied by, (2) allied with, or (3) established with the help of the Nazi government of Germany?	☐ Yes	☐ No
c. Any German, Nazi, or S.S. military unit, paramilitary unit, self-defense unit, vigilante unit, citizen unit, police unit, government agency or office, extermination camp, concentration camp, prisoner of war camp, prison, labor camp or transit camp?	☐ Yes	☐ No

▶ **EXPLANATION** If you were involved with Nazis, you usually are not allowed to enter the United States. If the USCIS finds out about Nazi activity you didn't tell them about before, they may deny your application and/or seek to remove you from the United States.

C. Continuous Residence.		
Since becoming a Lawful Permanent Resident of the United States:		
13. Have you **ever** called yourself a "nonresident" on a Federal, state or local tax return?	☐ Yes	☐ No
14. Have you **ever** failed to file a Federal, state or local tax return because you considered yourself to be a "nonresident"?	☐ Yes	☐ No

▶ **EXPLANATION** For these questions, the USCIS wants to know if you have lived in another country while you were a permanent resident of the United States. Filing taxes as a nonresident or not filing taxes (= failing to file) may tell them this. If you answer "Yes" to either question, they may decide that you are not currently eligible for United States citizenship. They may also determine that you have abandoned (= gave up) your permanent resident status if you have been out of the United States for more than one year, without permission from the United States government.

The USCIS Interview

Interview Skill: Asking for Clarification

You may not understand every question the USCIS interviewer asks. Here are some things you might want to say if you don't understand. Practice saying these expressions.

I didn't understand what you said.	What does that mean?
What do you mean?	I'm sorry, I don't understand.
Could you explain the question, please?	Could you give me an example?

 Go to the Interview Skills menu of the DVD to view examples of this skill.

TIP: When you ask the interviewer for clarification, he or she might rephrase the question using words that are easier for you to understand.

A. Complete the conversations below. Write one of the phrases above on the lines below.

1. A: Have you persecuted any person for whatever reason?

B: _____

2. A: In the United States or elsewhere, are you affiliated with any organization, party, or club?

B: _____

3. A: Have you had any association with the Nazi government of Germany?

B: _____

 B. Watch the DVD segments for this chapter. You can find them on the Chapters menu of the DVD.

 C. Part of the interview segment with Mr. Huang is included below. Practice it with a partner.

Interviewer: Mr. Huang, have you ever been a member of or associated with any organization, association, fund, foundation, party, club, society, or similar group in the United States or in any other place?

Mr. Huang: Sorry, that was long question! Could you repeat that slowly, please?

Interviewer: Sure. Have you ever been a member of any group— an organization or a club, for example?

Mr. Huang: In the United States?

Interviewer: Here or back in China.

Mr. Huang: I have been a member of the Chinese Progressive Association. That's all.

Interviewer: Okay. And have you ever persecuted anyone based on their race, religion, nation of origin, membership in a particular social group, or political opinion?

Mr. Huang: Another long question! Could you please explain the question, please?

Interviewer: Sure. I'll shorten it. Have you ever persecuted anyone for any reason? You do know what "persecute" means, don't you?

Mr. Huang: Sure. Treat bad ... *badly* ... because you don't like what that person does or believes.

Mr. Huang asks for clarification.

 D. Now, with a partner, practice the interview using correct information about yourself.

Reading and Writing Test Practice

 A. Answer the questions with a word from the vocabulary box. Then practice reading the questions and answers with a partner.

1. Who was the first President of the United States?

   _____.

2. Where does the President live? _____

   _____.

3. When is Presidents' Day? _____.

   _____.

 B. With a partner, take turns reading the questions below to each other and writing the answers. The answers can be found on page 148.

Example:

For the reading test, the interviewer asks you to read a question like this one:

When do we vote for President?

For the writing test, the interviewer reads a sentence like this one and asks you to write it:

We vote for President in November.

1. Who lives in the White House?

   _____.

2. Who is the Father of Our Country?

   _____.

3. Who was the second President?

   _____.

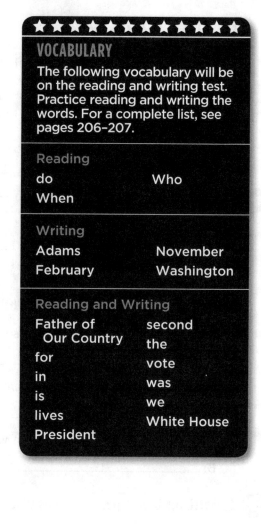

★★★★★★★★★★★★★★

VOCABULARY

The following vocabulary will be on the reading and writing test. Practice reading and writing the words. For a complete list, see pages 206–207.

Reading

do	Who
When	

Writing

Adams	November
February	Washington

Reading and Writing

Father of Our Country	second
for	the
in	vote
is	was
lives	we
President	White House

Grammar Review: *Can, Should, Had Better, Must,* and *Have to/Has to*

Sometimes, we use "helping verbs" to express our ideas. *Can, should, had better, must,* and *have/has to* are some of these helping verbs. For example:

Can means he or she has the ability to do this: he or she *is able* to do this.

> The President **can** sign bills to become laws.

Should and *had better* mean that this is good advice. If the President is smart, he or she will do these things.

> The President **should** be a good citizen.
> The President **had better** make good decisions.

Must and *have to* mean that something is necessary or required.

> The President **must** be at least 35 years old.
> The President **has to** be a U.S.-born citizen.

When we use these helping verbs in sentences, they are followed by the simple form of a verb. For example:

> We should **vote** in every election.
> We must **file** an income tax return every year.
> We have to **pay** a fee with our N-400.

A. Fill in the blanks with *can, should, had better, must,* or *have/has to*. The first one is done for you.

1. People in the United States _____ can _____ say what they want.

2. Citizens _____ be 18 years old to vote.

3. A person who wants to become President _____ be a good leader.

4. Citizens _____ vote for the best candidate for President.

5. A candidate for President _____ be a U.S.-born citizen.

B. Work with a partner to answer these questions. For Questions 1 and 2, check each other's answers. For Questions 3 and 4, use complete sentences, and be sure that you use the correct form of the verb.

1. Print your full name here: _____

2. Sign your full name here: _____

3. Name one thing you can do in the United States because of the Bill of Rights.

_____

4. Name one thing you must not do if you want to become a naturalized U.S. citizen.

_____

Civic Engagement
VOTING IN YOUR COMMUNITY

One of the benefits of citizenship is the right to vote. Find out the following information about voting in your community.

A. Name of your city or town: _____

B. List four places you could find out about voting in your city or town.

1. _____   2. _____

3. _____   4. _____

C. Answer the following questions about voting in your city or town.

1. I can register to vote at _____.

2. My voting place is at _____.

3. Some communities are divided into *precincts*. My precinct number is: _____.

4. When I vote, I must bring _____.

	True	False
5. When I move, I have to register to vote again.	☐	☐
6. If I change my name, I don't have to register to vote again.	☐	☐
7. If I go on vacation during voting time, I can vote early.	☐	☐
8. If I have filled out the N-400, I can vote.	☐	☐

D. Find two organizations that provide information about local politics and laws.

Example:

The League of Women Voters

1. _____
   _____

2. _____
   _____

When you register to vote, you must bring proof of U.S. citizenship.

8 The Legislative Branch of Government

Interview Focus:
Asking for a
Definition

Nancy Pelosi is sworn in as the first female Speaker of the House in 2007.

Connect to the Topic

ALBIO SIRES was born in 1951 in Bejucal, Cuba. With the help of family members in the United States, Sires and his family fled pre-Communist Cuba and came to the United States in 1962. He received degrees from St. Peter's College in New Jersey and from Middlebury College in Vermont. He was elected to the House of Representatives in 2006. He is a Democrat. Before that, he worked as a businessperson, a teacher, and a politician. He was the first Hispanic to serve as New Jersey Speaker of the General Assembly, a high-ranking political role.

Getting into the Reading

Answer the questions.

1. What does the legislative branch of government do?

2. What are members of Congress called?

3. What is the name of the building where they work?

4. What are the names of your senators and representatives in Congress?

5. Albio Sires, the subject of the *Connect to the Topic* profile above, is an immigrant from Cuba who became a member of the United States Congress. Do you think it is important for immigrants to hold government positions? Why or why not?

The Legislative Branch

The legislative branch of the U.S. government spends most of its time passing legislation, or making federal laws. It also has the power to declare war.

The legislative branch of the federal government is the Congress of the United States. Congress has two parts, or houses. One house is called the House of Representatives, and the other is called the Senate. Both the houses meet in the Capitol Building in Washington, D.C.

There are 100 members of the Senate. Each of the 50 states has two representatives called senators, so each state has equal power in the Senate. Senators are elected by the people of their state and represent the whole state. They are elected for a six-year term. There is no limit to the number of times a senator can be reelected. The Vice President is the leader of the Senate.

WORDS TO KNOW

amend
committee
debate
declare
defeated
district
legislation
majority
minority
pass
population
two-thirds

There are 435 voting members of the House of Representatives. In addition, there are five nonvoting members: representatives from Washington, D.C., and the U.S. territories of American Samoa, Guam, Puerto Rico, and the U.S. Virgin islands. The population of a state determines the number of representatives for that state. Every state has at least one representative; some states have more than 25. Each representative is elected by the people who live in a district (an area) of his or her state and represents the people of that district. Representatives serve a two-year term. There is no limit to the number of times a representative can be reelected.

The leader of the House of Representatives is called the Speaker of the House. The Speaker, who is elected by the House members, becomes the President of the United States if both the President and the Vice President can no longer serve.

Your senators and representatives have offices in your state and in Washington, D.C. Staff members in these offices can help you with federal law issues, such as immigration, social security benefits, income tax, and public housing.

A ceremony in the House of Representatives Chamber.

How a Bill Becomes a Law

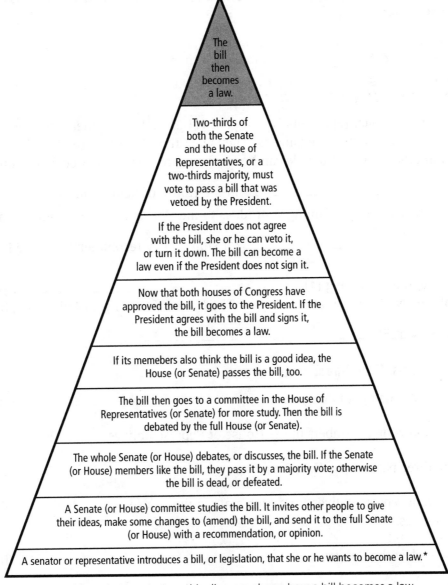

The bill then becomes a law.

Two-thirds of both the Senate and the House of Representatives, or a two-thirds majority, must vote to pass a bill that was vetoed by the President.

If the President does not agree with the bill, she or he can veto it, or turn it down. The bill can become a law even if the President does not sign it.

Now that both houses of Congress have approved the bill, it goes to the President. If the President agrees with the bill and signs it, the bill becomes a law.

If its memebers also think the bill is a good idea, the House (or Senate) passes the bill, too.

The bill then goes to a committee in the House of Representatives (or Senate) for more study. Then the bill is debated by the full House (or Senate).

The whole Senate (or House) debates, or discusses, the bill. If the Senate (or House) members like the bill, they pass it by a majority vote; otherwise the bill is dead, or defeated.

A Senate (or House) committee studies the bill. It invites other people to give their ideas, make some changes to (amend) the bill, and send it to the full Senate (or House) with a recommendation, or opinion.

A senator or representative introduces a bill, or legislation, that she or he wants to become a law.*

Viewed from bottom to top, this diagram shows how a bill becomes a law.

IRCA: A Federal Law

In 1986, a law that affected many immigrants was passed by Congress and signed by the President. It is the Immigration Reform and Control Act of 1986 (IRCA). Among many other changes, IRCA granted amnesty, or legalization, to many immigrants who did not have legal status.

IRCA also requires employers to check that their workers have the right papers to work in the United States legally. Employers can be fined for hiring people who do not have legal status. Many people dislike the effects of this law, so in 2007, a new immigration reform act was introduced in the Senate—The Comprehensive Immigration Reform Act. As of 2008, it had not yet been passed.

Getting Information from the Reading

A. Use the words in the box to fill in each blank below. You might not use all of the words in the box. The first one is done for you.

> amend   debate   legislation   minority
>
> committee   ~~district~~   majority

You are a congressional representative. In your (1) *district* , there are many immigrants who want to become citizens. They want the USCIS to hire more naturalization officers so that people can become citizens faster. You decide to introduce

(2) _____ in the House of Representatives.

You give a great speech explaining your ideas to the House, and the bill goes to a

(3) _____ for study. They recommend that the House pass the bill.

In the House, there is a long (4) _____ about your bill. Some people really like it, but others do not. The House amends your bill a little, but it

finally passes by a (5) _____ .

B. Read the sentences. Circle *True* or *False*.

1. There are 100 senators in Congress.	True	False
2. There are 400 voting members of the House of Representatives.	True	False
3. There are three parts of the U.S. Congress.	True	False
4. There are four representatives from each state in the House of Representatives.	True	False
5. The people elect the Congress.	True	False
6. Congress meets in the Capitol Building.	True	False
7. A representative's term is for four years.	True	False
8. The leader of the House of Representatives is called the Speaker of the House.	True	False
9. We elect a United States Representative to serve for eight years.	True	False

The 100 History and Government Questions

A. Look at the clues below. Write the letter on the line.

1. _____ It makes federal laws.

2. _____ The number of senators for each state

3. _____ The number of years for which we elect senators

4. _____ This person becomes President if the President and Vice President can no longer serve.

5. _____ This and the House of Representatives make up the legislative branch of government.

> a. two
>
> b. six
>
> c. the Senate
>
> d. the Speaker of the House
>
> e. the legislative branch

 B. 100 Questions Practice. These questions may be asked as part of the U.S. history and government test. Ask and answer the questions with a partner. Talk about the answers. There may be more than one correct answer. All 100 questions can be found on page 154. Go to the Quizzes menu of the DVD for more 100 Questions practice.

> 1. Name <u>one</u> branch or part of the government.
> 2. What are the <u>two</u> parts of the U.S. Congress?
> 3. How many U.S. senators are there?
> 4. We elect a U.S. senator for how many years?
> 5. Who is <u>one</u> of your state's U.S. senators now?
> 6. The House of Representatives has how many voting members?
> 7. Why do some states have more representatives than other states?
> 8. What is the name of the Speaker of the House of Representatives now?
> 9. If both the President and the Vice President can no longer serve, who becomes President?
> 10. Who makes federal laws?
> 11. Name your U.S. representative.
> 12. Who does a U.S. senator represent?
> 13. We elect a U.S representative for how many years?

The U.S. Senate Chamber

The N-400 Application: Passive Voice and Experience Questions: 1

Many questions on the N-400 application use the passive voice. These questions ask specific information about your life experience. Review the form of the passive and active voices.

Active Form	Subject	Verb	Object
	The police	arrested	the man.
Passive Form	Subject	*be* + past participle	Object
	The man	was arrested	by the police.

Active	Passive	Example	Explanation
arrest cite detain	be arrested be cited be detained	**Have** you **ever been arrested, cited,** or **detained?**	This question asks if anyone has ever arrested you, cited you (given you a ticket), or detained (held) you for doing something illegal.
charge	be charged	**Have** you ever **been charged with** committing any crime or offense?	This question asks if anyone has ever charged, or formally accused, you of doing something illegal.
convict	be convicted	**Have** you ever **been convicted of** a crime or offense?	This question asks if anyone has ever found you guilty of doing something illegal.
place in	be placed in	**Have** you ever **been placed** in a rehabilitative program?	This question asks if anyone has ever put you in a rehabilitative program.

A. Answer the questions. Use the chart above. The first one is done for you.

1. Have you ever been arrested, cited, or detained?

   Yes. I was arrested for driving without a driver's license.

2. Have you ever been charged with committing any crime or offense?

   _____

3. Have you ever been convicted of a crime or offense?

   _____

4. Have you ever been placed in a rehabilitative program?

   _____

B. Your Turn. Ask and answer the questions above with a partner.

The N-400 Application: Part 10D (Questions 15–24)

The USCIS wants to be sure that people applying for U.S. citizenship are of **good moral character.** You do not have good moral character if you did any of the following:

☐ lied to the USCIS when you got your permanent residence

☐ did not file federal tax returns every year as a permanent resident

☐ have been involved in illegal activity or were a member of the Communist or Nazi Party

☐ got married just to get your permanent residence

☐ did not register with the Selective Service (for men born after 1960 who lived in the United States between the ages of 18 and 25)

See the Legal Overview on page 182 for more information.

> **TIP:** It is important for you to answer questions honestly. The USCIS will check your information to see if you are being honest. If you answer "yes" to any of these questions, you should get legal advice. To make sure you understand the questions, read the Explanations below.

D. Good Moral Character.

15. Have you **ever** committed a crime or offense for which you were **not** arrested? ☐ Yes ☐ No

▶ **EXPLANATION** Did you ever commit a crime and **not** get arrested for it?

---

16. Have you **ever** been arrested, cited or detained by any law enforcement officer (including USCIS or former INS and military officers) for any reason? ☐ Yes ☐ No

▶ **EXPLANATION** *Cited* means given a written ticket by the police. *Detained* means that a police officer or immigration officer ordered a person held in a jail or detention facility but did not place that person under arrest. There are many reasons that a police officer or immigration officer could detain a person. Most often, immigration officers detain people who have broken immigration laws. Because most immigration laws are "civil" violations and not "criminal," people are "detained," not "arrested." The police can also detain a person for questioning about a crime, or while they investigate a crime. The process of being detained, or *detention,* is a formal process; it does not refer to a brief police stop or a border inspection.

---

17. Have you **ever** been charged with committing any crime or offense? ☐ Yes ☐ No

▶ **EXPLANATION** Were you arrested and held by the police and formally accused of committing a crime?

---

18. Have you **ever** been convicted of a crime or offense? ☐ Yes ☐ No

▶ **EXPLANATION** Were you convicted of a crime by a judge or jury even if it was later erased from your record?

19. Have you **ever** been placed in an alternative sentencing or a rehabilitative program (for example: diversion, deferred prosecution, withheld adjudication, deferred adjudication)? ☐ Yes ☐ No

▶ **EXPLANATION** Were you ever told by a judge or district attorney to participate in a program to reform your criminal behavior, such as unpaid community service, drug or alcohol abuse treatment, or rehabilitation of some other kind? This may also include paying a fine or staying at home under "house arrest."

20. Have you **ever** received a suspended sentence, been placed on probation, or been paroled? ☐ Yes ☐ No

▶ **EXPLANATION** A *suspended sentence* is when the judge does not make you go to jail or prison unless you commit another crime during a period of time set by the judge. A suspended sentence is like probation. *Probation* is when you are allowed to go home from jail if you follow certain rules. These may include staying away from certain people and places or not taking any illegal drugs or abusing alcohol.

21. Have you **ever** been in jail or prison? ☐ Yes ☐ No

▶ **EXPLANATION** *Jail* is generally where you go before the judge rules on your case, or if you are only serving a short sentence after you are convicted of a crime. *Prison* is for people who have been convicted or found guilty of a crime and are serving a longer sentence.

22. Have you **ever:**

a. Been a habitual drunkard? ☐ Yes ☐ No

b. Been a prostitute, or procured anyone for prostitution? ☐ Yes ☐ No

c. Sold or smuggled controlled substances, illegal drugs, or narcotics? ☐ Yes ☐ No

d. Been married to more than one person at the same time? ☐ Yes ☐ No

e. Helped anyone enter or try to enter the United States illegally? ☐ Yes ☐ No

f. Gambled illegally or received income from illegal gambling? ☐ Yes ☐ No

g. Failed to support your dependents or to pay alimony? ☐ Yes ☐ No

▶ **EXPLANATION**

a. Were you ever drunk every day?

b. Did you ever engage in sex for pay?

c. Did you ever sell narcotic drugs or marijuana?

d. Were you ever married to more than one person at a time?

e. Did you ever help someone enter the United States illegally?

f. Did you ever get money illegally from gambling?

g. Did you ever refuse to pay child support?

23. Have you **ever** given false or misleading information to any U.S. government official while applying for any immigration benefit or to prevent deportation, exclusion, or removal? ☐ Yes ☐ No

▶ **EXPLANATION** Did you ever lie about anything (for example, about your marriage or another family relationship) to get a visa to come to the United States, to extend your stay in the United States, to get your "green card," or to avoid being removed from the United States?

24. Have you **ever** lied to any U.S. government official to gain entry or admission into the United States? ☐ Yes ☐ No

▶ **EXPLANATION** Did you ever lie at an American consulate or embassy to get a visa to the United States, or at an airport or border to get into the United States, whether as a visitor or as an immigrant?

The USCIS Interview

Interview Skill: Asking for a Definition

You may not understand every question the USCIS interviewer asks you. Here are some ways you can ask for the definition of a word or phrase. Practice saying these expressions:

Question: Do you have multiple spouses?

Possible Responses: I'm sorry. What does **multiple** mean?
Does **multiple** mean the same as **more than one?**
Multiple? I forget what that means.
Multiple. Do you mean **more than one?**

 Go to the Interview Skills menu of the DVD to view examples of this skill.

A. Complete the conversations. Write one of the phrases above on the lines below. Ask for the meaning of the words in boldface.

1. **A:** When we talk about good moral character, can we assume you are a person of this **caliber?**

    B: _____

2. **A:** Did you ever commit a **terrorist** act?

    B: _____

3. **A:** Is **polygamy** something you practice?

    B: _____

> **TIP:** When you ask the interviewer the meaning of something, he or she may repeat the question in a different way.

 B. Watch the DVD segments for this chapter. You can find them on the Chapters menu of the DVD.

C. The interview segment with Mr. Huang is included below. Practice it with a partner.

Interviewer: Have you ever committed a crime or offense for which you were *not* arrested?
Mr. Huang: Does *offense* mean something I do to offend someone?
Interviewer: Not quite. An offense is something illegal or against the law.
Mr. Huang: Oh, I understand. No.
Interviewer: And have you ever gambled illegally or received income from illegal gambling?
Mr. Huang: No.
Interviewer: And have you ever failed to support your dependents or failed to pay alimony?
Mr. Huang: Alimony? I forget what that means.
Interviewer: Alimony is money you give to your ex-wife each month after a divorce.
Mr. Huang: Oh. After the Chinese divorce, the judge no make ... *did not* make me to pay the alimony.

Mr. Huang asks the interviewer to define a word he doesn't understand.

D. Now, with a partner, practice the interview using correct information about yourself. Ask the interviewer the meaning of a word in different ways.

Reading and Writing Test Practice

A. Match the words and phrases on the left with the words and phrases on the right. Write the correct letter on the line.

1. _____ Congress

2. _____ senators

3. _____ laws

4. _____ the people

5. _____ Washington, D.C.

6. _____ states

a. Two senators represent each of these.

b. The Senate and the House of Representatives

c. the executive branch is in this city

d. They elect the members of Congress.

e. Congress makes these.

f. There are 100 of these in Congress.

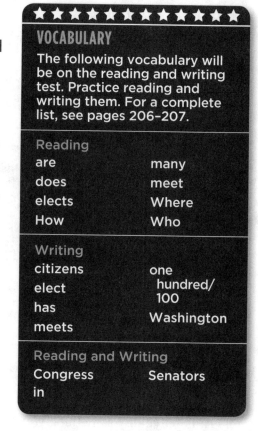

VOCABULARY

The following vocabulary will be on the reading and writing test. Practice reading and writing them. For a complete list, see pages 206–207.

Reading

are	many
does	meet
elects	Where
How	Who

Writing

citizens	one hundred/100
elect	
has	Washington
meets	

Reading and Writing

Congress	Senators
in	

B. With a partner, take turns reading the questions to each other and writing the answers. The answers can be found on page 149.

Example:

For the reading test, the interviewer asks you to read a question like this one:

How many U.S. senators does a state have?

For the writing test, the interviewer reads a sentence like this one and asks you to write it:

A state has two senators.

1. How many senators are in Congress?

_____

2. Who elects Congress?

_____

3. Where does Congress meet?

_____

Grammar Review: Articles

Articles are small words, such as *a, an,* and *the.* When we speak, we do not always say them clearly. This sometimes makes listening for them (and dictations) difficult.

Here are some general rules for article use:

A and *an* are used only before singular nouns and only when talking about something in general. Use *a* before words beginning with a consonant sound. For example:

> **A** President should be a great leader.

Use *an* before words beginning with a vowel sound. For example:

> **An** amendment is a change in the Constitution

The is used when talking about a specific thing. For example:

> **The** President of the United States must be at least 35 years old.
> **The** Thirteenth Amendment ended slavery in **the** United States.

Sometimes no article is used. This happens when we talk about something (a noun) that cannot be counted or the plural of something in general. For example:

> People can write to their senators and representatives.
> Presidents should be smart.

Practice with articles. Write *a, an, the,* or nothing in the blanks. The first one is done for you.

1. The President lives in _____*the*_____ White House.

2. The President is _____ elected official.

3. _____ representatives can be reelected many times.

4. _____ responsibilities of a President are many.

5. The Vice President serves _____ four-year term of office.

6. All people living in _____ United States are protected by _____ Bill of Rights

7. Washington, D.C., is _____ capital of _____ country.

8. _____ President's wife is called _____ First Lady.

9. Confidence is _____ important quality for a President to have.

10. Being a U.S.-born citizen is _____ requirement for the U.S. presidency.

Civic Engagement:

YOUR U.S. REPRESENTATIVE AND SENATORS

Secretary of State Hillary Clinton

Find out about your district's U.S. Representative in Congress and one of the U.S. Senators in your state.

A. What are some ways you could find out information about your state's district and its representative or senator?

Example:

On the Internet visit the following web sites:
http://www.house.gov/
and http://www.senate.gov/.

_____   _____

_____   _____

B. Write the information you find. Use one of the sources you listed above to help you.

Your state: _____

Your district in your state: _____

One of your state's U.S. senators: _____

The U.S. representative for your district: _____

C. Write three facts about your U.S. representative or U.S. senator.

1. _____

2. _____

3. _____

D. Talk about what you find out with a partner.

Congress in session

The Judicial Branch of Government

The U.S. Supreme Court is made up of nine justices, or judges. The Chief Justice is John Roberts.

Connect to the Topic

In 2003, SAMUEL DER-YEGHIAYAN was confirmed as a United States federal judge for the Northern District of Illinois. He is the first Armenian immigrant to serve as a federal judge in the United States. He was 19 years old when he immigrated to the United States. Der-Yeghiayan was born in Aleppo, Syria, in 1952 and studied law in Concord, New Hampshire. President Bill Clinton appointed him an immigration judge for the Department of Justice in 2000, and President George W. Bush nominated him for his current position in 2003.

Getting into the Reading

Answer the questions.

1. What is a judge? What does a judge do?

2. What are important qualities of a good judge?

3. Have you ever been to court in the United States? If so, what was it like?

4. What do you know about the U.S. Supreme Court?

5. Samuel Der-Yeghiayan, the subject of the *Connect to the Topic* profile above, is an Armenian immigrant. Do you know of any immigrants from your native country who hold a government position?

The Judicial Branch

The judicial branch of government is a system of courts that hears cases and interprets, or explains, the laws. There are courts at the local, state, and federal levels. Each level is responsible for a different kind of case. For example, federal courts hear cases involving federal laws. State courts hear all other cases.

The highest court in the United States is the U.S. Supreme Court. The Supreme Court decides whether the Constitution permits certain laws. All other courts must follow the decisions of the U.S. Supreme Court. If a person loses a case in a lower federal court, he or she can appeal to, or ask, a higher-level federal court to hear the case. In the end, a case may go to the Supreme Court for a final decision.

There are nine justices on the Supreme Court. They are nominated by the President and must be approved by the Senate. Supreme Court Justices are appointed to their jobs for life, or until they decide to retire. In 1981, Sandra Day O' Connor became the first female Supreme Court Justice. The leader of the Supreme Court is called the Chief Justice of the Supreme Court.

★ ★ ★ ★ ★ ★ ★
WORDS TO KNOW
appealed
case
guilty
hear
interpret
judge
judicial
punishable by
rights
ruled
systems

The Supreme Court building in Washington, D.C.

Famous Supreme Court Cases

Brown v. the Board of Education

In 1954, one of the most famous cases in the history of the Supreme Court was heard, *Brown v. the Board of Education of Topeka, Kansas.* In this case, the Supreme Court ruled that segregation, or the separation of blacks and whites, in public schools was illegal. Many historians say that this ruling was the event that started the civil rights movement, which lasted through the 1950s and 60s.

Gideon v. Wainwright

Gideon v. Wainwright **was an important Supreme Court case.** Clarence Gideon was arrested for breaking into a building in 1961. He was poor, so he could not afford a lawyer. He wanted the court to give him one for free, but the judge said he had to pay because the crime was not punishable by death. Gideon had to be his own lawyer, but he did not do very well at the trial. The jury found him guilty.

Gideon believed that anyone who could be sentenced to at least one year in jail should have a lawyer, even if he or she could not afford to pay for one. While he was in jail, Gideon asked the Supreme Court to hear his case. In 1963, the Supreme Court agreed with Gideon. It said the Constitution guaranteed poor people the right to have a free lawyer in criminal cases.

Miranda v. Arizona

Another very important Supreme Court case was *Miranda v. Arizona.* Ernesto Miranda was arrested in Arizona for the rape of an 18-year-old girl. Police officers asked Miranda many questions, and he answered them without his lawyer there to help him. He then signed a paper that said he was guilty. At the trial, the jury decided he should be in prison for 20 to 30 years.

Miranda appealed his case to the Supreme Court. He believed the Constitution guaranteed him the right to be told he could have a lawyer present before the police asked him questions. The police officers had not told him that. In 1963, the Supreme Court ruled in favor of Miranda.

Now, because of these two cases, police officers must read people their rights when they are arrested for a criminal act. Below are the "Miranda Rights."

Miranda Rights
1. You have the right to be silent.
2. Anything you say can and will be used against you in court.
3. You have the right to talk to a lawyer before you answer questions.
4. You have the right to have a lawyer with you while you answer questions.
5. If you cannot afford a lawyer, you can have one for free.

A police officer reads someone his Miranda Rights

Getting Information from the Reading

A. Read the following passage. Use the words in the box to fill in each blank. The first one is done for you.

appealed	constitutional	law	ruled
~~case~~	interpreted	people	states

In 1982, the Supreme Court heard *Plyler v. Doe*. This (1) ____case____ was about a law

passed in the state of Texas. The (2) _____ said that children of illegal aliens, or the

undocumented, could not go to public school. The Supreme Court (3) _____

the Constitution as saying that (4) _____ cannot make laws to stop undocumented

children from going to public schools. The court (5) _____
that the Texas law was not constitutional.

In November 1994, (6) _____ in California voted for Proposition 187. One part of
this law says that children who are undocumented cannot go to public schools in California.
The courts have stopped the state of California from putting this part of Proposition 187 into

effect because the case of *Plyler v. Doe* says this is not (7) _____.

The state of California (8) _____ this decision to the Court of Appeals.
However, after years of litigation, on July 29, 1999, California decided to drop the appeal.

B. Read each sentence. Circle *True* or *False*.

1.	The judicial branch of the government is the President, Vice President, and cabinet.	True	False
2.	The Supreme Court is the highest court in the United States.	True	False
3.	The are 435 members of the Supreme Court.	True	False
4.	Supreme Court justices are appointed for life.	True	False
5.	The leader of the U.S. Supreme Court is called the Chief Justice.	True	False
6.	There are ten justices on the Supreme Court.	True	False
7.	Supreme Court Justices are nominated by the President.	True	False
8.	The judicial branch of government interprets, or explains, the laws.	True	False

The 100 History and Government Questions

A. Choose the correct word or phrase to complete the statements. Circle the correct answer.

1. The _____ Court is the highest court in the land.
   a. Chief   b. Supreme   c. Judicial

2. There are nine _____ on the Supreme Court.
   a. senators   b. justices   c. Chief Justices

3. The judicial branch _____.
   a. hears cases and   b. makes laws and   c. appeals to higher courts
      interprets laws   enforces them

4. The _____ is the leader of the Supreme Court.
   a. President   b. Speaker of the House   c. Chief Justice

5. The _____ branch is one branch, or part, of the government.
   a. constitutional   b. judicial   c. supreme

B. 100 Questions Practice. These questions may be asked as part of the U.S. history and government test. Talk about the answers with a partner. All of the 100 questions can be found on page 154. Go to the Quizzes menu of the DVD for more 100 Questions practice.

1. What does the judicial branch do?
2. What is the highest court in the United States?
3. How many justices are on the Supreme Court?
4. Who is the Chief Justice of the United States now?
5. Name one branch or part of the government.

C. Word Search. Find the words in the box in the puzzle below.

```
R  E  D  J  J  L  C  A  B  I  N  E  T  W
E  K  L  L  J  U  H  G  V  W  E  K  W  R
P  U  E  Y  A  C  D  E  A  C  H  D  H  M
U  G  G  X  K  I  E  I  I  K  H  G  I  K
B  W  I  F  E  O  R  T  C  D  V  K  T  L
L  H  S  F  C  C  R  I  Q  I  M  J  E  T
I  S  L  C  P  K  U  W  E  M  A  P  H  I
C  K  A  P  J  U  S  T  I  C  E  L  O  S
A  S  T  W  K  Q  F  X  I  A  J  I  U  C
N  Y  I  I  F  J  F  Y  O  V  J  I  S  P
V  E  V  K  G  K  U  G  C  H  E  W  E  P
T  P  E  P  R  E  S  I  D  E  N  T  O  R
R  C  S  U  P  R  E  M  E  C  O  U  R  T
V  W  P  A  D  E  M  O  C  R  A  T  V  D
```

| judicial |
| legislative |
| executive |
| White House |
| President |
| Cabinet |
| Supreme Court |
| justice |
| Democrat |
| Republican |

The N-400 Application: Passive Voice and Experience Questions: 2

You learned on page 90 that many questions on the N-400 application use the passive voice. These questions ask specific information about your life experience. Passive-voice questions ask if something happened to you. Active-voice questions ask if *you* did something. Here are more examples of this form:

		Example	Explanation
Passive	be removed be excluded be deported	Have you ever **been removed, excluded,** or **deported** from the U.S.?	This question asks if anyone has ever moved you from the United States.
	be ordered to	Have you ever **been ordered to** be removed, excluded, or deported from the U.S.?	This question asks if anyone has ever formally told you to leave the United States.
Active	apply for	Have you ever **applied for** relief from removal?	This question asks if you have ever asked the USCIS to let you stay in the United States.
	serve	Have you ever **served** in the U.S. Armed Forces?	This question asks if you were ever in the United States military.
	leave	Have you ever **left** the U.S. to avoid being drafted?	This question asks if you ever left the United States so that you wouldn't have to serve in its military.

A. Answer the questions. Use the chart above. The first one is done for you.

1. Have you ever been deported from the United States?

   Yes. I was arrested for driving without a driver's license.

2. Have you ever applied for relief from a draft?

   _____

3. Have you ever served in the military of any country?

   _____

4. Have you ever been ordered to leave the United States?

   _____

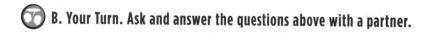 **B. Your Turn. Ask and answer the questions above with a partner.**

The N-400 Application: Part 10E, F, and G

E. Removal, Exclusion and Deportation Proceedings.

25. Are removal, exclusion, rescission, or deportation proceedings pending against you? ☐ Yes ☐ No

---

▶ **EXPLANATION Removal, exclusion, and deportation all mean basically the same thing.** (*Removal* is a newer word used by the government. *Exclusion* and *deportation* are older words.) *Rescission* means that the federal government is attempting to *rescind*, or revoke or take back, someone's permanent resident status. This is a much rarer process than a removal proceeding. Has any federal officer or federal judge told you that the United States government is currently trying to make you leave the country? This only applies if it comes from the **Federal** government—not from a local police officer or court.

---

26. Have you **ever** been removed, excluded, or deported from the United States? ☐ Yes ☐ No

---

▶ **EXPLANATION** Again, these words mean basically the same thing. Has any officer or judge from the U.S. government issued an order that says that you cannot enter the United States, or that you must leave the United States? This is not the same as a simple refusal of entry at an airport or land border. There must have been an official document with the words "Removal," "Deportation," or "Exclusion." Were you ever ordered to leave the United States and then came back? Sometimes people are asked to leave by a system called *Voluntary Departure*. This is different from deportation.

---

27. Have you **ever** been ordered to be removed, excluded, or deported from the United States? ☐ Yes ☐ No

---

▶ **EXPLANATION** This question means the same thing as Number 26. Did an officer or court ever give you paperwork that said that you were ordered to be removed (or excluded or deported)?

---

28. Have you **ever** applied for any kind of relief from removal, exclusion, or deportation? ☐ Yes ☐ No

---

▶ **EXPLANATION** Did you ever ask the USCIS to allow you to stay in the United States before you were ordered to be removed, or after an order was issued, but before you left the country? *Relief* is a legal remedy, which may allow you to remain in the United States when you are under removal proceedings. You may have asked to stay because you had strong family relationships, you had a good job, or for something else.

F. Military Service.

29. Have you **ever** served in the U.S. Armed Forces? ☐ Yes ☐ No

▶ **EXPLANATION** Were you ever in the United States Army, Navy, Air Force, or Marines?

30. Have you **ever** left the United States to avoid being drafted into the U.S. Armed Forces? ☐ Yes ☐ No

▶ **EXPLANATION** Did you ever leave the United States because you did not want to be drafted? Once someone is *drafted*, he is forced to join the military whether he wants to or not. The United States has not used the draft since 1973.

31. Have you **ever** applied for any kind of exemption from military service in the U.S. Armed Forces? ☐ Yes ☐ No

▶ **EXPLANATION** Did you ever request to **NOT** be drafted for some reason? If you tried to avoid being drafted into the U.S. Army for reasons such as being a conscientious objector, a student, or the only family support, this may be a bar to becoming a U.S. citizen. A conscientious objector is someone who refuses to join the military because of personal beliefs.

32. Have you **ever** deserted from the U.S. Armed Forces? ☐ Yes ☐ No

▶ **EXPLANATION** Did you ever leave the Army without permission? *Desert* is a verb that means "to leave without permission." When *desert* is a noun, it means "a vast, dry area of land" such as the Mojave Desert.

G. Selective Service Registration.

33. Are you a male who lived in the United States at any time between your 18th and 26th birthdays in any status except as a lawful nonimmigrant? ☐ Yes ☐ No

▶ **EXPLANATION** This question only applies to men who lived in the United States between age 18 and age 25. It does not apply to men who were here at that age and were here legally as visitors. For example, if you were here on a student, tourist, or working visa, this doesn't apply to you. It does apply to men who were in the United States illegally. If you did not register for the draft, you should try to register. The USCIS wants to know if you intentionally tried to avoid registering. You may need to explain this to the examiner at your interview. If you think you registered but do not have any proof of registration, you should get proof before a decision is made on your application.

There are two ways to contact the Selective Service regarding your registration. If you want to get proof of your registration, or obtain your selective service number, you can call (847) 688-6888, or visit the Web site at http://www.sss.gov. If you are not registered and would like to do so, you can register online at http://www.sss.gov or send your registration by mail to Selective Service System, Registration Information Office, P.O. Box 94638, Palatine, IL 60094-4638. For more information you can also visit the USCIS Web site, http://www.uscis.gov.

The USCIS Interview

Interview Skill: Stalling for Time and Expressing Uncertainty

When the USCIS interviewer asks you a question, you may need time to think about your answer. While you think, you can show you need more time, or **stall for time,** by using one of the phrases in the chart below.

You also might not be sure of or remember the answer to a question. You can let the interviewer know this by **expressing uncertainty.**

Stalling for Time	Expressing Uncertainty
Um, let me see.	I don't think so.
Hmm, let me think about that.	I think so.
Uh, give me a minute, please.	I'm not sure.
Let me think.	Maybe.

 Go to the Interview Skills menu of the DVD to view examples of this skill.

TIP: If you don't speak for five seconds after the interviewer asks you a question, he or she will think you don't know the answer. If you need time to think, say so.

A. Complete the conversations. First stall for time. Then express uncertainty. Write phrases from the chart above on the lines. The first one is done for you.

1. **A:** Did you register for the Selective Service?

    B: *Um, let me see.   I think so.*

2. **A:** Do you know your Selective Service number?

    B: _____

3. **A:** Have you ever been deported by immigration?

    B: _____

 B. Watch the DVD segments for this chapter. You can find them on the Chapters menu of the DVD.

 C. Part of the interview segment with Mr. Dada is included below. Practice it with a partner.

Interviewer: You're right about that, Mr. Dada. Now, are there removal, exclusion, rescission, or deportation proceedings pending against you?

Mr. Dada:　I'm not sure.

Interviewer: Why not?

Mr. Dada:　Because I don't know what reci ... means.

Interviewer: Oh, rescission. That means revoking or canceling your legal permanent resident status.

Mr. Dada:　Now I understand. No, there is no proceedings.

Interviewer: And have you ever left this country to avoid being drafted in the U.S. Armed Forces?

Mr. Dada:　I don't believe so. I left this country two ... no, three times. I told you that. But it was never to escape being put into the army.

D. Now, with a partner, practice the interview with correct information about yourself. Use different phrases to stall for time and express uncertainty.

Reading and Writing Test Practice

A. Complete the sentences with a word from the vocabulary box. You will not use all the words.

1. "You have the _____ to remain silent."

2. There is only one Supreme Court in the

   _____.

3. The justices of the Supreme Court are nominated

   by the _____.

4. The Supreme Court _____ in the Supreme Court Building in Washington, D.C.

5. Washington, D.C., is the _____ of the United States.

B. With a partner, take turns reading the questions to each other and writing the answers. The answers can be found on page 150.

Example:

The interviewer asks you to read this question:
What is the capital of the United States?

The interviewer says this sentence and asks you to write it:
The capital of the United States is Washington, D.C.

1. What is the capital of the United States?

   _____

2. What city was the first capital of the United States?

   _____

3. What was the first state?

   _____

★ ★ ★ ★ ★ ★ ★ ★ ★ ★ ★ ★ ★ ★

VOCABULARY

The following vocabulary will be on the reading and writing test. For a complete list, see pages 206–207.

Reading
city
What

Writing
Delaware
meets
New York City
President
right
Washington, D.C.

Reading and Writing
capital
first
is
of
of
state
the
the
United States
was

Grammar Review: *There is (not) / There are (not)*

Often, when we want to describe something, we use the words *there is* or *there are*.
For example:

> **There are** thirteen stripes on the American flag.
> **There is** one star on the flag for every state.

You have to decide whether to use *is* or *are*. Sometimes this is confusing in sentences with many extra words. These extra words are not important, but you have to know whether the subject of the sentences is singular (one) or plural (more than one). For example:

Singular:	**There is** one young senator from Florida who agrees.
Plural:	**There are** 50 white stars on the flag.

Singular:	**There isn't** a line at the voting booth.
Plural:	**There aren't** any chairs in the meeting room.

A. Write *is* or *are* in each of the sentences. The first one is done for you.

1. There _____*are*_____ 27 amendments to the Constitution.

2. There _____ ten amendments to the Bill of Rights.

3. There _____ not a limit for how many years a Supreme Court justice can serve.

4. There _____ three branches of the U.S. government.

5. There _____ one Chief Justice.

6. There _____ 435 members of the House of Representatives.

7. There _____ a presidential election every four years.

8. There _____ not any courts above the Supreme Court.

9. There _____ two senators from each state.

10. There _____ many kinds of courts.

11. There _____ nine justices on the U.S. Supreme Court.

12. There _____ not more than one U.S. Supreme Court.

Civic Engagement:
YOUR COMMUNITY'S COURT SYSTEM

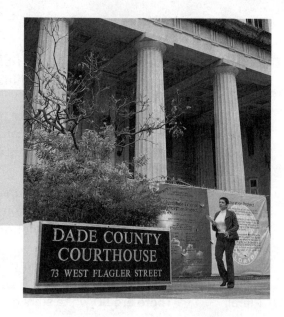

A. Do a search on the Web for information on the courts in your community. Use a search Web site such as http://www.google.com. Enter the name of your city + *courts*. Or look in the government section in the front of the local phone book. Write the information you find below.

The name of your city or town:

_____

The courthouses in or near your city or town:

1. _____

2. _____

3. _____

B. Write the names of two judges that work in these courthouses.

1. _____

2. _____

C. What are three types of minor crimes that someone might have to go to court for?

1. _____

2. _____

3. _____

D. Talk about what you find out with a partner.

10 State and Local Government

This is the California State Capitol building in Sacramento, California.

Connect to the Topic

ARNOLD SCHWARZENEGGER was born in Austria. He is a world-famous athlete and actor. When he was 20, he won the Mr. Universe bodybuilding contest. Then he moved to the United States. He became a U.S. citizen in 1983. He acted in many Hollywood films, but he was also interested in politics. President George H.W. Bush appointed him the Chair of the President's Council on Physical Fitness and Sports in 1990. In 2003, he was elected the 38th governor of the state of California. As governor, Schwarzenegger has worked on economic and environmental issues.

Getting into the Reading

Answer the questions.

1. Find your state on the map of the United States on page 48. What are some big cities in your state? What is the state capital?

2. Look at a large map of your state. Where is your city, town, or county?

3. What government buildings are close to your home?

4. Reread the *Connect to the Topic* profile above. Arnold Schwarzenegger is the governor of what state? What issues are important to him?

State and Local Government

Under our Constitution, some powers belong to the states. These powers include providing schooling and education, protection (as well as safety), giving driver's licenses, and approving zoning and land use. Zoning is how local governments say an area can be used (for example, for houses or for shopping).

State government, like the federal government, has three branches. They are the legislative branch, judicial branch, and executive branch.

The legislative branch of state government is often called the State Assembly or State Legislature. Most states have a Senate and a House of Representatives. Each state decides how many senators and representatives to have and how to choose them. The legislative branch is responsible for passing laws about state issues. It decides how much state income tax and sales tax people should pay and how tax money should be spent.

State legislatures receive millions of dollars from the federal government. State governments often combine federal money with state money to pay for such projects as new roads or housing for the poor.

The judicial branch of state government is the state court system. Each state has a Constitution, a Bill of Rights, and a Supreme Court that the state courts must obey. No state law can contradict, or go against, federal law or decisions of the U.S. Supreme Court. State courts hear all cases except cases about certain federal issues.

The governor is the leader of the executive branch of state government. He or she can propose, or give ideas for, new laws to the state legislature and can veto bills she or he does not like. The governor appoints judges to state courts and is the leader of the state's National Guard. The governor also has a group of advisors. This group is much like the President's Cabinet. Each advisor is responsible for one area of state government, such as education or transportation.

Your state senators and representatives have offices in the state capitol and near your community. Staff members in these offices may be able to help you with state issues such as driver's licenses, unemployment insurance, and services for the disabled.

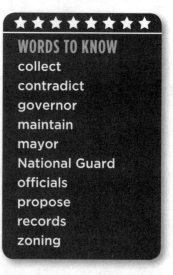

WORDS TO KNOW
collect
contradict
governor
maintain
mayor
National Guard
officials
propose
records
zoning

The Texas State Capitol building in Austin, Texas

Local Government

Local government includes county government and city, town, or village government. Each kind of government is organized, or set up, differently, and each has its own responsibilities.

County government is usually run by a board of commissioners or supervisors. County government also includes other county officials (people who hold offices), such as a sheriff and a county manager.

City government is usually run by an elected mayor and a city council, which acts like a legislature. Representatives on the city council represent their own areas called wards or boroughs. Some cities, towns, and villages do not have a mayor. Sometimes the city or town council hires a city or town manager. Still other cities, towns, and villages have an elected city commission instead.

Local government provides such services as police and fire protection, which are necessary to the local area. City and county governments charge local property and sales taxes, and they receive money from the state and federal government. They also collect money from fines that people pay, such as charges for parking tickets, and from fees and licenses. Local government has a court system to handle such local issues as traffic laws.

These people are all local government employees.

Your local county and city government representatives have offices in your community, in the county seat (the capital of your county), or at the city or village hall. Staff members there may be able to help you with local issues.

One of the local government's most important responsibilities is to manage the public schools. Local government must also provide and maintain parks and libraries; garbage collection; clean drinking water; public transportation; roads and bridges; safe streets; courthouses and jails; and marriage, birth, and death records.

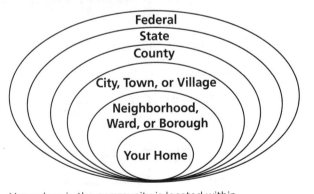

Your place in the community is located within many levels of government.

Just as the federal, state, and local government have responsibilities to their citizens, citizens have responsibilities to their government. When you become a citizen, you will take the Oath of Allegiance. You will promise to give up loyalty to other countries, to defend the Constitution and laws of the United States, to obey the laws, to serve in the U.S. military if needed, to serve the nation in other ways if needed, and to be loyal to the United States.

Getting Information from the Reading

A. Use the words in the box to complete the sentences below. The first one is done for you.

collect	mayor	propose
contradict	National Guard	records
~~governor~~	officials	zoning
maintain		

1. The _____ *governor* _____ is the head of the state.

2. State and local governments _____ money from residents through taxes, fees, and fines.

3. The head of city government is called a _____.

4. Local governments usually keep _____ of marriages, births, and deaths.

5. State laws cannot _____ federal laws.

6. The governor is the leader of the state's _____.

7. States must _____ roads and bridges.

8. People who hold political offices are called _____.

9. State governments approve _____, which tells how land can be used.

10. A governor can _____, or give ideas for, new laws.

B. Write *S* (state) or *F* (federal) to tell what level of government is responsible for each task. The first one is done for you.

1. to approve zoning and land use _____ *S* _____

2. to create an army _____

3. to declare war _____

4. to give a driver's license _____

5. to make treaties _____

6. to print money _____

7. to provide protection (police) _____

8. to provide safety (fire) _____

9. to provide schooling and education _____

10. to issue parking tickets _____

The 100 History and Government Questions

A. Check the answers to the following questions. More than one may be correct.

1. What powers belong to the states, NOT the federal government? (Check 5.)

   ☐ print money

   ☐ provide schooling and education

   ☐ make treaties

   ☐ declare war

   ☐ provide protection (police)

   ☐ provide safety (fire departments)

   ☐ give driver's licenses

   ☐ approve zoning and land use

   ☐ create an army

2. What promise do you make when you become a citizen and take the Oath of Allegiance? (Check six answers.)

   ☐ to give up loyalty to other countries

   ☐ to serve in the U.S. military if needed

   ☐ to vote in every election

   ☐ to defend the Constitution and laws of the United States

   ☐ to obey the laws

   ☐ to serve the nation in other ways if needed

   ☐ to go to school

   ☐ to be loyal to the United States

3. What is the capital of your state? Write it on the line. Check your spelling.

   _____

B. 100 Questions Practice. These questions may be asked as part of the U.S. history and government test. Talk about the answers with a partner. There may be more than one correct answer. All 100 questions can be found on page 154. Go to the Quizzes menu of the DVD for more 100 Questions practice.

> 1. Under our Constitution, some powers belong to the states. What is one power of the states?
> 2. Who is the Governor of your state now?
> 3. What is the capital of your state?
> 4. What is one promise you make when you become a United States citizen?

The N-400 Application: Paraphrasing

Some vocabulary on the N-400 application is difficult. If you know what the difficult words mean, you can think of them or say them in a way that is easier to understand. When you say something in different words, we say that you *paraphrase*. Here are some examples:

Words/Phrases	Meaning	Words/Phrases	Meaning
allegiance	loyalty	mental reservation	doubt
bear arms on behalf	fight for	oath	promise
conviction	belief	renounce	give up
full	complete		

A. Read the first sentence. Then complete the paraphrase. Use synonyms of the underlined words.

1. New citizens of the United States must <u>renounce</u> their <u>allegiance</u> to other governments.

    Paraphrase: When you become a citizen of the United States you must _____ your _____ to other countries.

2. Do the Constitution and the form of the U.S. government follow your <u>convictions</u>?

    Paraphrase: Are your _____ in support of the U.S. Constitution and form of government?

3. Are you willing to take the <u>full</u> Oath of Allegiance to the United States?

    Paraphrase: Will you take the _____ Oath of Allegiance to the United States?

4. I will <u>bear arms on behalf of</u> the United States.

    Paraphrase: I will _____ the United States.

B. Read the Oath of Allegiance that you will say when you become a citizen. For each section of the oath on the left, match the correct paraphrase on the right. The first one is done for you.

The Oath of Allegiance

I hereby declare, on oath,

1. that I absolutely and entirely renounce and abjure all allegiance and fidelity to any foreign prince, potentate, state, or sovereignty, of whom or which I have heretofore been a subject or citizen; ___*b*___

2. that I will support and defend the Constitution and laws of the United States of America against all enemies, foreign and domestic; _____

3. that I will bear true faith and allegiance to the same; _____

4. that I will bear arms on behalf of the United States when required by the law; that I will perform noncombatant service in the armed forces of the United States when required by the law; _____

5. that I will perform work of national importance under civilian direction when required by the law; _____

6. and that I take this obligation freely, without any mental reservation or purpose of evasion; so help me God. _____

Paraphrase (in simpler words)

I promise that:

a. I believe in the Constitution and will defend it.

b. I will give up any loyalty to any other country.

c. I will be loyal to the United States.

d. I will serve (or fight) in the U.S. military if needed.

e. I agree to this freely and without any doubts.

f. I will serve (or do other important work for) the United States. if needed.

The N-400 Application: Parts 10H (Questions 34–39), 11, and 12

Below is the last part of the N-400 application with some simple explanations, or paraphrases, that will help you understand the questions.

---

34. Do you support the Constitution and form of government of the United States? ☐ Yes ☐ No

▶ **EXPLANATION** Do you believe in what the Constitution says? Do you support the republican form of government?

---

35. Do you understand the full Oath of Allegiance to the United States? ☐ Yes ☐ No

▶ **EXPLANATION** Do you understand all of the Oath of Allegiance to the United States? (The Oath of Allegiance is on page 114.)

---

36. Are you willing to take the full Oath of Allegiance to the United States? ☐ Yes ☐ No

▶ **EXPLANATION** Will you take all of the oath (see page 114)? You can request to take a slightly different oath if your religion does not allow you to bear arms (fight with guns). Will you request a different oath? Do you have a disability that makes it difficult for you to take the oath (for example, a speech problem)?

---

37. If the law requires it, are you willing to bear arms on behalf of the United States? ☐ Yes ☐ No

▶ **EXPLANATION** Will you serve in the U.S. military and use a weapon to fight for the United States if necessary?

---

38. If the law requires it, are you willing to perform noncombatant services in the U.S. Armed Forces? ☐ Yes ☐ No

▶ **EXPLANATION** Will you serve in the U.S. military but without using a weapon? This means will you serve in a medical unit or do any other work that does not require combat

---

39. If the law requires it, are you willing to perform work of national importance under civilian direction? ☐ Yes ☐ No

▶ **EXPLANATION** Will you do work to help the country, such as helping put down sandbags in a flood?

Part 11. Your signature.

Write your USCIS "A"- number here:
A

I certify, under penalty of perjury under the laws of the United States of America, that this application, and the evidence submitted with it, are all true and correct. I authorize the release of any information that the USCIS needs to determine my eligibility for naturalization.

Your Signature

Date *(mm/dd/yyyy)*

▶ **EXPLANATION** By signing this application, you are promising that you told the complete truth for every question. You are also saying that you give permission to the USCIS to use all documents they already have about you and to look for additional information about you (from the FBI or police, for example) to find out if you are eligible to become a U.S. citizen.

Part 12. Signature of person who prepared this application for you. *(If applicable.)*

I declare under penalty of perjury that I prepared this application at the request of the above person. The answers provided are based on information of which I have personal knowledge and/or were provided to me by the above named person in response to the *exact questions* contained on this form.

Preparer's Printed Name

Preparer's Signature

Date *(mm/dd/yyyy)*

Preparer's Firm or Organization Name *(If applicable)*

Preparer's Daytime Phone Number

Preparer's Address - Street Number and Name

City

State

Zip Code

▶ **EXPLANATION** If you did not fill out your own application, the person who filled it out for you will sign it.

After you send in your N-400 Form, you may need to wait several months before your interview, then another few months for the naturalization ceremony.

The USCIS Interview

Interview Skill: Responding to Requests for Clarification

The USCIS interviewer may not understand something you say and may ask you to repeat or clarify your words. Be sure to repeat what you said slowly or say it more clearly. Practice saying the expressions.

A. Read the ways you can respond to requests for clarification. Practice saying the expressions.

Interviewer: What did you say? / What? / I don't understand what you just said.

You: I'm sorry; I said _____

Oh, I made a mistake. I meant to say _____.

Oh, I wasn't clear. I meant _____.

 Go to the Interview Skills menu of the DVD to view examples of this skill.

 B. Watch the DVD segments for this chapter. You can find them on the Chapters menu of the DVD.

C. The interview segment with Mr. Dada is included below. Practice it with a partner.

Interviewer: Now, do you support the Constitution of the United States?

Mr. Dada: By *support* do you want to know if I am for them rather than against them?

Interviewer: Yes, that's what I mean by *support*.

Mr. Dada: Then yes, I totally support the Constitution and this kind of government.

Interviewer: And are you willing to take the full Oath of Allegiance to the United States?

Mr. Dada: Sure.

Interviewer: What did you say?

Mr. Dada: I'm sorry. I was mistaken. I meant to say, yes, I am willing to take the Oath of Allegiance.

Interviewer: Good. And if the law requires it, are you willing to perform noncombatant services for the U.S. armed forces?

Mr. Dada: Are you saying that I would not have to carry a rifle, but I would have to follow military orders? Yes?

Interviewer: Yes.

Mr. Dada: Then yes, I would do that.

I meant to say that yes, I am very willing to take the Oath of Allegiance.

D. Now, with a partner, practice the interview using correct information about yourself. Tell the interviewer what you meant to say if he or she didn't understand what you said.

Reading and Writing Test Practice

A. Complete the sentences with a word from the box.

> capital   state
> is   what

1. What _____ the capital of the United States?

2. Washington, D.C., is the _____ of the United States.

3. _____ is the capital of your state?

4. Sacramento is the capital of the _____ of California

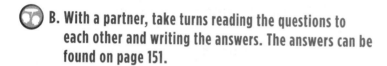 **B. With a partner, take turns reading the questions to each other and writing the answers. The answers can be found on page 151.**

Example:

The interviewer asks you to read this question:

What is the capital of the United States?

The interviewer says this sentence and asks you to write it:

Washington, D.C., is the capital of the United States.

1. What do we pay to the government? _____

2. What is the name of the largest state? _____

3. What state has the most people? _____

The city in the United States with the most people is New York City. Over 8.2 million people live there.

★ ★ ★ ★ ★ ★ ★ ★ ★ ★ ★ ★ ★ ★

VOCABULARY

The following vocabulary will be on the reading and writing test. For a complete list, see pages 206–207.

Reading

do	of
government	to
name	What

Writing

Alaska
California
taxes

Reading and Writing

has	people
is	state
largest	the
most	we
pay	

Grammar Review: Future Tense

There are two ways to talk about the future in English: first, with *be going to* and second, with *will*.

For *be going to*, use the correct present tense of the verb *be*. Then use *going to* plus the base form of the verb. For example:

> You **are going to** apply for U.S. citizenship.
> I **am going to** apply for U.S. citizenship.

For *will*, use *will* + the base verb. For example:

> You **will apply for** U.S. citizenship.
> I **will apply for** U.S. citizenship.

To form the negative, add the word *not*. *Won't* is the contraction, or shortened form, of *will not*. For example:

> I am **not** going to be nervous.
> He **will not** be nervous. You **won't** be nervous either.

Sometimes *be going to* and *will* have different meanings. *Be going to* is used when you talk about a plan you have for the future. *Will* is used when you are willing or happy to help. For example:

> After he is naturalized, he **is going to** bring his parents here from Peru.
> He **will** help them learn English.

Write the future tense of the verb in parentheses. Use either a form of *be going to* or *will*. The first one is done for you.

1. You (sign) ___*are going to sign*___ an oath of allegiance.

2. He (need) _____ his green card at the swearing-in ceremony.

3. She (go) _____ to the courthouse for the swearing-in ceremony.

4. The USCIS interviewer (ask) _____ you some difficult questions.

5. You (ask) _____ for clarification if necessary.

6. If there is a war, you (help) _____ protect the United States.

7. We (be) _____ good citizens.

8. I (fight)_____ for the United States if necessary.

9. If the interviewer doesn't understand you, you (have to) _____ repeat your answer.

10. After the ceremony, we (have) _____ a party.

Civic Engagement:
LEARNING RULES AND LAWS

A. Work with a partner. Brainstorm, or think of, a list of rules you have to follow at your school. Use the topic ideas below.

Topic	Rule
Attendance	
Returning library books	
Smoking and eating	
Parking	
Noise	

B. Work with a partner. Brainstorm, or think of, a list of five laws you have to follow in your community. Use the topic ideas below and think of one of your own.

Topic	Law
Traffic	
Work	
Home	
Bill payment	
Your idea: _____ _____	

11 Making Your Voice Heard

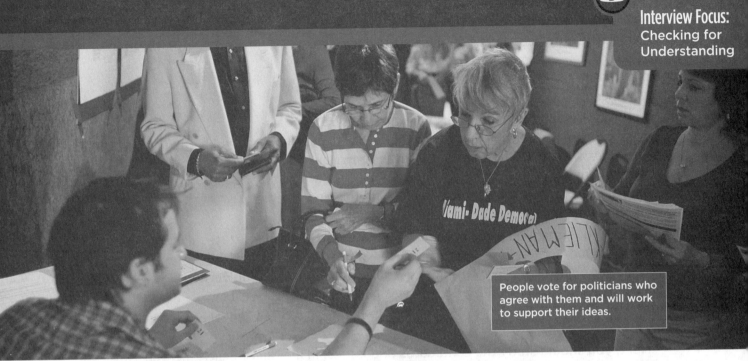

People vote for politicians who agree with them and will work to support their ideas.

Connect to the Topic

RASHIL MAJONGADOL and TABESA YUOL are friends who met in Sudan. Both left their country because of the fighting there and came to the United States separately. Rashil arrived in San Diego, California, in 1999, and Tabesa in 2000. They met each other again there at school. Both women want to help people in Sudan. They traveled to Washington, D.C., to ask Congress to help the people suffering in the Darfur region of Sudan. Both women are now U.S. citizens.

Getting into the Reading

Answer the questions.

1. Many kinds of officials are elected in the United States. Which ones can you name?
2. Did you ever vote in your native country? If so, what was it like? Was it important to vote in your native country?
3. Do you think it is important for U.S. citizens to vote? Why?
4. Voting is one way to make your voice heard. What are some other ways you can make your voice heard by the government?
5. Reread the *Connect to the Topic profile* above. What did Tabesa and Rashil do to make their voices heard?

Voting

The United States is a representative democracy.
Citizens elect representatives to speak for them in the federal, state, and local governments.

Voting is the most important right of U.S. citizenship.
When people study the candidates, understand the issues, and think carefully about their choices, they elect high-quality representatives. The more people vote, the stronger our government is.

In the United States, all citizens who are at least 18 years old can vote. That was not always true. In the past, voters had to be 21 years old and be able to read. African Americans and women of any race could not vote. Sometimes citizens even had to pay a tax to vote. Amendments to the Constitution and other legislation have changed all that.

WORDS TO KNOW
ballot
candidates
endorse
neighborhood
participation
political party
protest
register
Selective Service
special-interest
 group

Before you vote, you must register, or sign up, to vote in all states except North Dakota. In most states, you must be registered at least 30 days before the next election. You may be able to register to vote at public libraries, at the Board of Elections offices, or at the Department of Motor Vehicles. After registering, you will receive a voter's registration card. You do not have to register again unless you have moved, not voted for a long time, or changed your name.

Next, you should study the candidates and issues. In the United States, there are two major political parties—the Republican Party and the Democratic Party. Candidates often represent these two parties, as well as smaller political parties. Newspapers and television provide a lot of information on the candidates, as do candidate debates and other public meetings. Project Vote Smart is a website at http://www.vote-smart.org that provides information about candidates' positions on the issues.

Special-interest groups are organizations of people who agree on certain issues. They endorse, or approve, specific candidates and explain why they think people should vote for them. There are special-interest groups for people who want to protect the environment, for those interested in women's rights, for certain religious groups, and for people who have a similar way of thinking.

When you go to vote, the election judge may ask to see a photo ID (identification) or your voter's registration card. The judge will give you a ballot, or sheet of paper used for voting, and show you where to go to vote. You can ask for help or bring a friend to help you. All voting is secret: no one can know how you voted. When you are finished voting, you will place your ballot in the locked box. If you are voting electronically, follow instructions provided for you.

Voting is an important way to make your voice heard. Officials work hardest for communities that vote for them in elections, and they listen carefully to the needs of people in areas with a lot of voter participation. Legal permanent residents should not register to vote or vote in an election.

Other Ways to Make Your Voice Heard

In the United States, people are often successful at getting what they want from the government when they organize with other people. You can work together with people in your community or with a special-interest group.

Many communities have neighborhood organizations that work to make their area a better place to live. These organizations can ask for money to improve their neighborhood schools or for park programs. They can work with local government to fix streetlights or roads. They can ask for help from the police for safer streets or bring together a group of citizens who report any unusual activity in the neighborhood.

Special-interest groups work to improve things they think are important. For example, a group of immigrants may work for more English as a Second Language classes or for a quicker naturalization process.

There are many different ways to make your voice heard and participate in a democracy:

a. You can vote.

b. You can join a political party.

c. You can help with an election campaign for a specific candidate.

d. You can join a civic group.

e. You can join a community or neighborhood group.

f. You can give an elected official your opinion on an issue.

g. You can call your senators and representatives.

h. You can publicly support or oppose an issue or policy.

i. You can run for office.

j. You can write to a newspaper.

In addition to making your voice heard, you have other important responsibilities. You must send in your federal income tax forms by April 15 every year; and men must register for the Selective Service (draft for the military services) when they turn 18, or between the ages of 18 and 26.

How are these people making their voices heard?

Getting Information from the Reading

A. Use the words in the box to complete the sentences. You will not use all of the words in the box. The first one is done for you.

> ballot   ~~candidates~~   endorse   neighborhood
>
> participation   protest   register

1. People who run for office are called _____ *candidates* _____.

2. When you go to vote, you will get a _____, which shows you who is running for each office.

3. In most states, you have to _____ 30 days before an election if you want to vote.

4. Newspapers often _____, or approve, certain candidates before the election.

5. Some people become involved in their communities by joining _____ organizations that work to make the area where they live safer.

B. Choose the correct answer.

1. You must be _____ years old or older to vote.
   a. 18   b. 21   c. 25

2. _____ is the most important right of U.S. citizenship.
   a. Getting a passport   b. Joining the army   c. Voting

3. You must _____ in your state before you can vote.
   a. pay a tax   b. get a driver's license   c. register

4. The two major political parties are the _____.
   a. Board of Elections and public library
   b. Republicans and Democrats
   c. Democrats and Independents

5. You may need to _____ when you go to vote.
   a. show identification   b. pay a fee   c. take an oath

6. Before you vote, you should _____.
   a. be a permanent legal resident   b. get your passport   c. learn about candidates

7. You must register for _____ if you are male and between 18 and 26 years old.
   a. college   b. the Selective Service   c. office

8. The latest date that you can file your federal income tax is _____.
   a. April 15   b. January 1   c. November 11

Getting into the Reading

 **Look at the picture. Discuss with a partner.**

What event is in the picture below? What can Tabesa and Rashil from the *Connect to the Topic* profile on page 121 do as citizens that they cannot do if they are only residents? How does being a citizen make their voices stronger?

A swearing-in or naturalization ceremony

The Swearing-In Ceremony

Before the Ceremony

The last step in the naturalization process is the hearing or swearing-in ceremony. You will get a piece of paper with the date, time, and location for your swearing-in ceremony either at the end of your USCIS interview or in the mail after your interview. The paper will also give you ideas about what to wear to the ceremony.

You should arrive on time with your Permanent Resident Card (your green card) and your completed Notice of Naturalization Oath Ceremony (Form N-445). You will need to talk with an USCIS employee to turn in your papers.

WORDS TO KNOW
ceremony
court clerk
gavel
judge
swearing in

At the Ceremony

The people at the ceremony might include a judge, a court clerk (the judge's assistant), USCIS employees, candidates for naturalization, and families of the candidates. Here is an abbreviated version of what might happen at a typical swearing-in ceremony.

USCIS Employee: May I have your green card and N-445?

Candidate: Sure. Here they are.

USCIS Employee: Have there been any changes since your interview?

Candidate: No.

USCIS Employee: OK. Thank you. Please find a seat in the front. Your family can sit over there.

Court Clerk: The ceremony will begin in a moment. Please stand up. (The clerk bangs the gavel.) This court is now in session.

USCIS Employee: There are 235 people who are applying for naturalization here. They all meet the requirements. I recommend that the oath be given so that they can become citizens.

The Judge: Will the candidates please stand while I read the oath? (The judge reads the entire oath.) Say "I do" and you will become U.S. citizens.

Candidates: I do.

The Judge: Now shake hands. You are now in this together as U.S. citizens.

(The candidates shake hands. Families applaud.)

Congratulations! This day is important for you but also for our country. This nation was founded by immigrants and is based on the rights of the individuals. It is your responsibility to vote and to be informed citizens. Do not give up your past and your heritage. Make it a part of our nation. This country is now your country. I congratulate each one of you and wish you happiness. God bless you. God bless America.

Court Clerk: All rise. (The clerk bangs the gavel.) This court is adjourned. When I say your name, please come and get your certificate. If there is a mistake on it, please tell us before you leave today.

New citizens with their Certificates of Naturalization

Getting Information from the Reading

A. Read the sentences. Circle *True* or *False*.

1. Each person is sworn in as a new citizen one at a time.   True   False

2. A judge swears in new citizens.   True   False

3. Your family is invited to the ceremony.   True   False

4. You get a certificate when you become a citizen.   True   False

5. You become a citizen right after your interview.   True   False

B. Answer the questions.

1. What is the last step in the naturalization process?

   _____

2. What does every new citizen have to agree to?

   _____

Susan B. Anthony

Susan B. Anthony was born in Massachusetts in 1820. In her twenties, she was part of the temperance movement, which tried to prevent the suffering of women and children because of alcohol abuse. She also was involved in the anti-slavery movement. Susan B. Anthony is best known for her work in getting women the right to vote (suffrage). She campaigned for the rights of both blacks and women to vote. She was disappointed when only black men were given that right in the Fourteenth and Fifteenth Amendments. In 1872, she demanded that women be allowed to vote, and she led a group of women to the polls to vote. She was arrested. However, she never stopped fighting for women's suffrage. She died before the Nineteenth Amendment was passed in 1920.

C. For or Against? Susan B. Anthony supported some things and fought against others. Write *F* (for) for the things she supported and *A* (against) for the things she didn't like.

1. women's right to vote _____

2. slavery _____

3. drinking too much alcohol _____

4. civil rights for blacks and women _____

The 100 History and Government Questions

A. Check the correct answer or answers.

1. What are ways that Americans can participate in their democracy?

☐ vote

☐ join a political party

☐ help with a campaign

☐ join a civic group

☐ join a community group

☐ give an official your opinion

☐ call your senator or representative

☐ support or oppose issues

☐ run for office

☐ write to a newspaper

2. What did Susan B. Anthony do? (Check two answers.)

☐ fought for women's rights

☐ fought for civil rights

☐ ran for office

3. What is the last day you can file your income tax returns?

☐ January 1

☐ April 15

☐ July 4

4. When must all men be registered for the Selective Service?

☐ when they are 18

☐ when they are 35

☐ when they are 21

B. 100 Questions Practice. These questions may be asked as part of the U.S. history and government test. Talk about the answers with a partner. There may be more than one correct answer. All 100 questions can be found on page 154. Go to Quizzes menu of the DVD for more 100 Questions practice.

1. What is the last day you can send in your federal income tax forms?
2. How old do citizens have to be to vote for President?
3. What are two ways that Americans can participate in their democracy?
4. What did Susan B. Anthony do?
5. When must all men register for the Selective Service?

The USCIS Interview

Interview Skill: Checking for Understanding

The interviewer may not always understand your answer. You can check to make sure he or she understands you by asking questions. For example:

Did you understand me?   Is that what you meant?
Was that what you were asking / looking for?   Is my answer clear?

 Go to the Interview Skills menu of the DVD to view examples of this skill.

A. Answer the interviewer's question. Then write a question on the line to check for understanding.

1. Interviewer: What are two ways you can participate in a democracy?

   You: *I can vote and I can write to my senator. Is that what you meant?*

2. Interviewer: What did Susan B. Anthony do?

   You: _____

3. Interviewer: When is the last day you can file your income tax returns?

   You: _____

4. Interviewer: When must men register with the Selective Service?

   You: _____

B. Watch the DVD segments for this chapter. You can find them on the Chapters menu of the DVD.

C. Part of the interview segment with Mr. Dada is included below. Practice it with a partner.

Interviewer: I assume you studied the 100 American government and history questions?

Mr. Dada: Yes, I have.

Interviewer: Now I'm going to ask you a few of them to see how well you understand.

Narrator: This part of the interview is difficult for some people. You may forget an answer—even one you know. That's OK. Just stay calm.

Interviewer: All right. What are two Cabinet-level positions?

Mr. Dada: The President's Cabinet? The Secretary of Defense and State.

Did you understand me?

Interviewer: Could you say that again?

Mr. Dada: I'm sorry, the Secretary of Defense and the Secretary of State.

Interviewer: Good. Now what did the Declaration of Independence do?

Mr. Dada: It said to Great Britain that the colonies wanted freedom.

Interviewer: Excellent. Let's see... how many U.S. senators are there?

Mr. Dada: Um... 50. No, 100.

Interviewer: And can you say who lived in America before the Europeans arrived?

Mr. Dada: The American Indians. Was that what you were looking for?

Reading and Writing Test Practice

A. Complete the sentences with a word from the box.

citizen	senators
citizens	states
November	tax forms
President	vote
right	vote for

1. A _____ can vote.

2. In an election, people _____ the candidate they like best.

3. Voting is the most important _____ citizens have.

4. We vote for the _____ in _____.

5. You must be at least 18 years old to _____.

6. We must send in our _____ by April 15.

7. Only _____ can vote.

8. _____ represent _____.

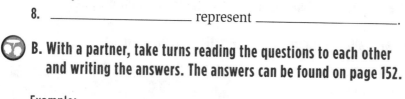 **B. With a partner, take turns reading the questions to each other and writing the answers. The answers can be found on page 152.**

Example:

The interviewer asks you to read this question:

When do we elect the President?

The interviewer says this sentence and asks you to write it:

We elect the President in November.

1. When do people vote for President? _____

2. What is one right of a U.S. citizen? _____

3. Who can vote? _____

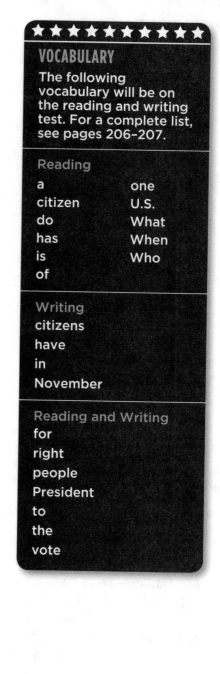

★ ★ ★ ★ ★ ★ ★ ★ ★ ★ ★

VOCABULARY

The following vocabulary will be on the reading and writing test. For a complete list, see pages 206–207.

Reading

a	one
citizen	U.S.
do	What
has	When
is	Who
of	

Writing

citizens
have
in
November

Reading and Writing

for
right
people
President
to
the
vote

Grammar Review: Modals of Possibility and Obligation

We use the modals *can* and *may* to talk about things that we are allowed to do.

> Citizens **can** run for office.
> Citizens **may** run for office.

We use the modals *must* and *have to* to talk about things we are required to do.

> Citizens **must** serve on a jury if they are called to do so.
> Citizens **have to** serve on a jury if they are called to do so.

We use the negative forms *cannot, may not,* and *must not* for things we are not allowed to do. *Must not* is stronger than the others.

> Permanent legal residents who are not citizens **must not** vote.
> Permanent legal residents who are not citizens **cannot** vote.
> Permanent legal residents who are not citizens **may not** vote.

Complete these sentences with the correct form in parentheses.

1. Citizens _____ (can/can't) get a U.S. passport.

2. Citizens _____ (must/must not) serve in the army if required.

3. Permanent legal residents _____ (can/must) apply to become citizens.

4. Candidates, or people who want to become citizens, _____ (can/cannot) invite their families to the swearing-in ceremony.

5. Citizens _____ (can/must) vote.

6. If you're not a citizen, you _____ (can/can't) run for office.

7. You _____ (must/must not) be at least 18 years old to vote.

8. Permanent legal residents _____ (must/must not) vote.

9. Anyone _____ (may/must) learn about political issues.

10. Men who are 18 years old _____ (may/must) register for the Selective Service.

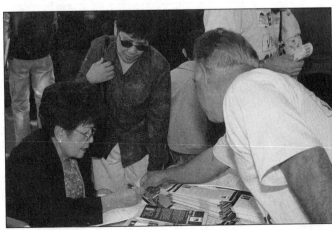

Citizens must register to vote at least six weeks before an election if they want to vote in that election.

Civic Engagement:
ELECTIONS IN YOUR COMMUNITY

A. Answer the questions about elections in your community.

1. When is the next election in your community? _____

2. What offices will people be voting for? _____

3. What are the names of two candidates running for office? _____

_____

B. Rank the issues below in order of their importance to you. Put *1* next to the most important issue and *10* next to the issue that is least important to you. Discuss your ideas with a partner.

_____ restriction on immigration   _____ neighborhood safety

_____ education for children (K–12)   _____ museums and public art

_____ roads and highways   _____ drunk driving

_____ community colleges and adult education   _____ racial tolerance

_____ parks and recreation   _____ health care

C. Online Research. Choose one of the issues in Part B. Learn about the issue online. Use a search engine and enter the name of your city and the issue (for example, "Medford and education"). You may need to add the words "election issues" to your search if you don't find anything. You may also read your city or town's newspaper to find out the information. List three facts you learned about the issue.

Name of issue: _____

1. _____

2. _____

3. _____

D. Find one argument on each side of an issue. Discuss the ideas with a partner.

Part A: U.S. Geography

Work with a partner on this activity. Decide who will be Student A and Student B. Student A will use this page. Student B will use page 134.

Student A

Some of the 100 History and Government Questions ask about U.S. geography. You and your partner have all of the information you need to answer those geography questions, but you must work together. You will ask your partner for the information that is missing from your map.

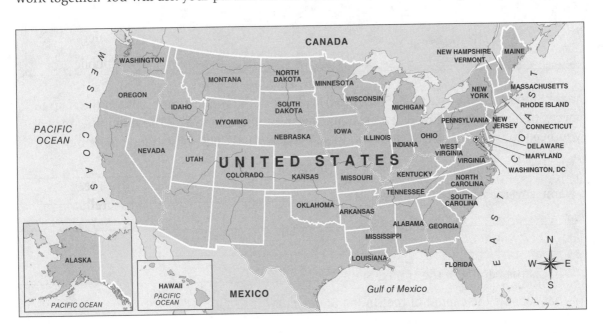

You are Student A. Ask the first question to Student B. Write down the answer. Then look on the map to answer Student B's question. If you need to, you can ask: "Could you please repeat that?" OR: "How do you spell that?"

1. What are the two longest rivers in the United States? _____

   _____

3. What ocean is on the east coast of the United States? _____

5. Name several states that border Mexico. _____

   _____

7. Where is the Statue of Liberty? _____

Student B

Some of the 100 History and Government Questions ask about U.S. geography. You and your partner have all of the information you need to answer those geography questions, but you must work together. You will ask your partner for the information that is missing from your map.

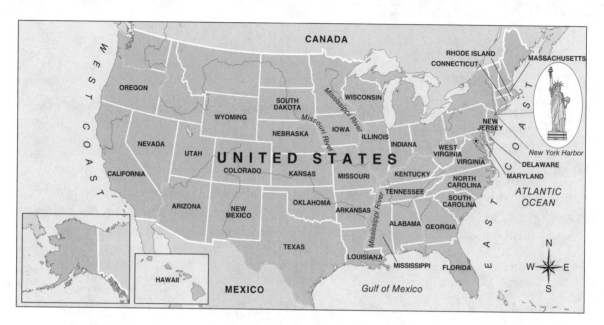

You are Student B. Your partner (Student A) will ask the first question. Look on the map to answer Student A's question. Then ask your question to Student A. Write down the answer. If you need to, you can ask: "Could you please repeat that?" OR: "How do you spell that?"

2. What ocean is on the west coast of the United States? _____

4. Name several states that border Canada. _____

_____

_____

6. What is the capital of the United States? _____

8. What coast is the capital of the United States near? _____

Part B: U.S. Holidays

Question 100 of the 100 History and Government Questions list asks you to name two U.S. national holidays. Although you only have to name two, it is important to know about American holidays so that you can understand why Americans celebrate them.

New Year's Day *January 1* This celebrates the beginning of the new year.	**Labor Day** *September–First Monday* This day honors workers in the United States.
Martin Luther King, Jr., Day *January–Third Monday* This day honors Martin Luther King, Jr., who fought for civil rights.	**Columbus Day** *October–Second Monday* This day honors the arrival of Christopher Columbus in North America.
Presidents' Day *February–Third Monday* This day honors U.S. Presidents.	**Veterans Day** *November 11* This day honors the men and women who have served in the U.S. military.
Memorial Day *May–Last Monday* This day remembers the U.S. soldiers who fought or died in wars.	**Thanksgiving** *November–Fourth Thursday* This day commemorates a celebration between colonists and Native Americans in 1621.
Independence Day *July 4th* This day celebrates the anniversary of the day the U.S. declared independence from Great Britain (England).	**Christmas** *December 25* This day honors the birth of Jesus Christ in the Christian religion.

Discuss the following questions with a partner.

1. How is New Year's Day celebrated in your country? Do you know how it is celebrated in the United States? If so, is it different or the same as in your country?

2. Does your country have an Independence Day? When is it? How did your country gain independence?

3. Which holiday above would you like to learn more about? Where can you look for more information about it?

Turkey is often served for Thanksgiving dinner.

Part C: Important People in U.S. History

Look at these people who have shaped our country. Think about what they did.

American Indians	Africans	Thomas Jefferson	Benjamin Franklin
George Washington	Abraham Lincoln	Susan B. Anthony	Woodrow Wilson
Franklin Roosevelt	Dwight D. Eisenhower	Martin Luther King, Jr.	New U.S. Citizens

Fill in the blanks with the name of a person or group of people. The first one has been done for you.

1. *Thomas Jefferson* wrote the Declaration of Independence.

2. _____ was a general in World War II before he was President.

3. _____ was the first President of the United States and is the "Father of Our Country."

4. _____ fought for civil rights and equality for all Americans.

5. _____ freed the slaves and saved the Union.

6. _____ was a U.S. diplomat, the oldest member of the Constitutional Convention, and a writer.

7. _____ fought for women's rights and civil rights.

8. _____ was President during World War I.

9. _____ were taken to America and sold as slaves.

10. _____ lived in America before the Europeans arrived.

11. _____ was President during the Great Depression and World War II.

12. Which of the people were U.S. Presidents? _____ _____

_____

13. Which two people are famous for fighting for civil rights? _____ and

_____

14. Which group of people will you join once you pass your citizenship test? _____

Part D: Review: U.S. History

Important points and events in U.S. history are listed on the right. Match each description on the left with the name of the point or event. Write the letter on the line. The first one is done for you.

___e___ 1. Thomas Jefferson wrote this important paper in 1776.

_____ 2. The Founding Fathers wrote this important paper in 1787.

_____ 3. Thomas Jefferson bought this land from France in 1803.

_____ 4. These wars were fought in the 1800s.

_____ 5. This war was also called the War Between the States.

_____ 6. Abraham Lincoln signed this important paper that freed the slaves.

_____ 7. These wars were fought in the 1900s.

_____ 8. The United States fought these countries in World War II.

_____ 9. The main concern of the United States was communism during this war.

_____ 10. This movement tried to end racial discrimination.

_____ 11. Terrorists attacked the United States on this day.

_____ 12. This is the day the United States celebrates its independence.

a. World War I, World War II, the Korean War, the Vietnam War, and the Gulf War

b. the Cold War

c. Japan, Germany, and Italy

d. the Constitution

e. the Declaration of Independence

f. September 11, 2001

g. the Civil War

h. the War of 1812, the Mexican-American War, the Civil War, the Spanish-American War

i. the Louisiana Territory

j. the civil rights movement

k. the Emancipation Proclamation

l. July 4

A July 4th parade

Part E: Review: Board Game

Play this game with one or more partners to see how well you have learned the information in this book. Each player should use a different U.S. coin as a game piece. Place the coins on START. The first person will roll a die (singular of *dice*) and move the amount of spaces rolled. Then that person will read the question aloud and answer it. If the question is not answered correctly, the person will lose a turn.

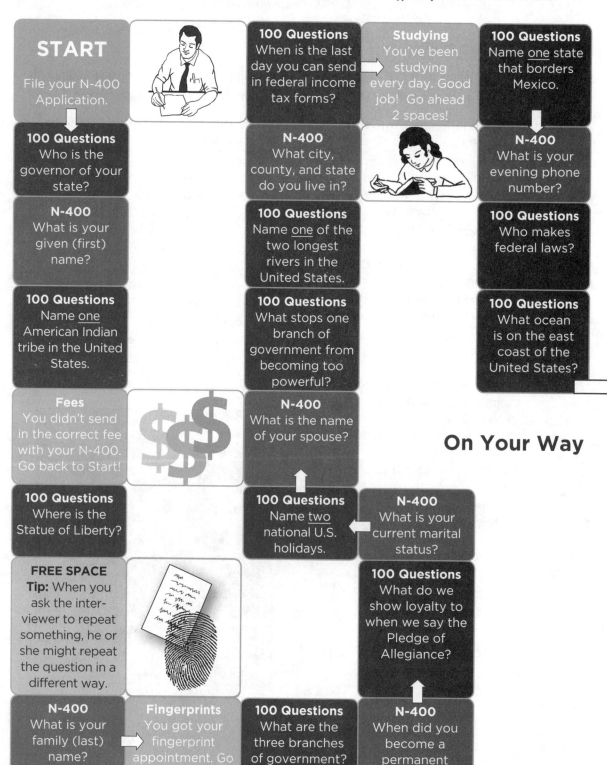

START
File your N-400 Application.

100 Questions
Who is the governor of your state?

N-400
What is your given (first) name?

100 Questions
Name one American Indian tribe in the United States.

Fees
You didn't send in the correct fee with your N-400. Go back to Start!

100 Questions
Where is the Statue of Liberty?

FREE SPACE
Tip: When you ask the interviewer to repeat something, he or she might repeat the question in a different way.

N-400
What is your family (last) name?

Fingerprints
You got your fingerprint appointment. Go ahead 3 spaces!

100 Questions
What are the three branches of government?

100 Questions
When is the last day you can send in federal income tax forms?

N-400
What city, county, and state do you live in?

100 Questions
Name one of the two longest rivers in the United States.

100 Questions
What stops one branch of government from becoming too powerful?

N-400
What is the name of your spouse?

100 Questions
Name two national U.S. holidays.

N-400
What is your current marital status?

N-400
When did you become a permanent resident?

Studying
You've been studying every day. Good job! Go ahead 2 spaces!

100 Questions
What do we show loyalty to when we say the Pledge of Allegiance?

100 Questions
Name one state that borders Mexico.

N-400
What is your evening phone number?

100 Questions
Who makes federal laws?

100 Questions
What ocean is on the east coast of the United States?

On Your Way

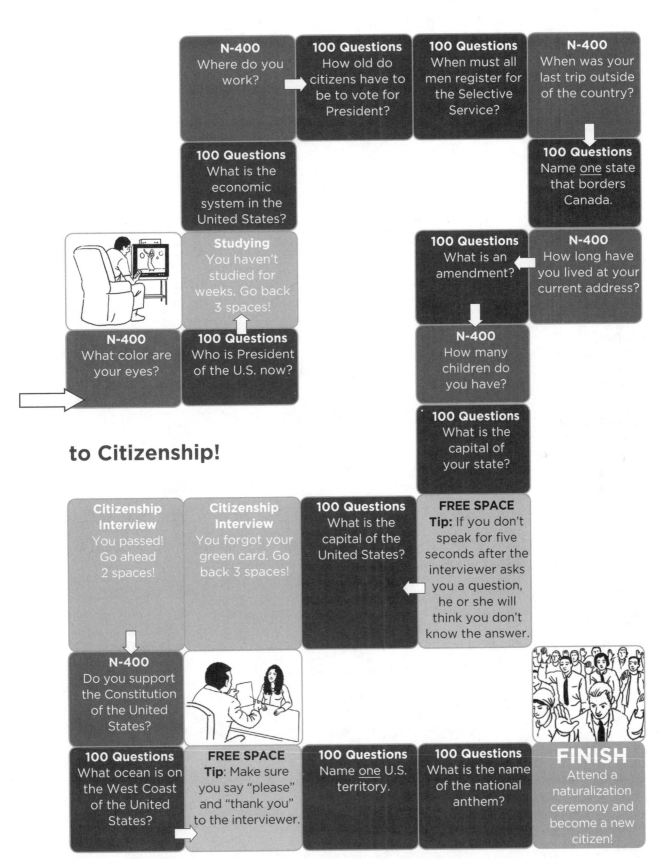

N-400
Where do you work?

100 Questions
How old do citizens have to be to vote for President?

100 Questions
When must all men register for the Selective Service?

N-400
When was your last trip outside of the country?

100 Questions
What is the economic system in the United States?

100 Questions
Name <u>one</u> state that borders Canada.

Studying
You haven't studied for weeks. Go back 3 spaces!

100 Questions
What is an amendment?

N-400
How long have you lived at your current address?

N-400
What color are your eyes?

100 Questions
Who is President of the U.S. now?

N-400
How many children do you have?

to Citizenship!

100 Questions
What is the capital of your state?

Citizenship Interview
You passed! Go ahead 2 spaces!

Citizenship Interview
You forgot your green card. Go back 3 spaces!

100 Questions
What is the capital of the United States?

FREE SPACE
Tip: If you don't speak for five seconds after the interviewer asks you a question, he or she will think you don't know the answer.

N-400
Do you support the Constitution of the United States?

100 Questions
What ocean is on the West Coast of the United States?

FREE SPACE
Tip: Make sure you say "please" and "thank you" to the interviewer.

100 Questions
Name <u>one</u> U.S. territory.

100 Questions
What is the name of the national anthem?

FINISH
Attend a naturalization ceremony and become a new citizen!

Part F: Review: The Three Branches

A. Answer each question about the three branches of government. The answers are written under the question word. Copy the answer under the correct branch. The first one is done for you.

	Executive Branch	Legislative Branch	Judicial Branch
Who? ~~Chief Justice~~ Representatives, Vice President, Cabinet, Senators, Supreme Court Justices, President	• • •	• •	• Chief Justice •
What? Makes Federal laws, signs laws, explains laws, vetoes laws	• •	•	•
Where? White House, Supreme Court Building, Capitol Building	•	•	•
When? appointed for life, 6 2 4	• Presidents are elected for ____ years.	• Senators are elected for ____ years. • Representatives are elected for ____ years.	• Supreme Court Justices are ____
How Many? 100 1 435 15 1 9	• Presidents: ____ • Vice Presidents: ____ • Cabinet Departments: ____	• Senators: ____ • Representatives: ____	• Supreme Court Justices: ____
Need help? Review:	Chapter 7, Pages 73—84	Chapter 8, Pages 85—96	Chapter 9, Pages 97—108

B. Think of current members of the three branches of government. Fill in the blanks with the names of the people who hold these offices now.

1. Who is <u>one</u> of your state's U.S. senators? _____

2. Name your U.S. representative. _____

3. What is the name of the President of the United States? _____

4. What is the name of the Vice President of the United States? _____

5. Who is the Chief Justice of the U.S. Supreme Court now? _____

Answer Key

Chapter 1

Getting into the Reading (page 1)

Answers will vary but may include:

1. They are at a naturalization ceremony. They are taking the oath of allegiance. They feel happy because they are becoming U.S. citizens.

2. To be with family, for opportunities, to be free

3. Because of the opportunities

Getting Information from the Reading (page 4)

A. 1. True
   2. False
   3. False
   4. True
   5. True
   6. True
   7. False
   8. False
   9. False

B. a. 3, b. 2, c. 5, d. 1, e. 4

C. 1. USCIS
   2. apply
   3. naturalization
   4. fingerprints
   5. oath of allegiance
   6. naturalization ceremony
   7. federal
   8. jury

D. Answers will vary.

The 100 History and Government Questions (page 6)

A. 1. right
   2. both
   3. right
   4. right
   5. responsibility

B. Answers will vary.

C. *Each question has more than one correct answer:*
   1. vote in a federal election, run for federal office
   2. serve on a jury, vote in a federal election
   3. New York Harbor, Liberty Island.

The Pledge of Allegiance (page 7)

1. the United States
2. the American flag

The N-400 Application (page 7)

1. Answers will vary.

The USCIS Interview (page 9)

C. Answers will vary.

Reading and Writing Test Practice (page 10)

A. 1. U.S., vote
   2. right
   3. jury
   4. President

B. 1. People want to be free.
   2. Mexico is south of the United States.
   3. Canada is north of the United States.

Grammar Review: Questions Words (page 11)

A. 1. e
   2. d
   3. b
   4. f
   5. c
   6. a

B. Answers will vary.

C. 1. What
   2. When
   3. Where
   4. Why
   5. Who
   6. Why
   7. How

Chapter 2

Getting into the Reading (page 13)

Answers will vary but may include:

1. Christopher Columbus was the first European to come to America

2. Yes

3. Explorers wanted to come to the New World to find gold and wealth. Other Europeans came to America for freedom and economic opportunities.

4. Juan Carlos Hernandez came to the United States to better his life.

Getting Information from the Reading (page 16)

A. 1. Europeans, colonies

2. American Indians

3. England

4. Pilgrims

5. Atlantic

6. Pacific

B. 1. **b.** Massachusetts
c. New Hampshire

2. **a.** New York
d. Pennsylvania

3. **b.** Maryland
d. Georgia

C. *Answers will vary but may include:*

1. freedom of religion: people can worship as they please

2. freedom from persecution: people cannot be punished for being different

3. political freedom: people are free to have any political belief

4. economic opportunity: people can do many things to earn money.

The 100 History and Government Questions (page 17)

A. 1. *Answers may include:* Navajo, Cherokee, Sioux, Chippewa, Pueblo, Apache, Iroquois, Creek, Blackfeet, Seminole, Cheyenne, Shawnee, Mohegan, Huron, Lakota, Crow, Inuit

2. religious freedom, escape persecution, political liberty, economic opportunity

3. New Hampshire, Massachusetts, Rhode Island, Connecticut, New York, New Jersey, Pennsylvania, Delaware, Maryland, Virginia, North Carolina, South Carolina, Georgia

B. 1. *Any of the following is correct:* freedom, political liberty, religious freedom, economic opportunity, practice their religion, escape persecution

2. American Indians OR Native Americans

3. New Hampshire, Massachusetts, Rhode Island, Connecticut, New York, New Jersey, Pennsylvania, Delaware, Maryland, Virginia, North Carolina, South Carolina, Georgia

4. Atlantic (Ocean)

5. *Any of the following is correct:* Cherokee, Navajo, Sioux, Chippewa, Choctaw, Pueblo, Apache, Iroquois, Creek, Blackfeet, Seminole, Cheyenne, Arawak, Shawnee, Mohegan, Huron, Oneida, Lakota, Crow, Teton, Hopi, or Inuit

The N-400 Application (page 18)

A. 1. 12/10/1998

2. 07/04/2001

3. 02/15/1998

4. 10/05/1982

B. and C. Answers will vary.

Reading and Writing Test Practice (page 22)

A. 1.c; 2. a; 3. b.

B. 1. American Indians lived here first.

2. Columbus Day is in October.

3. Thanksgiving is in November.

4. People come to be free.

Grammar Review (page 23)

A. 1. is

2. are

3. is

4. am, am

B. 1. was

2. were

3. was

4. were

Civic Engagement (page 24)

Answers will vary. Some answers include: look in the yellow pages of a telephone book, ask people who were helped by lawyers or consultants, ask your teachers.

Chapter 3

Getting into the Reading (page 25)

Answers will vary but may include:

2. Congo, Eritrea, India, Pakistan, Philippines, Vietnam, Mexico, all South American countries
3. Congo, Kenya, Cape Verde, Mexico
4. have an independent government
5. the right to make many choices and to improve his life

Getting Information from the Reading (page 28)

A. 1. tax
   2. self-government
   3. Revolutionary War
   4. Declaration of Independence
   5. "The Star-Spangled Banner"

B. 1. c
   2. b
   3. b

C. Answers will vary.

D. *Answers will vary but may include:*
   1. right to not be killed
   2. right to be free and to make own choices
   3. right to make lives better

The 100 History and Government Questions (page 29)

A. 1. a, b, c, d
   2. b, c, d
   3. b, c, d, f, g
   4. a, c, e, h

B. *Each question has more than one correct answer:*

1. because of high taxes (taxation without representation), because the British army stayed in their houses (boarding, quartering), because they didn't have self-government
2. The 13 original states are: New Hampshire, Massachusetts, Rhode Island, Connecticut, New York, New Jersey, Pennsylvania, Delaware, Maryland, Virginia, North Carolina, South Carolina, Georgia
3. (Thomas) Jefferson
4. July 4, 1776
5. July 4
6. announced our independence (from Great Britain), declared our independence (from Great Britain), said that the United States is free (from Great Britain)
7. life, liberty, pursuit of happiness
8. U.S. diplomat, oldest member of the Constitutional Convention, first Postmaster General of the United States, writer of "Poor Richard's Almanac", started the first free libraries
9. (George) Washington
10. (George) Washington
11. "The Star-Spangled Banner"

The N-400 Application (page 30)

B. Practice:
   1. From 01/03/2001 to 11/15/2003
   2. From 10/04/1998 to 12/01/2004
   3. From 04/15/1992 to 05/11/2005

The USCIS Interview (page 33)

A. 1. c
   2. d
   3. b
   4. a
   5. f
   6. e

Reading and Writing Test Practice (page 34)

A. 1. Washington was the first President of the United States.
   2. The colors of the American flag are red, white, and blue.
   3. Independence Day is in July.
   4. George Washington/Washington/President Washington is the "Father of Our Country."

B. 1. Washington was the first President of the United States.

  2. Independence Day is in July.

  3. Washington is on the dollar bill.

Grammar Review (page 35)

A. 1. Yes, I am. No, I am not (I'm not).

  2. Yes, it is. No, it is not (isn't).

  3. Yes, she/he is. No, he/she is not (isn't).

  4. Yes, I am. No, I am not.

  5. Yes, I was. No, I was not (wasn't).

B. 1. Yes, I do. No, I do not.

  2. Yes, I can. No, I cannot (can't).

  3. Yes, I do. No, I do not (don't).

  4. Yes, they do. No, they do not (don't).

  5. Yes, I do. No, I do not (don't).

C. 1. Yes, it is. No, it is not (isn't).

  2. Yes, he was. No, he was not (wasn't).

  3. Yes, I was. No, I was not (wasn't).

  4. Yes, I am. No, I am not (I'm not).

  5. Yes, they were. No, they were not (weren't).

  6. Yes, I am. No, I am not (I'm not).

  7. Yes, it is. No, it is not (isn't).

  8. Yes, I am. No, I am not (I'm not).

Civic Engagement (page 36)

Answers will vary.

Chapter 4

Getting into the Reading (page 37)

Answers will vary. Some suggestions:

1. for economic opportunity, for religious freedom, to be with family

2. for religious freedom, for opportunity, because they had no choice as slaves

3. a war within one country.

4. The United States got bigger/got more territory.

5. because of the Civil War in her country

Getting Information from the Reading (page 40)

A. 1. True

  2. True

  3. False

  4. True

  5. False

  6. False

  7. True

  8. False

B. 1. slave

  2. expand

  3. captured

  4. assassinated

  5. territory

  6. federal

C. a. 7

  b. 2

  c. 6

  d. 4

  e. 8

  f. 1

  g. 5

  h. 3

D. 1. *Suggested answers:* slavery, economic reasons, states' rights

  2–6. Answers will vary.

The 100 History and Government Questions (page 42)

A. 1. c

  2. f

  3. a

  4. b

  5. g

  6. d

  7. e

B. 1. 50

  2. There are 50 stars because there is one star for each state.

  3. 13

  4. There are 13 stripes because there were 13 original colonies.

C. *Questions have more than one answer:*

  1. Africans, people from Africa

  2. the Louisiana Territory, Louisiana

3. War of 1812, Mexican-American War, Civil War, Spanish-American War

4. the Civil War, the War Between the States

5. slavery, economic reasons, states' rights

6. freed the slaves (Emancipation Proclamation), saved (or preserved) the Union, led the United States during the Civil War

7. freed the slaves, freed slaves in the Confederacy, freed slaves in the Confederate states, freed slaves in most Southern states

8. because there were 13 original colonies, because the stripes represent the original colonies

9. because there is one star for each state, because each star represents a state, because there are 50 states

The N-400 Application (page 43)

A. Answers will vary.

B. Answers will vary.

The USCIS Interview (page 45)

A. 1. married
2. divorced
3. went
4. left
5. came

Reading and Writing Test Practice (page 46)

A. 1. red, white
2. red, white, blue
3. Abraham Lincoln
4. fifty/50

B. 1. Lincoln was President during the Civil War.
2. The flag is red, white, and blue.
3. The United States has fifty states.

Grammar Review (page 47)

A. 1. reached
2. called
3. wanted
4. ended

B. 1. stopped
2. saved
3. expanded
4. worried
5. signed

Chapter 5

Getting into the Reading (page 49)

Answers will vary. Possible answers:

1. afraid, worried, excited

2. a war fought by many countries

3. two, to stop Germany and other countries from invading and controlling other nations

4. Both wars involved the United States and concerned communism.

5. The Vietnam War; She came to the United States for more security.

Getting Information from the Reading (page 52)

A. 1. Woodrow Wilson
2. Italy, Japan
3. The Great Depression
4. general
5. Cold War
6. terrorists, Pentagon, World Trade Center

B. 1. c
2. g
3. a
4. d
5. f
6. b
7. e

The 100 History and Government Questions (page 53)

A. 1. World War I, World War II, the Vietnam War, the Korean War, the (Persian) Gulf War
2. Woodrow Wilson
3. Franklin Delano Roosevelt
4. Germany, Japan, Italy
5. World War II
6. communism
7. Terrorists attacked the United States.

B. 1. World War I, World War II, the Vietnam War, the Korean War, or the Gulf War
2. (Woodrow) Wilson
3. (Franklin) Roosevelt

4. Germany, Japan, and Italy

5. World War II

6. Communism

7. Terrorists attacked the United States.

The N-400 Application (page 54)

1. applicable
2. lawful
3. annulled
4. given
5. previous/prior
6. previous, prior

USCIS Interview (page 57)

Answers will vary.

Reading and Writing Test Practice (page 58)

A. 1. d
   2. b
   3. g
   4. f
   5. c
   6. a
   7. e

B. 1. Memorial Day is in May.
   2. Flag Day is in June.
   3. Labor Day is in September.

Grammar Review (page 59)

Answers will vary. Possible answers:

1. No, I wasn't. This is my first marriage.
2. No, they weren't. They were citizens of Russia.
3. No, I didn't.
4. No, she didn't.

5. No, I didn't.
6. No, I didn't.
7. No, I haven't. I don't believe in communism.
8. Yes, I do.
9. No, I wasn't. I was never arrested.
10. No, I wasn't.
11. No, I didn't. I never got deported.
12. Yes, I was.

Civic Engagement (page 60)

A. 1. The memorials help people remember wars and other important events in U.S. history.
   2. a. Vietnam War
      b. World War II
      c. Korean War
      d. September 11 attack

Chapter 6

Getting into the Reading (page 61)

Answers will vary. Possible answers:

1. A law is a rule that citizens must obey. Some laws say that you cannot kill, or steal, or sell drugs.
2. A constitution sets up the government of the country.
3. Answer may vary.
4. A right is something that you are allowed to do. For example, in the United States people can practice any religion they want, they can express their opinions, and they can have an attorney if they get arrested.

The Rizvanollis probably think that freedom of religion is important.

Getting Information from the Reading (page 63)

A. 1. branch
   2. beliefs
   3. supreme
   4. ratified
   5. checks and balances
   6. amendment
   7. power

B. 1. a
   2. b
   3. c
   4. c
   5. b
   6. a

Getting Information from the Reading (page 65)

A. 1. 1
   2. 6
   3. 4
   4. 2
   5. 5
   6. 1
   7. 6
   8. 10
   9. 5
   10. 9
   11. 24
   12. 19

B. 1. The Bill of Rights
   2. the freedom of religion, press, assembly, or speech, or to petition the government

3. 27

4. the right to practice any religion you want or not practice a religion

5. any two of the rights listed on page 64

The 100 History and Government Questions (page 66)

A. 100 Questions Practice

1. c

2. a

3. b

4. a

5. c

6. a

7. b

B. 1. The Constitution

2. sets up the government OR defines the government OR protects basic rights of Americans

3. We the People

4. a change or addition (to the Constitution)

5. The Bill of Rights

6. speech, religion, assembly, press, petition the government

7. 27

8. You can practice any religion, or not practice a religion.

9. checks and balances OR separation of powers

10. Citizens 18 and older can vote, you don't have to pay (a poll tax) to vote, any citizen can

vote (men and women can vote), and a male citizen of any race can vote.

11. The Constitution was written OR The Founding Fathers wrote the Constitution.

12. 1787

13. (James) Madison, (Alexander) Hamilton, (John) Jay, and Publius

14. Everyone must follow the law. OR Leaders must obey the law. OR Government must obey the law. OR No one is above the law.

N-400 Application (page 67)

A. *Answers may vary. Possible answers:*

1. No, I haven't.

2. No, I haven't.

3. No, I haven't.

4. Yes, I have. I was married once before, but was divorced.

5. No, I haven't. I have always filed my income taxes.

USCIS Interview (page 69)

A. 1. What is your spouse's country of origin? What is my spouse's country of origin?

2. When were you born? When was I born?

3. What is your country of birth? What is my country of birth?

4. Where did your marriage take place? Where did my marriage take place?

Reading and Writing Test Practice (page 70)

A. 1. Citizens, vote

2. people, country, free

3. freedom of speech

B. 1. Citizens can vote in the United States.

2. People in the United States have the right to be free.

3. People have the freedom of speech.

Grammar Review (page 71)

Answers may vary. Probable answers:

1. Yes, I am.

2. Yes, it was.

3. Yes, I have.

4. No, I haven't.

5. Yes, I was.

6. Yes, I did.

7. Yes, I am.

8. Yes, I do.

9. No, I don't.

10. No, I haven't.

Civic Engagement (page 72)

Photo 1: Right to vote
Photo 2: Freedom of religion
Photo 3: Freedom of the press or freedom of speech
Photo 4: Right to a fair trial and an attorney

Chapter 7

Getting into the Reading (page 73)

1. John F. Kennedy, George Bush, Abraham Lincoln, the current President
2. the current President
3. Answers will vary.
4. Answers will vary.

Getting Information from the Reading (page 76)

A. 1. elects
   2. The White House
   3. bill
   4. advise, responsibilities
   5. Democratic, Republican
   6. requirements

B. 1. c
   2. c
   3. b
   4. a
   5. b

The 100 History and Government Questions (page 77)

A. 1. c
   2. e
   3. d
   4. b
   5. a

B. 1. *All of these are correct:* Congress, legislative, President, executive, the courts, judicial
   2. the President
   3. the current President
   4. the current Vice President

5. four (4)
6. November
7. the Vice President
8. the President
9. Democratic and Republican
10. the President
11. the President
12. the political party of the current President
13. Secretary of Agriculture, Secretary of Commerce, Secretary of Defense, Secretary of Education, Secretary of Energy, Secretary of Health and Human Services, Secretary of Homeland Security, Secretary of Housing and Urban Development, Secretary of the Interior, Secretary of Labor, Secretary of State, Secretary of Transportation, Secretary of the Treasury, Secretary of Veterans Affairs, Attorney General, Vice President
14. advises the President
15. 18 years old

The N-400 Application (page 78)

Answers will vary. Some suggestions:

1. Yes, I was a member of the Communist Party for five years. It was required by law in my country.
2. No. I have never been associated with a union or any organization.

3. No, I have never been associated with people who have committed crimes.
4. Yes, I was associated with a children's health group. We gave food to homeless children.

The USCIS Interview (page 81)

A. *Answers will be one of the following:*
   1. What does that mean?
   2. Could you explain the question, please?
   3. I didn't understand what you said. What do you mean?

Reading and Writing Test Practice (page 82)

A. 1. Washington was the first President.
   2. The President lives in the White House.
   3. Presidents' Day is in February.

B. 1. The President lives in the White House.
   2. Washington is the Father of our Country.
   3. Adams was the second President.

Grammar Review (page 83)

A. 1. can
   2. must/have to
   3. should/had better/ must/has to
   4. should
   5. must/has to

B. Answers will vary.

Chapter 8

Getting into the Reading (page 85)

1. The legislative branch makes laws.

2. Members of Congress are called representatives and senators.

3. They work in the Capitol building.

4. Answers will vary.

5. Answers will vary.

Getting Information from the Reading (page 88)

A.
1. district
2. legislation
3. committee
4. debate
5. majority

B.
1. True   6. True
2. False   7. False
3. False   8. True
4. False   9. False
5. True

The 100 History and Government Questions (page 89)

A.
1. e
2. a
3. b
4. d
5. c

B.
1. Congress, legislative, President, executive, the courts, judicial
2. the House of Representatives and the Senate
3. 100

4. six

5. Answers will vary.

6. 435

7. (because of) the state's population, (because) they have more people, (because) some states have more people

8. the current Speaker of the House

9. the Speaker of the House

10. Congress, the Senate and House (of Representatives), (U.S. or national) legislature

11. Answers will vary.

12. all people of the state

13. two years

The N-400 Application (page 90)

A. *Answers will vary. Some suggestions:*

1. Yes, I was arrested for driving without a driver's license.

2. No. I have never been charged with committing a crime.

3. No, I have never been convicted of a crime or offense.

4. No, I have never been placed in a rehabilitative program.

The USCIS Interview (page 93)

A. *Answers will vary but may include:*

1. Does **caliber** mean the same as **quality**?

2. I'm sorry. What does **terrorist** mean?

3. **Polygamy.** Do you mean married to more than one person?

Reading and Writing Test Practice (page 94)

A.
1. b
2. f
3. e
4. d
5. c
6. a

B.
1. Congress has 100 senators.
2. Citizens elect Congress.
3. Congress meets in Washington, D.C.

Grammar Review (page 95)

1. the
2. an
3. nothing
4. The
5. a
6. the, the
7. the, a/the
8. The, the
9. an
10. a

Chapter 9

Getting into the Reading (page 97)

1. A judge is a court official who interprets the law.

2. *Answers may include:* honesty, good judgment,

knowledge of the law, common sense

3–5. Answers will vary.

Getting Information from the Reading (page 100)

A. 1. case

2. law

3. interpreted

4. states

5. ruled

6. people

7. constitutional

8. appealed

B. 1. False

2. True

3. False

4. True

5. True

6. False

7. True

8. True

The 100 History and Government Questions (page 101)

A. 1. b

2. b

3. a

4. c

5. b

B. 1. reviews laws, explains laws, interprets laws, resolves disputes, decides if a law goes against the Constitution

2. the Supreme Court

3. nine

4. John Roberts

5. Congress, legislative, President, executive, the courts, judicial

C.

```
R E D J J L C A B I N E T W
E K L L J U H G V W E K W R
P U E Y A C D E A C H D H M
U G G X K I E I I K H G I K
B W I F E O R T C D V K T L
L H S F C C R I Q I M J E T
I S L C P K U W E M A P H I
C K A P J U S T I C E L O S
A S T W K Q F X I A J I U C
N Y I I F J F Y O V J I S P
V E V K G K U G C H E W E P
T P E P R E S I D E N T O R
R C S U P R E M E C O U R T
V W P A D E M O C R A T V D
```

The N-400 Application (page 102)

A. *Answers will vary. Some suggestions:*

1. Yes, I was arrested for driving without a driver's license.

2. No, I have never applied for relief from a draft.

3. Yes, I served in the military in Mexico.

4. No, I have never been ordered to leave the United States.

The USCIS Interview (page 105)

A. *Answers can be any combination of the phrases in the boxes on the page.*

Reading and Writing Test Practice (page 106)

A. 1. right

2. United States

3. President

4. meets

5. capital

B. 1. The capital of the United States is Washington, D.C.

2. New York City was the first capital of the United States.

3. Delaware was the first state.

Grammar Review (page 107)

A. 1. are

2. are

3. is

4. are

5. is

6. are

7. is

8. are

9. are

10. are

11. are

12. is

Chapter 10

Getting Into the Reading (page 109)

1–3. *Answers will vary.*

4. Arnold Schwarzenegger is governor of California. Economic and environmental issues are important to him.

Getting Information from the Readings (page 112)

A. 1. governor
   2. collect
   3. mayor
   4. records
   5. contradict
   6. National Guard
   7. maintain
   8. officials
   9. zoning
   10. propose

B. 1. S
   2. F
   3. F
   4. S
   5. F
   6. F
   7. S
   8. S
   9. S
   10. S

The 100 History and Government Questions (page 113)

A. 1. provide schooling and education, provide protection (police), provide safety (fire departments), give driver's licenses, approve zoning and land use.

   2. to give up loyalty to other countries, to defend the Constitution and laws of the United States, to obey the laws, to serve in the U.S. military if needed, to serve the nation in other ways if needed.

   3. *Answers will vary.* [District of Columbia residents should answer that D.C. is not a state and does not have a capital. Residents of U.S. territories should name the capital of the territory.]

B. 1. *One of the following:* provide schooling and education, provide protection, provide safety, give driver's licenses, approve zoning and land use

   2. Answers will vary.

   3. Answers will vary.

   4. *One of the following*: to give up loyalty to other countries, to defend the Constitution and laws of the United States, to obey the laws, to serve in the U.S. military if needed, to serve the nation in other ways if needed

The N-400 Application (page 114)

A. 1. give up, loyalty
   2. beliefs
   3. complete
   4. fight for

B. 1. b
   2. a
   3. c
   4. d
   5. f
   6. e

Reading and Writing Test Practice (page 118)

A. 1. is
   2. capital
   3. What
   4. state

B. 1. We pay taxes.
   2. Alaska is the largest state.
   3. California has the most people.

Grammar Review (page 119)

A. 1. are going to sign/will sign
   2. is going to need/will need
   3. is going to go/will go
   4. is going to ask/will ask
   5. are going to ask/will ask
   6. are going to help/will help
   7. are going to be/will be
   8. am going to fight/will fight
   9. are going to have to/will have to
   10. are going to have/will have

Chapter 11

Getting into the Reading (page 121)

1. *Answers will vary. Examples:* a mayor, governor, senator, President

2. *Answers will vary.*

3. to make your voice heard

4. Students will learn this in the reading.

5. They traveled to Washington, D.C. to ask Congress to help the Sudanese people.

Getting Information from the Reading (1) (page 124)

A. 1. candidates
   2. ballot
   3. register
   4. endorse
   5. neighborhood

B. 1. A   5. A
   2. C   6. C
   3. C   7. B
   4. B   8. A

Getting Information from the Reading (2) (page 127)

A. 1. False   4. True
   2. True   5. False
   3. True

B. 1. swearing-in ceremony
   2. the Oath of Allegiance

Susan B. Anthony (page 127)

1. F
2. A
3. A
4. F

The 100 History and Government Questions (page 128)

A. 1. All answers should be checked.
   2. fought for women's rights, fought for civil rights
   3. April 15
   4. when they are 18

B. 1. April 15
   2. 18
   3. *any two:* vote, join a political party, help with a campaign, join a civic group, join a community group, give an elected official your opinion on an issue, call senators and representatives, publicly support or oppose an issue or policy, run for office, write to a newspaper
   4. fought for women's rights, fought for civil rights
   5. at age 18/between 18 and 26

The USCIS Interview (page 129)

A. *Answers will vary. Possible answers:*

   1. I can vote and I can write to my senator. Is that what you meant?

   2. She fought for civil rights. Is that what you were looking for?

   3. April 15. Is my answer clear?

   4. When they are 18. Is that what you meant?

Reading and Writing Test Practice (page 130)

A. 1. citizen
   2. vote for
   3. right
   4. President, November
   5. vote
   6. tax forms
   7. citizens
   8. Senators, states

B. 1. People vote for President in November.
   2. Citizens have the right to vote.
   3. Citizens can vote.

Grammar Review (page 131)

A. 1. can
   2. must
   3. can
   4. can
   5. can
   6. can't
   7. must
   8. must not
   9. may
   10. must

Chapter 12

Part A: U.S. Geography Student A (page 133)

1. Missouri River and Mississippi River
3. Atlantic Ocean
5. California, Arizona, New Mexico, Texas
7. New York Harbor
8. east coast

U.S. Geography: Student B (page 134)

2. Pacific Ocean
4. Maine, New Hampshire, Vermont, New York, Pennsylvania, Ohio, Michigan, Minnesota, North Dakota, Montana, Idaho, Washington, Alaska
6. Washington, D.C.

Part B: U.S. Holidays (page 135)

Answers will vary.

Part C: Important People in History (page 136)

1. Thomas Jefferson
2. Dwight D. Eisenhower
3. George Washington
4. Martin Luther King, Jr. and Susan B. Anthony
5. Abraham Lincoln
6. Benjamin Franklin
7. Susan B. Anthony
8. Woodrow Wilson
9. Africans
10. American Indians
11. Franklin Roosevelt
12. Washington, Jefferson, Lincoln, Wilson, Roosevelt, Eisenhower
13. Martin Luther King, Jr., and Susan B. Anthony
14. New U.S. citizens

Part D: U.S. History Review (page 137)

1. e
2. d
3. i
4. h
5. g
6. k
7. a
8. c
9. b
10. j
11. f
12. l

Part E: Final Review: Board Game (page 138)

Answers will vary.

Part F: Review The Three Branches and Five Questions (page 140)

A.

	Executive Branch	Legislative Branch	Judicial Branch
Who?	• President • Vice President • Cabinet	• Senators • Representatives	• Chief Justice • Supreme Court Justices
What?	• Signs laws • Vetoes laws	• Makes Federal Laws	• Explains laws
Where?	• White House	• Capitol Building	• Supreme Court Building
When?	• Presidents are elected for 4 years.	• Senators are elected for 6 years. • Representatives are elected for 2 years.	• Supreme Court Justices are appointed for life.
How Many?	• Presidents: 1 • Vice Presidents: 1 • Cabinet Departments: 15	• Senators: 100 • Representatives: 435	• Supreme Court Justices: 9

B.
1. Answers will vary.
2. Answers will vary.
3. current U.S. President
4. current U.S. Vice President
5. John Roberts

100 History and Government Questions and Answers

AMERICAN GOVERNMENT

A: Principles of American Democracy

1. What is the supreme law of the land?

   - *the Constitution*

2. What does the Constitution do?

   - *sets up the government*
   - *defines the government*
   - *protects basic rights of Americans*

3. The idea of self-government is in the first three words of the Constitution. What are these words?

   - *We the People*

4. What is an amendment?

   - *a change (to the Constitution)*
   - *an addition (to the Constitution)*

5. What do we call the first ten amendments to the Constitution?

   - *the Bill of Rights*

6. What is <u>one</u> right or freedom from the First Amendment?*

   - *speech*
   - *religion*
   - *assembly*
   - *press*
   - *petition the government*

7. How many amendments does the Constitution have?

   - *twenty-seven (27)*

8. What did the Declaration of Independence do?

   - *announced our independence (from Great Britain)*
   - *declared our independence (from Great Britain)*
   - *said that the United States is free (from Great Britain)*

9. What are <u>two</u> rights in the Declaration of Independence?

   - *life*
   - *liberty*
   - *pursuit of happiness*

10. What is freedom of religion?

    - *You can practice any religion, or not practice a religion.*

11. What is the economic system in the United States?*

    - *capitalist economy*
    - *market economy*

12. What is the "rule of law"?

    - *Everyone must follow the law.*
    - *Leaders must obey the law.*
    - *Government must obey the law.*
    - *No one is above the law.*

B: System of Government

13. Name <u>one</u> branch or part of the government.*

    - *Congress*
    - *legislative*
    - *President*
    - *executive*
    - *the courts*
    - *judicial*

14. What stops <u>one</u> branch of government from becoming too powerful?

    - *checks and balances*
    - *separation of powers*

15. Who is in charge of the executive branch?

    - *the President*

16. Who makes federal laws?

    - *Congress*
    - *Senate and House (of Representatives)*
    - *(U.S. or national) legislature*

* If you are 65 years old or older and have been a legal permanent resident of the United States for 20 or more years, you may study just the questions that have been marked with an asterisk.

17. What are the <u>two</u> parts of the U.S. Congress?*

    - *the Senate and House (of Representatives)*

18. How many U.S. Senators are there?

    - *one hundred (100)*

19. We elect a U.S. Senator for how many years?

    - *six (6)*

20. Who is <u>one</u> of your state's U.S. Senators now?*

    - *Answers will vary. [District of Columbia residents and residents of U.S. territories should answer that D.C. (or the territory where the applicant lives) has no U.S. Senators.]*

21. The House of Representatives has how many voting members?

    - *four hundred thirty-five (435)*

22. We elect a U.S. Representative for how many years?

    - *two (2)*

23. Name your U.S. Representative.

    - *Answers will vary. [Residents of territories with nonvoting Delegates or Resident Commissioners may provide the name of that Delegate or Commissioner. Also acceptable is any statement that the territory has no (voting) Representatives in Congress.]*

24. Who does a U.S. Senator represent?

    - *all people of the state*

25. Why do some states have more Representatives than other states?

    - *(because of) the state's population*
    - *(because) they have more people*
    - *(because) some states have more people*

26. We elect a President for how many years?

    - *four (4)*

27. In what month do we vote for President?*

    - *November*

28. What is the name of the President of the United States now?*

    - *the current President*

29. What is the name of the Vice President of the United States now?

    - *the current Vice President*

30. If the President can no longer serve, who becomes President?

    - *the Vice President*

31. If both the President and the Vice President can no longer serve, who becomes President?

    - *the Speaker of the House*

32. Who is the Commander in Chief of the military?

    - *the President*

33. Who signs bills to become laws?

    - *the President*

34. Who vetoes bills?

    - *the President*

35. What does the President's cabinet do?

    - *advises the President*

36. What are <u>two</u> cabinet-level positions?

    - *Secretary of Agriculture*
    - *Secretary of Commerce*
    - *Secretary of Defense*
    - *Secretary of Education*
    - *Secretary of Energy*
    - *Secretary of Health and Human Services*
    - *Secretary of Homeland Security*
    - *Secretary of Housing and Urban Development*

* If you are 65 years old or older and have been a legal permanent resident of the United States for 20 or more years, you may study just the questions that have been marked with an asterisk.

- *Secretary of the Interior*
- *Secretary of Labor*
- *Secretary of State*
- *Secretary of Transportation*
- *Secretary of the Treasury*
- *Secretary of Veterans Affairs*
- *Attorney General*
- *Vice President*

37. What does the judicial branch do?

- *reviews laws*
- *explains laws*
- *resolves disputes (disagreements)*
- *decides if a law goes against the Constitution*

38. What is the highest court in the United States?

- *the Supreme Court*

39. How many justices are on the Supreme Court?

- *nine (9)*

40. Who is the Chief Justice of the United States now?

- *John Roberts (John G. Roberts, Jr.)*

41. Under our Constitution, some powers belong to the federal government. What is <u>one</u> power of the federal government?

- *to print money*
- *to declare war*
- *to create an army*
- *to make treaties*

42. Under our Constitution, some powers belong to the states. What is <u>one</u> power of the states?

- *provide schooling and education*
- *provide protection (police)*
- *provide safety (fire departments)*
- *give a driver's license*
- *approve zoning and land use*

43. Who is the Governor of your state now?

- *Answers will vary. [District of Columbia residents should answer that D.C. does not have a Governor.]*

44. What is the capital of your state?*

- *Answers will vary. [District of Columbia residents should answer that D.C. is not a state and does not have a capital. Residents of U.S. territories should name the capital of the territory.]*

45. What are the <u>two</u> major political parties in the United States?*

- *Democratic and Republican*

46. What is the political party of the President now?

- *the political party of the current President*

47. What is the name of the Speaker of the House of Representatives now?

- *the current Speaker of the House of Representatives*

C: Rights and Responsibilities

48. There are four amendments to the Constitution about who can vote. Describe <u>one</u> of them.

- *Citizens eighteen (18) and older (can vote).*
- *You don't have to pay (a poll tax) to vote.*
- *Any citizen can vote. (Women and men can vote.)*
- *A male citizen of any race (can vote).*

49. What is <u>one</u> responsibility that is only for United States citizens?*

- *serve on a jury*
- *vote in a federal election*

* If you are 65 years old or older and have been a legal permanent resident of the United States for 20 or more years, you may study just the questions that have been marked with an asterisk.

50. Name <u>one</u> right only for United States citizens.

- *vote in a federal election*
- *run for federal office*

51. What are <u>two</u> rights of everyone living in the United States?

- *freedom of expression*
- *freedom of speech*
- *freedom of assembly*
- *freedom to petition the government*
- *freedom of worship*
- *the right to bear arms*

52. What do we show loyalty to when we say the Pledge of Allegiance?

- *the United States*
- *the flag*

53. What is <u>one</u> promise you make when you become a United States citizen?

- *give up loyalty to other countries*
- *defend the Constitution and laws of the United States*
- *obey the laws of the United States*
- *serve in the U.S. military (if needed)*
- *serve (do important work for) the nation (if needed)*
- *be loyal to the United States*

54. How old do citizens have to be to vote for President?*

- *eighteen (18) and older*

55. What are <u>two</u> ways that Americans can participate in their democracy?

- *vote*
- *join a political party*
- *help with a campaign*
- *join a civic group*
- *join a community group*
- *give an elected official your opinion on an issue*
- *call Senators and Representatives*

- *publicly support or oppose an issue or policy*
- *run for office*
- *write to a newspaper*

56. When is the last day you can send in federal income tax forms?*

- *April 15*

57. When must all men register for the Selective Service?

- *at age eighteen (18)*
- *between eighteen (18) and twenty-six (26)*

AMERICAN HISTORY

A: Colonial Period and Independence

58. What is <u>one</u> reason colonists came to America?

- *freedom*
- *political liberty*
- *religious freedom*
- *economic opportunity*
- *practice their religion*
- *escape persecution*

59. Who lived in America before the Europeans arrived?

- *American Indians*
- *Native Americans*

60. What group of people was taken to America and sold as slaves?

- *Africans*
- *people from Africa*

61. Why did the colonists fight the British?

- *because of high taxes (taxation without representation)*
- *because the British army stayed in their houses (boarding, quartering)*
- *because they didn't have self-government*

* If you are 65 years old or older and have been a legal permanent resident of the United States for 20 or more years, you may study just the questions that have been marked with an asterisk.

62. Who wrote the Declaration of Independence?

- *(Thomas) Jefferson*

63. When was the Declaration of Independence adopted?

- *July 4, 1776*

64. There were 13 original states. Name <u>three</u>.

- *New Hampshire*
- *Massachusetts*
- *Rhode Island*
- *Connecticut*
- *New York*
- *New Jersey*
- *Pennsylvania*
- *Delaware*
- *Maryland*
- *Virginia*
- *North Carolina*
- *South Carolina*
- *Georgia*

65. What happened at the Constitutional Convention?

- *The Constitution was written.*
- *The Founding Fathers wrote the Constitution.*

66. When was the Constitution written?

- *1787*

67. The Federalist Papers supported the passage of the U.S. Constitution. Name <u>one</u> of the writers.

- *(James) Madison*
- *(Alexander) Hamilton*
- *(John) Jay*
- *Publius*

68. What is <u>one</u> thing Benjamin Franklin is famous for?

- *U.S. diplomat*
- *oldest member of the Constitutional Convention*

- *first Postmaster General of the United States*
- *writer of "Poor Richard's Almanac"*
- *started the first free libraries*

69. Who is the "Father of Our Country"?

- *(George) Washington*

70. Who was the first President?*

- *(George) Washington*

B: 1800s

71. What territory did the United States buy from France in 1803?

- *the Louisiana Territory*
- *Louisiana*

72. Name <u>one</u> war fought by the United States in the 1800s.

- *War of 1812*
- *Mexican-American War*
- *Civil War*
- *Spanish-American War*

73. Name the U.S. war Between the North and the South.

- *the Civil War*
- *the War Between the States*

74. Name <u>one</u> problem that led to the Civil War.

- *slavery*
- *economic reasons*
- *states' rights*

75. What was <u>one</u> important thing that Abraham Lincoln did?*

- *freed the slaves (Emancipation Proclamation)*
- *saved (or preserved) the Union*
- *led the United States during the Civil War*

* If you are 65 years old or older and have been a legal permanent resident of the United States for 20 or more years, you may study just the questions that have been marked with an asterisk.

76. What did the Emancipation Proclamation do?

- *freed the slaves*
- *freed slaves in the Confederacy*
- *freed slaves in the Confederate states*
- *freed slaves in most Southern states*

77. What did Susan B. Anthony do?

- *fought for women's rights*
- *fought for civil rights*

C: Recent American History and Other Important Historical Information

78. Name <u>one</u> war fought by the United States in the 1900s.*

- *World War I*
- *World War II*
- *Korean War*
- *Vietnam War*
- *(Persian) Gulf War*

79. Who was President during World War I?

- *(Woodrow) Wilson*

80. Who was President during the Great Depression and World War II?

- *(Franklin) Roosevelt*

81. Who did the United States fight in World War II?

- *Japan, Germany, and Italy*

82. Before he was President, Eisenhower was a general. What war was he in?

- *World War II*

83. During the Cold War, what was the main concern of the United States?

- *Communism*

84. What movement tried to end racial discrimination?

- *civil rights (movement)*

85. What did Martin Luther King, Jr., do?*

- *fought for civil rights*
- *worked for equality for all Americans*

86. What major event happened on September 11, 2001, in the United States?

- *Terrorists attacked the United States.*

87. Name <u>one</u> American Indian tribe in the United States. *[USCIS Officers will be supplied with a list of federally recognized American Indian tribes.]* Tribes include:

- *Cherokee*
- *Navajo*
- *Sioux*
- *Chippewa*
- *Choctaw*
- *Pueblo*
- *Apache*
- *Iroquois*
- *Creek*
- *Blackfeet*
- *Seminole*
- *Cheyenne*
- *Arawak*
- *Shawnee*
- *Mohegan*
- *Huron*
- *Oneida*
- *Lakota*
- *Crow*
- *Teton*
- *Hopi*
- *Inuit*

INTEGRATED CIVICS

A: Geography

88. Name <u>one</u> of the two longest rivers in the United States.

- *Missouri (River)*
- *Mississippi (River)*

---

* If you are 65 years old or older and have been a legal permanent resident of the United States for 20 or more years, you may study just the questions that have been marked with an asterisk.

89. What ocean is on the west coast of the United States?

- *Pacific (Ocean)*

90. What ocean is on the east coast of the United States?

- *Atlantic (Ocean)*

91. Name <u>one</u> U.S. territory.

- *Puerto Rico*
- *U.S. Virgin Islands*
- *American Samoa*
- *Northern Mariana Islands*
- *Guam*

92. Name <u>one</u> state that borders Canada.

- *Maine*
- *New Hampshire*
- *Vermont*
- *New York*
- *Pennsylvania*
- *Ohio*
- *Michigan*
- *Minnesota*
- *North Dakota*
- *Montana*
- *Idaho*
- *Washington*
- *Alaska*

93. Name <u>one</u> state that borders Mexico.

- *California*
- *Arizona*
- *New Mexico*
- *Texas*

94. What is the capital of the United States?*

- *Washington, D.C.*

95. Where is the Statue of Liberty?*

- *New York (Harbor)*
- *Liberty Island*

[Also acceptable are New Jersey, near New York City, and on the Hudson (River).]

B: Symbols

96. Why does the flag have 13 stripes?

- *because there were 13 original colonies*
- *because the stripes represent the original colonies*

97. Why does the flag have 50 stars?*

- *because there is one star for each state*
- *because each star represents a state*
- *because there are 50 states*

98. What is the name of the national anthem?

- *"The Star-Spangled Banner"*

C: Holidays

99. When do we celebrate Independence Day?*

- *July 4*

100. Name <u>two</u> national U.S. holidays.

- *New Year's Day*
- *Martin Luther King, Jr. Day*
- *Presidents' Day*
- *Memorial Day*
- *Independence Day*
- *Labor Day*
- *Columbus Day*
- *Veterans Day*
- *Thanksgiving*
- *Christmas*

* If you are 65 years old or older and have been a legal permanent resident of the United States for 20 or more years, you may study just the questions that have been marked with an asterisk.

DVD Interview Scripts

Ms. Garcia Interview Script

Chapter 1

Interviewer: Come in. You must be… Ms. Garcia.

Ms. Garcia: Yes. Good to meet you.

Interviewer: Please, have a seat.

Ms. Garcia: Thank you.

Interviewer: Who came with you here today?

Ms. Garcia: My … spouse.

Interviewer: I will be asking you some questions. You need to answer them truthfully … to tell the truth.

Ms. Garcia: The truth. *La verdad.* Of course.

Interviewer: Yes. Please stand and raise your right hand. Do you promise to tell the truth, the whole truth, and nothing but the truth?

Ms. Garcia: I promise.

Interviewer: Please sit down again. Do you understand what you promised?

Ms. Garcia: Yes. To tell the truth. All the truth.

Interviewer: Could you show me your passport, your permanent resident card, and your photos? Your passport and permanent resident card.

Ms. Garcia: Oh *mi pasaporte.* Yes, here.

Interviewer: Please tell me your name.

Ms. Garcia: My name is Maria Elena Garcia.

Interviewer: How long have you been a permanent resident of the U.S.?

Ms. Garcia: Resident? I don't understand.

Interviewer: You are a resident of the United States, yes?

Ms. Garcia: Resident? Yes.

Interviewer: When did you come here?

Ms. Garcia: Six … six year … years.

Chapter 2

Interviewer: Six years. And what country are you from? What nationality?

Ms. Garcia: Nationality. El Salvador.

Interviewer: Were you born in El Salvador?

Ms. Garcia: I was born in San Miguel.

Interviewer: San Miguel, El Salvador? Are you married?

Ms. Garcia: Married? *Casada*, yes.

Interviewer: Do you see the line that says "home address"?

Ms. Garcia: Yes.

Narrator: Your body language is important. You don't need to be nervous, so don't *look* nervous. Just relax, sit up straight, but comfortably. And keep good eye contact.

Interviewer: And your phone number is 415-555-6776?

Ms. Garcia: *Sí.* Yes, it is.

Chapter 3

Interviewer: Are you Hispanic or Latino?

Ms. Garcia: Yes, I am Latina.

Interviewer: Is your hair black?

Ms. Garcia: Yes, it is.

Interviewer: Is your height five feet two inches?

Ms. Garcia: It is.

Interviewer: It says here that you live here.

Ms. Garcia: Yes.

Interviewer: And you have lived there for five years. Is this true?

Ms. Garcia: Yes, it is.

Interviewer: And do you work at Portola Fashions?

Ms. Garcia: Yes, I do.

Interviewer: What do you do there? What is your job?

Ms. Garcia: Ahh … garment worker … I am a garment worker.

Narrator: Sometimes, if you aren't sure of a word in English, you can use body language to express the idea.

Chapter 4

Interviewer: And in the last five years, how many trips outside the U.S. did you take?

Ms. Garcia: *No entiendo.* I don't understand.

Interviewer: You traveled … outside … the United States?

Ms. Garcia: Yes. I travel.

Interviewer: Traveled. Before now.

Ms. Garcia: Yes. I … I traveled.

Interviewer: How many times?

Ms. Garcia: One time. Two week … weeks.

Interviewer: You went to El Salvador?

Ms. Garcia: Yes. El Salvador. I went to El Salvador.

Interviewer: Okay … how many times have you been married?

Ms. Garcia: Married? *Casada.* One … one time.

Interviewer: When did you get married? What year?

Ms. Garcia: I … I … I can't say in English.

Interviewer: Was it 1999?

Ms. Garcia: Yes, it was.

Chapter 5

Interviewer: Is your spouse a U.S. citizen?

Ms. Garcia: I don't understand. Please say again.

Interviewer: Is your spouse—your husband—a citizen of the U.S.?

Ms. Garcia: No.

Interviewer: What country is he a citizen of?

Ms. Garcia: El Salvador.

Interviewer: And how many times has your husband been married?

Ms. Garcia: Sorry. A little nervous. Could you please repeat the question?

Interviewer: Your husband … was he married before he married you?

Ms. Garcia: No.

Interviewer: Do you have children?

Ms. Garcia: Yes.

Interviewer: How many?

Ms. Garcia: Two.

Interviewer: And what are their names?

Ms. Garcia: Alejandro is my son. Esperanza is my daughter.

Chapter 6

Interviewer: Have you ever voted in any federal, state, or local election in the U.S.?

Ms. Garcia: Have I ever voted?

Interviewer: You understand "vote," right?

Ms. Garcia: *Si. Votar.*

Interviewer: Did you ever vote?

Ms. Garcia: Yes. In El Salvador.

Interviewer: And here, in the U.S.?

Ms. Garcia: No.

Interviewer: Do you owe any taxes that are overdue?

Ms. Garcia: Over … due? Taxes that are … overdue?

Interviewer: Yes, taxes you should have paid before now.

Ms. Garcia: No, I pay all my taxes.

Chapter 7

Interviewer: Have you ever been a member of a terrorist organization?

Ms. Garcia: I'm … I'm sorry. Could you please say again slowly?

Interviewer: Have you ever been a member …

Ms. Garcia: A member …

Interviewer: … of a terrorist organization?

Ms. Garcia: *Terrorista.* Oh, no, I am no terrorist.

Interviewer: Have you ever advocated the overthrow of any government by force or violence?

Ms. Garcia: I don't understand. Can you please explain the question for me?

Interviewer: Did you ever try to make people get rid of a government …

Ms. Garcia: Ah …

Interviewer: … by force or violence?

Ms. Garcia: No. Never.

Chapter 8

Interviewer: Have you been convicted of a crime?

Ms. Garcia: Convicted? Could you please tell me what does "convicted" mean?

Interviewer: "Convicted" means that a judge or a jury found that you did something against the law.

Ms. Garcia: Oh. Not convicted. Never.

Interviewer: Have you ever been in jail or prison?

Ms. Garcia: No.

Interviewer: Have you ever been a prostitute?

Ms. Garcia: *Prostituta?* Prostitute. No. Never.

Interviewer: Have you ever lied to an official of the government so that you could get into the United States?

Ms. Garcia: "Lied" means no tell truth, no?

Interviewer: Yes.

Ms. Garcia: No. I never lie to get into United States.

Chapter 9

Interviewer: Have you ever been removed or excluded or deported from the United States?

Ms. Garcia: Let me think … deported?

Interviewer: Removed, excluded, or deported.

Ms. Garcia: No.

Interviewer: Have you ever served in the U.S. Armed Forces?

Ms. Garcia: I'm not sure. Armed Forces is like army, no? … No.

Chapter 10

Interviewer: Do you understand the full Oath of Allegiance to the United States?

Ms. Garcia: You are asking me about allegiance I take to be citizen?

Interviewer: What did you say?

Ms. Garcia: You are asking me about allegiance … oath that I take to be citizen?

Interviewer: Yes.

Ms. Garcia: Yes, I understand this oath.

Interviewer: Are you willing to take the full Oath of Allegiance?

Ms. Garcia: You ask me if I will take this oath?

Interviewer: Yes, are you willing to take it?

Ms. Garcia: Yes, I will take this oath.

Chapter 11

Interviewer: Have you studied the 100 history and government questions?

Ms. Garcia: Yes, I study … studied very much.

Interviewer: Okay, now I'm going to ask you …

Narrator: You've probably studied the 100 history and government questions a lot, but even so, you might be nervous. Remember, you only have to answer six out of ten questions correctly.

Interviewer: What do we call the first ten amendments to the Constitution?

Ms. Garcia: The Rights of Bills.

Interviewer: Ahh ….

Ms. Garcia: Was that OK?

Interviewer: Let's try it again. What do we call the first ten amendments to the Constitution?

Ms. Garcia: The Bill of Rights? … Did you understand what I say?

Interviewer: Yes, that's fine. Next, how many terms can the President serve? *(Ms. Garcia does not answer.)* Let's try another. Who was the first President?

Ms. Garcia: George Wash… Washington.

Interviewer: How many justices are on the Supreme Court?

Ms. Garcia: Nine justices. Nine.

Interviewer: What color are the stars on our flag?

Ms. Garcia: The stars? Mmm … white.

Interviewer: How many states are there in the United States today?

Ms. Garcia: Fifteen … I mean fifty.

Interviewer: Finally … what is the 4th of July?

Ms. Garcia: Independence Day.

Interviewer: Good. Now here's a question for you. Please read it for me.

Ms. Garcia: "What country … is north … of the United States?"

Interviewer: Good. Now, please write the sentence I say. Canada … is… north … of … the … United … States. *(Ms. Garcia writes the sentence.)* Very good, Ms. Garcia. I see that you've worked very hard.

Ms. Garcia: Thank you very much.

Interviewer: Now, we are done with the questions. The only thing you need to do is sign the forms here….

Ms. Garcia: Okay. Here.

Interviewer: … and here.

Ms. Garcia: Okay.

Interviewer: Congratulations, Ms. Garcia. I can tell that you will be a very good citizen of the United States.

Ms. Garcia: Did I … did … did I pass?

Interviewer: Yes. You passed.

Ms. Garcia: Thank you. Thank you for your help to make me a citizen.

Interviewer: You're very welcome. So, are you going out to celebrate …?

Mr. Huang Interview Script

Chapter 1

Mr. Huang: Excuse me. Are you Ms. Davis, for the interview?

Interviewer: Yes. You must be Mr. Huang.

Mr. Huang: Yes, I am.

Interviewer: It's good to meet you.

Mr. Huang: Thank you.

Interviewer: Please, have a seat. How do you like the weather today?

Mr. Huang: It's a bit hot, but I like it.

Interviewer: I do too. Now, Mr. Huang, I'm going to go through your N-400 form with you. And then I'm going to ask you a few questions about U.S. government and history, and then I'm going to ask you to read and write a sentence. Okay?

Mr. Huang: Yes.

Interviewer: You'll need to tell the truth.

Mr. Huang: Yes.

Interviewer: Okay. Please stand up and raise your right hand. Do you promise to tell the truth, the whole truth, and nothing but the truth?

Mr. Huang: I do.

Interviewer: Good, you may sit down again.

Mr. Huang: Thank you.

Interviewer: Now, please show me your passport, your alien registration card, and your photos.

Mr. Huang: Here they are.

Interviewer: Thanks. Very good.

Mr. Huang: Thank you.

Interviewer: All right. What is your full name, please?

Mr. Huang: Xiang Hua Huang.

Interviewer: And when did you become a permanent resident of the United States?

Mr. Huang: Ten year ago … almost.

Interviewer: Ten years?

Chapter 2

Interviewer: Can you tell me where were you born—what country?

Mr. Huang: China.

Interviewer: Are your parents U.S. citizens?

Mr. Huang: They are not alive today.

Interviewer: Oh, I see. What's your current marital status?

Mr. Huang: Current? Now?

Interviewer: Yes, now. Are you married?

Mr. Huang: Yes, I am.

Interviewer: Will you look at this form and tell me if this is your correct address?

Narrator: During the interview, think about body language: Relax, but sit up straight. And make good eye contact with the interviewer.

Interviewer: And is this still your e-mail address?

Mr. Huang: Yes, it is. For e-mail this address is good.

Chapter 3

Interviewer: Is your race Asian?

Mr. Huang: Yes, it is.

Interviewer: And do you have blonde hair?

Mr. Huang: No, I don't.

Interviewer: Black hair?

Mr. Huang: Yes, I do.

Interviewer: What is your eye color?

Mr. Huang: Brown.

Interviewer: Are these addresses the only places you've lived in the past five years?

Mr. Huang: Yes, they are.

Interviewer: And you're an engineer, right?

Mr. Huang: Yes, mechanical engineer.

Interviewer: Are Jones Engineering and Chelsea Corporation the only places you have worked in the past five years?

Mr. Huang: Yes, those two.

Chapter 4

Interviewer: How many trips have you taken outside of the United States in the past five years?

Mr. Huang: In the past five years? Let me see … I go … I went to China … once. I visited family.

Interviewer: Is that the only trip?

Mr. Huang: No, one more trip.

Interviewer: Where did you go?

Mr. Huang: I traveled to Singapore. I visited family. Some family who live there.

Interviewer: Okay. And how many times have you been married?

Mr. Huang: I have been married two times. Twice. I am married now, and I was married in China.

Interviewer: Were you divorced?

Mr. Huang: Yes, in China.

Interviewer: When?

Mr. Huang: I got divorced in … 1989.

Chapter 5

Interviewer: Okay. Now please tell me, is your wife a U.S. citizen?

Mr. Huang: No, she is Chinese.

Interviewer: And what's her immigration status?

Mr. Huang: Sorry. I don't understand. Say it again, please.

Interviewer: Yes, I asked about her immigration status. Is she a lawful, permanent U.S. resident?

Mr. Huang: Yes, she have her green card.

Interviewer: Okay. And how many times has your wife been married, including annulled marriages?

Mr. Huang: What kind of marriage? Could you repeat that, please?

Interviewer: Yes. Annulled marriages are marriages that have been declared void or invalid. Do you understand?

Mr. Huang: Yes, I understand. My wife has been only married to me.

Interviewer: And I see one child listed on your form. Ming Mei, is she your only child?

Mr. Huang: Yes, she is.

Interviewer: That's a very pretty name!

Mr. Huang: I think so, too.

Chapter 6

Interviewer: And have you ever registered to vote in any election in the U.S.?

Mr. Huang: Have I ever registered to vote *here*, in the U.S.? No, I have never registered.

Interviewer: And since getting your permanent resident card—your green card—have you ever failed to file a required federal, state, or local tax return?

Mr. Huang: Have I ever *failed* to file a tax return?

Interviewer: Yes, have you ever *not* filed a tax return?

Mr. Huang: No, I always pay my taxes.

Interviewer: Good. And do you owe any overdue taxes?

Mr. Huang: I no owe … I do not owe any money.

Interviewer: Good.

Chapter 7

Interviewer: Mr. Huang, have you ever been a member of or associated with any organization, association, fund foundation, party, club, society, or similar group in the United States or in any other place?

Mr. Huang: Sorry, that was long question! Could you repeat that slowly, please?

Interviewer: Sure. Have you ever been a member of any group—an organization or a club, for example?

Mr. Huang: In the United States?

Interviewer: Here or back in China.

Mr. Huang: I have been a member of the Chinese Progressive Association. That's all.

Interviewer: Okay. And have you ever persecuted anyone based on their race, religion, nation of origin, membership in a particular social group, or political opinion?

Mr. Huang: Another long question. Could you please explain that question, please?

Interviewer: Sure. I'll shorten it. Have you ever persecuted anyone for any reason? You do know what "persecute" means, don't you?

Mr. Huang: Sure. Treat bad … *badly* … because you don't like what that person does or believes.

Interviewer: Exactly.

Mr. Huang: No, I never persecute nobody … I mean, *any*body.

Chapter 8

Interviewer: Have you ever committed a crime or offense for which you were *not* arrested?

Mr. Huang: Does *offense* mean something I do to offend someone?

Interviewer: Not quite. An offense is something illegal or against the law.

Mr. Huang: Oh, I understand. No.

Interviewer: And have you ever gambled illegally or received income from illegal gambling?

Mr. Huang: No.

Interviewer: And have you ever failed to support your dependents or failed to pay alimony?

Mr. Huang: Alimony? I forget what that means.

Interviewer: Alimony is money you give to your ex-wife each month after a divorce.

Mr. Huang: Oh. After the Chinese divorce, the judge no make … *did not* make me to pay the alimony.

Chapter 9

Interviewer: Have you ever been ordered to be removed, excluded, or deported from the United States?

Mr. Huang: Give me a moment, please. Ordered to be removed … or excluded?

Interviewer: Excluded, do you know what that means?

Mr. Huang: Left out. I never was ordered to be left out or deported.

Interviewer: Okay. And have you ever applied for an exemption from the military service of the U.S. Armed Forces?

Mr. Huang: Let me think. I have never applied. I'm much too old for the Army or the Navy!

Chapter 10

Interviewer: Do you support the Constitution and form of government of the United States?

Mr. Huang: When you say "form of government," you mean something like democracy?

Interviewer: Yes, that's close enough.

Mr. Huang: Then … I support our government form.

Interviewer: Can you repeat that, please?

Mr. Huang: Then I support our form of government.

Interviewer: Thank you. And do you understand the Oath of Allegiance to the United States?

Mr. Huang: Yes. I read it many times, so I understand.

Interviewer: Good. And if the law requires it, are you prepared to bear arms on behalf of the United States?

Mr. Huang: To fight for the U.S.?

Interviewer: Yes.

Mr. Huang: I would carry weapons … if they want a old guy like me!

Chapter 11

Interviewer: And have you studied the 100 government and history questions?

Mr. Huang: Yes.

Narrator: This part of the interview can be hard. People sometimes forget answers, even answers they know. The best thing to do is just *relax*.

Interviewer: Whom did the United States fight in World War II?

Mr. Huang: Germany … Japan … and one more … Italy, I think.

Interviewer: You're right. Now, what is freedom of religion?

Mr. Huang: You can practice any religion … or you're not practicing a religion. You understand me?

Interviewer: Yes, that was fine. Now, who is the Commander in Chief of the military?

Mr. Huang: The President.

Interviewer: And who elects the President of the United States?

Mr. Huang: It's the … the word "college" is in it … the Electoral College.

Interviewer: Very good. And what is the White House?

Mr. Huang: The official home of the President.

Interviewer: Good. Finally, who was the main writer of the Declaration of Independence?

Mr. Huang: Jefferson? Thomas Jefferson.

Interviewer: Excellent. Now, will you please read this question back to me?

Mr. Huang: "When is Flag Day?"

Interviewer: Good. Will you please write this sentence? Flag Day … is in June. *(Mr. Huang writes the sentence.)* Excellent. You certainly understand English very well, Mr. Huang.

Mr. Huang: Well, easy to understand, hard to speak.

Interviewer: Well, there are no more questions, and you've passed, so all that's left now is to sign your name.

Mr. Huang: Where?

Interviewer: Here and here.

Mr. Huang: Okay.

Interviewer: Congratulations!

Mr. Huang: Thank you, Ms. Davis. It's not as scary as I thought.

Interviewer: I knew you'd do well. And I know you'll be a wonderful American citizen.

Mr. Huang: Thank you.

Mr. Dada Interview Script

Chapter 1

Interviewer: Come in.

Mr. Dada: Are you Ms. Davis?

Interviewer: Yes. And you must be Mr. Dada.

Mr. Dada: Yes, that is me … That is I.

Interviewer: Good to meet you. Have a seat.

Mr. Dada: Thank you.

Interviewer: Is it still raining?

Mr. Dada: No, it stopped.

Interviewer: Oh, good. How long did it take you to get here?

Mr. Dada: About one hour.

Interviewer: Not too much traffic?

Mr. Dada: No.

Interviewer: Good. Now, I'll be asking you a lot of questions. And, of course, I expect you to be truthful.

Mr. Dada: Of course.

Interviewer: Please stand and raise your right hand. Do you promise to tell the truth, the whole truth, and nothing but the truth?

Mr. Dada: I do.

Interviewer: You may sit down again. Do you know what kind of promise you just made?

Mr. Dada: An oath. I believe it is called an oath.

Interviewer: Exactly. And can you tell me why you have come here today.

Mr. Dada: Why? Because I hope to become a citizen of the United States.

Interviewer: Very good. Do you have identification with you, and your passport photos?

Mr. Dada: Yes. Here is my green card. And here is my passport from Togo.

Interviewer: Very good. Now … what is your full name?

Mr. Dada: My first name is Ola. My middle name is Yinka. And my last name is Dada. Ola Yinka Dada.

Interviewer: Very good. And when did you become a permanent resident of the U.S.?

Mr. Dada: Almost eight years ago.

Chapter 2

Interviewer: Excellent. Are you or have you ever been married?

Mr. Dada: No, I not … I am not married. I have never been …

Narrator: Body language is important. So remind yourself to sit up straight … to smile sometimes … and to look the interviewer in the eye.

Interviewer: Is the address on your application correct?

Mr. Dada: Yes, it is.

Interviewer: On the form we have your phone number as 212-555-2824. Is this correct?

Mr. Dada: Yes. That is my only phone. And my e-mail address is correct, also.

Chapter 3

Interviewer: Good. Now, here are some easy questions. Are you male?

Mr. Dada: Yes.

Interviewer: Are you black or African American?

Mr. Dada: Yes, I am.

Interviewer: What color is your hair?

Mr. Dada: Black.

Interviewer: And do you have brown eyes?

Mr. Dada: Yes, I do.

Interviewer: Good. Your application says that you have had two addresses in the last five years: where you live now and one other address. Is this true?

Mr. Dada: Yes, it is. I live … I *lived* … with my brother and my cousin my first four years in America.

Interviewer: And did you attend college in Togo?

Mr. Dada: No, I did not. I received my bachelor's degree in the United States, in accounting.

Interviewer: And since graduating from college you've worked at the same company?

Mr. Dada: Yes, it is a very good company. I recently received a promotion.

Interviewer: Very good.

Chapter 4

Interviewer: I see you traveled outside the United States three times in the last five years.

Mr. Dada: Yes, I took three trips.

Interviewer: Can you tell me about those trips, please.

Mr. Dada: Yes. My first trip, my uncle sended … *sent* me a plane ticket, and I visited him in London. I stayed nine … no, wait, ten days.

Interviewer: Good. By the way, there's no need to be nervous …. You are *allowed* to travel outside of the United States.

Mr. Dada: Thank you.

Interviewer: And you visited Mexico, too. Was that a vacation?

Mr. Dada: Yes, last winter I went to Cancun with my brother and my cousin.

Interviewer: That sounds like fun.

Mr. Dada: It was. I really like Cancun.

Interviewer: What about this two-day trip to Canada?

Mr. Dada: I drove to Toronto for work with my boss.

Interviewer: Before we go on I just want to make sure of one thing: You've never been married before, right?

Mr. Dada: Right. Never. I have never been married.

Chapter 5

Interviewer: Okay, then the next part of the application doesn't apply to your case.

Mr. Dada: Doesn't … ? Can you say that again, please?

Interviewer: I said the next part of the application doesn't apply in your case. That's because you've never been married.

Mr. Dada: Ah, yes. Because I do not have a wife.

Interviewer: What about children? How many sons and daughters have you had? Even though you've never been married, you *might* have children.

Mr. Dada: How many? I'm sorry, can you please repeat the question exactly?

Interviewer: Sure. How many sons and daughters have you had?

Mr. Dada: I do not have any children.

Interviewer: Okay. Let's move on to the next part.

Mr. Dada: Okay.

Chapter 6

Interviewer: Have you ever claimed to be a citizen of the United States, in writing or in any other way?

Mr. Dada: Have I ever claimed to be a citizen? Ah, no. I no … I have not.

Interviewer: Okay. You haven't ever voted in this country, have you?

Mr. Dada: No. I no … I did not vote, ever. I can't. I am not a citizen.

Interviewer: You don't have any title of nobility in a foreign country, do you?

Mr. Dada: No, I am not a noble … a nobleman.

Interviewer: Have you ever been declared legally incompetent or been confined to a mental institution within the last five years?

Mr. Dada: Have I ever been declared legally incompetent?

Interviewer: Right, have you?

Mr. Dada: No.

Interviewer: And you weren't ever a patient in a mental institution, were you?

Mr. Dada: No. I do not have any mental problems.

Chapter 7

Interviewer: By the way, you're doing fine. Your answers are all very good.

Mr. Dada: Oh good.

Interviewer: Now, have you ever been a member of or associated with any organization, association, fund, foundation, party, society, club, or any similar group in the United States or any other place?

Mr. Dada: I'm sorry. I must be a little bit nervous. I do not understand. Could you please say that more slowly?

Interviewer: No need to be nervous. I asked about groups you have belonged to or been associated with.

Mr. Dada: Oh yes. I remember. My brother told me to join a group that is for peace in my country.

Interviewer: And did your brother also tell you you had to join the chess club?

Mr. Dada: No, that was my idea. I am a very good chess player.

Interviewer: Since becoming a permanent U.S. resident, have you ever failed to file a tax return because you considered yourself a "nonresident"?

Mr. Dada: I'm sorry. Nonresident? Do you mean saying that I do not live in the United States?

Interviewer: Yes, saying you're not a resident.

Mr. Dada: No, I know I must always pay my taxes.

Interviewer: Yes, you need to pay them Mr. Dada.

Chapter 8

Interviewer: Have you ever been arrested, cited, or detained by any law enforcement officer for any reason?

Mr. Dada: Excuse me, what does "cited" mean?

Interviewer: "Cited" means told to appear in court.

Mr. Dada: Oh, no.

Interviewer: So, you have never been put in jail?

Mr. Dada: No, I have never been put in jail.

Interviewer: Have you ever sold or smuggled a controlled substance or illegal drugs or narcotics?

Mr. Dada: Does "controlled substance" mean the same as "illegal substance"?

Interviewer: Almost. A "controlled substance" is a drug that a doctor might prescribe, but is otherwise illegal to buy or sell.

Mr. Dada: No. No drugs.

Interviewer: Have you ever lied to a U.S. government official to get into the United States?

Mr. Dada: No. It is not a good idea to lie to the officials.

Chapter 9

Interviewer: You are right about that, Mr. Dada. Now, are there removal, exclusion, rescission or deportation proceedings pending against you?

Mr. Dada: I'm not sure.

Interviewer: Why not?

Mr. Dada: Because I don't know what resci … means.

Interviewer: Oh, rescission. That means revoking or canceling your legal permanent resident status.

Mr. Dada: Now I understand. No, there is no proceedings.

Interviewer: And have you ever left this country to avoid being drafted in the U.S. Armed Forces?

Mr. Dada: I don't believe so. I left this country two … no, three times. I told you that. But it was never to escape being put into the army.

Interviewer: I'm sure it wasn't.

Mr. Dada: No. Not at all.

Chapter 10

Interviewer: Now, do you support the Constitution of the United States?

Mr. Dada: By "support" do you want to know if I am for them rather than against them?

Interviewer: Yes, that's what I mean by "support."

Mr. Dada: Then yes, I totally support the Constitution and this kind of government.

Interviewer: And are you willing to take the full Oath of Allegiance to the United States?

Mr. Dada: Sure.

Interviewer: What did you say?

Mr. Dada: I'm sorry. I was mistaken. I meant to say, yes, I am willing to take the Oath of Allegiance.

Interviewer: Good. And if the law requires it, are you willing to perform noncombatant services for the U.S. Armed Forces?

Mr. Dada: Are you saying that I would not have to carry a rifle, but I would have to follow military orders? Yes?

Interviewer: Yes.

Mr. Dada: Then yes, I would do that.

Chapter 11

Interviewer: I assume you've studied the 100 American history and government questions.

Mr. Dada: Yes, I have.

Interviewer: Now, I'm going to ask you a few of them to see how well you ....

Narrator: This part of the interview is difficult for some people. You may forget an answer—even one you know. That's okay. Just stay calm.

Interviewer: All right. What are two Cabinet-level positions?

Mr. Dada: The President's Cabinet? The Secretary of Defense and State.

Interviewer: Could you say that again?

Mr. Dada: I'm sorry. The Secretary of Defense and the Secretary of State.

Interviewer: Good. Now, what did the Declaration of Independence do?

Mr. Dada: It said to Great Britain that the colonies wanted freedom.

Interviewer: Excellent. Let's see ... How many U.S. Senators are there?

Mr. Dada: 50 ... no, 100.

Interviewer: And can you say who lived in America before the Europeans arrived?

Mr. Dada: The American Indians. Was that what you were looking for?

Interviewer: Yes. In what month do we vote for President?

Mr. Dada: In November?

Interviewer: Yes. And what are the three branches of government?

Mr. Dada: Executive, Legislative ... and Judicious?

Interviewer: Could you repeat that last one?

Mr. Dada: Oh, Judiciary.

Interviewer: Very good. That's enough questions. Could you take this and please read this question back to me.

Mr. Dada: "Who was the second President of the United States?"

Interviewer: And please write this sentence. Adams ... was ... the ... second ... President. *(Mr. Dada writes the sentence.)* I'm impressed. You have done an excellent job. I can see that you've worked hard to learn English, and you've prepared very well for this interview.

Mr. Dada: I really appreciate you telling me this.

Interviewer: So congratulations. You've passed. Now all you need to do is sign this form here and here. Thank you. I know you're going to be a *great* American citizen.

Mr. Dada: Thank you very much. You are very kind.

Interviewer: It's my pleasure, Mr. Dada.

Variations on Typical Interview Questions

The following questions and requests show different ways that an interviewer might ask questions about you and your N-400 application.

1.
   - Give your full name.
   - I need your family name and given name.
   - State your name.
   - Your name: first, middle, and last, please.

2.
   - Give the name on your Alien Registration Card.
   - What is the name listed on your green card?
   - I need the name shown on your Alien Card.
   - On your Alien Registration Card, what is the name that appears?

3.
   - Give your Alien Registration number.
   - What is the number on your Green Card?
   - I need your alien number, please.
   - Can you state your Alien Registration number?

4.
   - Give me your Social Security number, now.
   - What's your social?
   - Give your Social Security number.
   - Tell me your Social Security number, please.

5.
   - Previous names?
   - What other names have you had?
   - Have you had other names?
   - Can you list any names you've had before, if any?

6.
   - Give your maiden name.
   - Maiden name, please?
   - What was your unmarried name?
   - Can you give me your unmarried name?

7.
   - State your date of birth.
   - Date of birth: month, day, and year, please.
   - When were you born?
   - Tell me the date of your birth.

8.
   - In what place were you born?
   - So… where are you from? What place?
   - Give your place of origin.
   - Where were you born?

9.
   - Give the city or town of your birth.
   - You were born in what city or town?
   - What city or town are you from?
   - State your city or town of origin.

10.
   - Give the country where you were born.
   - What country are you from originally?
   - You were born in what country?
   - What is your country of birth?

11.
   - Was either of your parents naturalized here in the U.S.A.?
   - I need to know if your mother or father was ever a U.S. citizen.
   - Can you tell me if any of your parents were citizens of the U.S.?
   - Was either of your parents U.S. citizens?

12.
   - Can you read and write fully in English?
   - Is it safe to assume that you can read and write in English?
   - Do you read and write English?
   - Are you able to read and write in English?

13.
   - Can you speak English?
   - Can you talk to me in English?
   - Do you speak any English?
   - Can you communicate in English orally?

14. • Please, sign in English.
    • Are you able to sign your name in English?
    • In English, please, sign your name.
    • Give your signature in English.

15. • What is your date of admission to become a permanent resident?
    • State the date of admission for permanent residency.
    • When were you admitted for permanent residency?
    • When did you get admitted for your permanent residential status?

16. • What is the time frame of your continuous residency in this country?
    • How long have you lived here?
    • For how long have you resided in the U.S.?
    • How long have you resided here continually?

17. • Do you plan to live in the U.S. permanently?
    • Are you going to reside in the United States indefinitely?
    • You will be residing permanently in this country?
    • Do you have intentions of residing here on a permanent basis?

18. • Were you ever a member of the United States armed forces/military?
    • Have you or have you not served in this country's armed forces/military?
    • Have you served in the armed forces/military of the United States?
    • Did you ever serve in the armed forces of the United States?

19. • List the addresses where you've resided for the last five years.
    • During the last five years, what addresses have you had?

    • Where have you lived for the last five years?
    • Where have you resided during the last five years?

20. • Currently, where do you live?
    • Presently, you live at … ?
    • What is your address right now?
    • What is your address at the present time?

21. • List places of employment for the last five years.
    • What jobs have you had in the last five years?
    • For the last five years, where have you worked?
    • For the last five years, where were you employed?

22. • What employment do you have right now?
    • Where do you work now?
    • What job do you have right now?
    • Who is your employer at the moment?

23. • Can you tell me where you work?
    • At what place do you work?
    • Where is your job?
    • Where are you employed?

24. • For six months or less, have you been absent from the U.S.?
    • Did you leave the country for less than six months?
    • Were you outside U.S. territory for exactly six months or less?
    • Have you left the U.S. for a time span of six months or less?

25. • For a period of six months or more have you been absent from the U.S.?
    • Did you leave the country for more than six months?

- Were you outside U.S. borders for exactly six months or more than six months?
- Have you left the U.S. for a time span of six months or more?

26.
- Can you explain your absences?
- Why did you leave the country?
- Give reasons for your absences.
- What are the reasons for your absences?

27.
- What is your marital status at the present time?
- What is your martial status, right now?
- Tell me your marital status at the moment.
- Presently, what marital status do you hold?

28.
- Can you tell me if you are married?
- You are married, correct?
- You are married at this time?
- Are you married?

29.
- Can you tell me if you're widowed?
- Are you widowed?
- Are you widowed right now?
- At this time are you widowed?

30.
- Can you tell me if you are divorced?
- Are you divorced?
- Are you divorced now?
- Presently, are you divorced?

31.
- Can you tell me if you are single?
- You are single, correct?
- Are you single right now?
- Are you single at this time?

32.
- Can I have the first name of your husband/wife?
- What is your husband's/wife's first name?
- Give your spouse's first name.
- What is the first name of your spouse?

33.
- Where did your marriage take place?
- Where did you get married?
- What is the place where you wed?
- Where were you wed?

34.
- What is the birth date of your spouse?
- What is your spouse's birth date?
- What is the date of birth of your husband/wife?
- What is the date of birth of your spouse?
- When was your husband/wife born?

35.
- What is your spouse's country of origin?
- Where is your husband/wife from originally?
- Where was your spouse born?
- What is the country where your spouse was born?

36.
- Where did your spouse enter this country?
- Where did your husband/wife enter the U.S.?
- Where did your spouse enter the U.S.?
- What place marked the entrance to the U.S. for your spouse?

37.
- Can you supply the date of entry to the U.S. for your spouse?
- Give me the date of entrance to the U.S. for your spouse.
- When did your spouse enter the U.S.?
- What was the date in which your husband/wife entered this country?

38.
- Can you give me the Alien number for your spouse?
- Do you know your spouse's Alien number?
- What is your spouse's Alien number?
- Do you recall your husband's/wife's Alien number?

39.
- Give the current immigration status for your husband/wife.
- What is your spouse's status, as an immigrant, right now?
- What is the present immigration status of your spouse?
- Can you cite the immigration status of your spouse now?

40.
- Do you know if your spouse is a citizen in this country?
- Here in the United States, is your spouse a citizen?
- Is your husband/wife a U.S. citizen?
- Is your spouse a citizen of the U.S.?

41.
- When did your husband/wife become a United States citizen?
- When did your husband/wife become naturalized?
- With regard to U.S. citizenship, when did your spouse obtain it?
- What is the date on which your spouse became naturalized?

42.
- Give the city or country where your husband/wife was naturalized.
- Your spouse's naturalization took place in what city or country?
- What is the city or country where your spouse became naturalized?
- In what city or country did your spouse obtain citizenship?

43.
- Did you ever marry before?
- Have you been married before?
- Have there been any other marriages in the past?
- Were you married prior to your current status?

44.
- Give me the name of your previous spouse.
- What was the name of your other husband/wife?
- What was the name of your spouse?
- Could you state the name of your previous spouse?

45.
- Give the date of your previous marriage.
- When were you previously married?
- When did your earlier marriage occur?
- On what date did your previous marriage take place?

46.
- On what date did that marriage officially end?
- When did you finally divorce?
- When did you divorce?
- When was your divorce finalized?

47.
- Was your present spouse married before?
- Was your husband/wife married before?
- Has your present spouse been married before?

48.
- How many times did your husband/wife marry before?
- What is the number of times your spouse married before?

49.
- Do you have any children?
- Have you got kids?
- Do you have kids?
- Are there any children of your own?

50. • Your children have what names?
    • What are the names of your kids?
    • What are the kid's names?
    • What are the children's names?

51. • Give each child's date of birth.
    • What was each child's date of birth?
    • On what date was each child born?
    • When was each of your children born?

52. • Each child was born in what country?
    • In what place was each child born?
    • Where was each child born?
    • What was the place of birth for each child?

53. • What is the entry date into this country for each child?
    • Give me each child's entry date into the U.S.
    • What is the entry date for each of your children into the U.S.?
    • What is the date of entry to the U.S. for each child?

54. • Give the Alien Registration numbers for each of your children.
    • What are your children's green card numbers?
    • What is the Alien number for each of your children?
    • What is the Alien Registration number for each child?

55. • Are you considered nobility in a foreign country?
    • Did you ever have a title of nobility?
    • Do you have a title of nobility from any foreign country?
    • Were you born with a title of nobility or did you acquire one in any foreign country?

56. • Have you been found legally incompetent?
    • Did you ever get labeled "legally incompetent"?
    • Are you legally incompetent?
    • Were you ever declared legally incompetent?

57. • Were you ever isolated as a patient in a mental institution?
    • Were you ever a patient in an institution for the mentally ill?
    • Were you ever secluded in an institution for mental patients?
    • Was there ever an instance when you were confined in a mental institution?

58. • In the U.S. or elsewhere, are you affiliated with any organization, party, or club?
    • Are you affiliated with any group in the U.S. or outside of it?
    • Do you have any affiliations with any group in the U.S. or in any other place?
    • Are you affiliated with any organization anywhere in the world?

59. • Have you had any kind of relation with the Communist Party wherever you have been?
    • Have you had anything to do with the Communist Party here or anywhere else?
    • While being in the U.S. or in any other place, have you been involved with the Communist Party?
    • Did you associate with the Communist Party while in the U.S. or in any other place?

60. • Tell me whether you are a communist or not.
- Are you a communist?
- Do you belong to the Communist Party?
- Are you a member of the Communist Party?

61. • Can you state whether or not you've had associations with the Nazi government of Germany?
- Have you had any association with the Nazi government of Germany?
- Did you have any involvement with the Nazis in Germany?
- Did you partake in association with the German Nazis?

62. • Did you ever participate in any way in the persecution of a person from 1933 to 1945?
- Have you persecuted any person for whatever reason?
- Between 1933 and 1945, did you participate in any form of persecution?
- Did you partake in active persecution toward any person between 1933 and 1945?

63. • Are you mentally ill, presently?
- Have you got a mental illness?
- Do you suffer from mental illness?
- Is mental illness one of your ailments?

64. • Did you ever commit any crimes?
- Are you guilty of committing any crime?
- Were any crimes ever committed by you?
- Have you ever engaged in any crime?

65. • Have you been arrested?
- Did you ever get arrested?
- Do you have an arrest record here?
- Have you ever been arrested?

66. • While you were outside U.S. territory, did you ever get arrested?
- Did you ever get arrested outside the U.S.?
- Were you ever arrested outside this country?
- Were you arrested anywhere outside the United States?

67. • When we talk about good moral character, can we assume you are a person of this caliber?
- Would you say you are someone of good moral character?
- Are you a person of good moral character?
- Can you be considered a person of good moral character?

68. • Is polygamy something you practice?
- Are you polygamous?
- Are you a polygamist?
- Do you engage in polygamy?
- Do you partake in polygamy?

69. • Do you have multiple spouses?
- Do you have more than one wife or husband?
- Do you have two or more spouses at once?
- Are you married to more than once person at the same time?

70. • Did you ever work as a prostitute?
- Were you ever a prostitute?
- Have you worked as a prostitute?
- Have you ever engaged in prostitution?

71. • Did you contribute to any alien's illegal entrance?
- Have you helped anyone enter the U.S. illegally?
- Did you ever help an alien enter the country illegally?
- Did you make illegal entries possible for aliens?

72. • Have you been a trafficker of narcotics or marijuana?
    • Did you ever traffic in narcotic drugs or marijuana?
    • Are you an illicit drug trafficker?
    • Did you ever take part in drug trafficking?

73. • Has the bulk of your income been due to illegal gambling?
    • Did you make most of your money by gambling illegally?
    • Has illegal gambling been your greatest source of income?
    • Did illegal gambling become your primary source of income?

74. • Is there an order for deportation that awaits you?
    • Are there any deportation proceedings pending against you?
    • Are you waiting for deportation proceedings to become final?
    • Do deportation proceedings pend on your behalf?

75. • Did you ever get deported?
    • Were you deported?
    • Have you been ordered deported?
    • Was deportation or an order for deportation ever imposed on you?

76. • Did you ever complete a "suspension of deportation" application?
    • Did you apply so that deportation in your case would be suspended?
    • Have you submitted an application for suspension of deportation?
    • Did you ever apply so that your order for deportation would be suspended?

77. • On what date did you file income taxes?
    • Your last income tax return was filed on what date?
    • When did you file your last income tax return?
    • What is the date in which you filed your most recent income tax return?

78. • As a permanent resident, did you file your income taxes stating you were a nonresident?
    • Did you file your taxes as if you were not a resident, when in reality you were?
    • Did you file your income tax return as a nonresident while you were a permanent resident?
    • Did you ever file an income tax return as a nonresident while being a permanent resident?

79. • While being a permanent resident, did you ever fail to file your income tax return?
    • Did you ever decide to ignore your income tax return?
    • Did you ever not file income taxes?
    • Have you ever failed to file your income tax return while being a permanent resident?

80. • Did you ever claim, by any means, to be a U.S. citizen?
    • Have you ever claimed to be a citizen of the United States?
    • Did you ever make false claims about your U.S. citizenship?
    • Have you lied or given false testimony regarding your immigration status?

81. • Are you a deserter of the armed forces in this country?
    • Have you ever deserted our armed forces?
    • Have you deserted from the United States armed forces?
    • Did you ever desert from the military, air, or naval forces here?

82. • In order to avoid being drafted, did you ever leave the country?
    • Did you leave the country in order to escape a draft?
    • Did you exit the United States in order to avoid a draft?
    • Have you fled the country in hopes of avoiding a draft into the United States Armed Forces?

83. • Do the Constitution and form of government of the U.S. follow your convictions?
    • Do you believe in our Constitution and form of government?
    • Are your beliefs in support of the U.S. Constitution and form of government?
    • Are the U.S. Constitution and form of government in accordance with your beliefs?

84. • Are you willing to take the complete oath of allegiance to the U.S.?
    • Do you want to take the full oath of allegiance to the U.S.?
    • Will you take the full oath of allegiance to the United States?
    • Are you willingly going to take the complete oath of allegiance to our country?

85. • On behalf of the U.S., would you bear arms?
    • Would you bear arms for our country?
    • Are you willing to bear arms on behalf of our country, if required by the law?
    • If the law requires that you do so, will you bear arms on behalf of our country?

86. • Would you be willing to perform non-combative services in the Armed Forces if required by law?
    • Would you perform noncombative services in the Armed Forces, if the law said you must?
    • Are you willing to perform peaceful services in the Armed Forces, if the law requires you to do so?
    • If the law says you must, would you engage in peaceful services in the Armed Forces of the U.S.?

87. • Under civilian direction, would you be willing to perform work of national importance?
    • Will you perform work under civilian direction, for our country?
    • Are you willing to perform work for this country under civilian direction?
    • Are you willing to perform work of national importance under the direction of a civilian?

88. • Have you ever applied in order to be excused from the military?
    • Did you apply for exclusion from the military?
    • Did you ever apply for exemption from military service for any reason?
    • Have you filled out an application in order to be exempt from military service in our country?

89.
- Is registration for U.S. Selective Service something that you've done?
- Did you register for the U.S. Selective Service?
- Have you registered under the Selective Service law or draft law of the United States?
- With regard to the U.S. Selective Service law or draft law, did you ever complete registration?

90.
- Is your name something you want to change?
- Do you want your name changed?
- Will you be changing your name now?
- Would you want to change your name?

Legal Overview of the Naturalization Process

The Process

Becoming a naturalized citizen of the United States of America involves numerous steps, but most fall within three general areas:

1. filing the naturalization application with USCIS;

2. demonstrating a basic knowledge of English and United States civics during an interview/test given by a USCIS interviewer; and

3. taking an oath of allegiance to the United States.

The application and supporting documents are filed with USCIS along with a $595 fee, plus an additional biometrics (electronic fingerprinting) fee of $80, for a total of $675. USCIS waives the biometrics fee for people over 75 years of age and for those serving in the military. Applicants should send the completed N-400 to the USCIS Service Center that serves their place of residence.

Citizenship Requirements

There are a variety of general rules for applicants, which are all subject to exceptions depending on age, marital status, military status, etc. However, in general an applicant must:

1. be a lawful permanent resident, or "green card" holder (a permanent resident is a person who receives an immigrant visa or adjusts to permanent residence status after living in the United States);

2. be at least 18 years of age;

3. have made a home in the United States for at least five years;

4. have been physically present in the United States for at least half of the five years proceeding the date of application;

5. be able to speak, read, and write words in ordinary usage in the English language;

6. be able to pass a civics test, which consists largely of United States history and government questions;

7. have good moral character, keeping in mind certain bars to naturalization; and

8. take an oath of loyalty to the United States.

Each of these requirements is explained below.

1. Lawful Permanent Residence

The general rule is that a person must be a permanent resident for at least five years to be eligible for naturalization. However, a permanent resident can apply for citizenship if she or he has been married to a United States citizen for three years and is not divorced or legally separated from the United States citizen spouse.

Applicants can look under the "Resident Since" heading on their Permanent Resident Card (also called an "I-551," "I-151," or a "green card") to find their date adjustment or admission, from which the USCIS counts the five- or three-year period. Permanent residents can file their Application for Naturalization (N-400) three months before the date of eligibility.

The USCIS considers refugees legal permanent residents as of the date of entry, provided they have adjusted to lawful permanent residence. The USCIS considers asylees permanent residents as of one year before their adjustment to lawful permanent residence status, which effectively shortens their permanent residency requirement to four years.

2. Age

An applicant must be at least 18 years old to naturalize.

Minor children (those under 18 years old) may automatically become United States citizens through their United States citizen parent. Minor children with a claim to United States citizenship will use Form N-600 to apply for citizenship. USCIS regulations state that minor children of United States citizens are eligible to automatically become citizens if they:

- have one United States citizen parent (native born or naturalized), and

- are under 18, and

- are living permanently in the United States in the legal and physical custody of the United States citizen parent, and

- are a lawful permanent resident.

In addition, an adopted child could be a United States citizen if the child was adopted by the United States citizen parent before the child turned 16 years old.

3. Continuity of Residence/Abandonment of Residence

As stated above, applicants must have resided in the United States for either five years as a lawful permanent resident, or for three years if she or he is the spouse of and resides with a United States citizen. Residence is defined as "general abode and principal dwelling place."

Generally, an applicant must live in the state or the USCIS district in which she or he files the petition for at least three months before filing the N-400. An applicant must reside continuously in the United States from the date of application to the time of the naturalization. As is explained below, an applicant can only leave the United States for short periods of time without abandoning their residence for citizenship purposes. However, the USCIS makes numerous exceptions for those with ties to the military and/or United States government. If an applicant has resided outside the United States for military or government service, he or she should check with the USCIS to see if they qualify for an exception.

The applicant must not have abandoned her or his residence in the United States. This means that the person must show that she or he has not only maintained a home in the United States, but actually lives at that home.

If a person has left the United States for more than six months at one time but for less than one year, the the USCIS will deem her or him to have abandoned residence for naturalization purposes, unless the person can prove otherwise. Absences of six months or less will not cause a person to abandon her or his residence. If the applicant left the United States for one year or longer, the applicant has disrupted their continuous residence (even if they have a re-entry permit) and the USCIS may deem that the applicant has abandoned his or her residence. No one with an absence of more than one year should apply for citizenship without first consulting with legal counsel or an accredited representative.

4. Physical Presence

The applicant must have been physically present in the United States for at least half (30 months) of the five-year residence period discussed above. The spouse of a United States citizen needs to have been here for half of the three-year residence period (18 months).

It is important to note that an applicant **must disclose all absences since becoming a lawful permanent resident,** not just the absences within the five years prior to filing their application.

5. English Language

Most applicants must be able to read, write, and speak basic English. Unless special circumstances exist, the USCIS will conduct the naturalization interview in English.

There are a number of exemptions to the English requirement. The USCIS makes exemptions for applicants who, on the day of filing:

1. are over 50 years old and have lived in the United States for at least 20 years since becoming a lawful permanent resident; or

2. are over 55 years old and have lived in the United States for at least 15 years since becoming a lawful permanent resident; or

3. are over 65 years old and have lived in the United States as a lawful permanent resident for periods totaling at least 20 years; or

4. cannot comply with the requirement because of a mental, physical, or developmental disability. In this instance, an applicant must file Form N-648 with the N-400 application. A licensed medical or osteopathic doctor or a licensed clinical psychologist must complete the N-648.

6. Civics

An applicant must understand basic aspects of United States civics. An applicant who fails the United States civics test is given an opportunity to retake the test within about 90 days.

USCIS waives the civics test requirement for those who <u>on the day of filing</u> are unable to comply because of a physical or developmental disability or mental impairment.

The USCIS also makes allowances for applicants who <u>on the day of filing</u>:

1. are over 50 years old and have lived in the United States for at least 20 years since becoming lawful permanent residents; or

2. are over 55 years old and have lived here for at least 15 years since becoming lawful permanent residents.

3. Applicants over 65 years of age can take a simpler version of the test in a language of their choosing. This modified civics test is a sample of 20 civics questions from the list of 100.

These groups will be tested on United States civics in their own language and should bring an interpreter.

Some applicants for naturalization may have fulfilled the United States civics requirements as part of the legalization program to become lawful permanent residents through the January 1, 1982, amnesty program under the Immigration Reform and Control Act.

In order to have fulfilled the United States civics requirement for naturalization at the same time an applicant fulfilled the legalization requirement for amnesty, the applicant must have either:

1. passed a test on English/civics at the Phase II interview, also called the "312" test, given by an immigration official; or

2. passed a standardized test of English and civics given by a staff person at certain community agencies. Examples of standardized tests are those provided by the Educational Testing Service (ETS) or the Comprehensive Adult Student Assessment System (CASAS).

A person who fulfilled the amnesty legalization programs' English and civics requirement in any other way will need to pass the USCIS citizenship test to fulfill the citizenship requirement. This applies, for example, to a person who fulfilled the legalization requirement with a United States high school diploma or with a Certificate of Satisfactory Pursuit stating that she or he had taken at least 40 hours of an English/civics class.

Special agricultural worker (SAW) applicants did not have to meet the English/civics requirement to obtain permanent resident status, so they must fulfill the normal English and civics requirements for naturalization.

7. Good Moral Character

Applicants for naturalization must have good moral character as defined by immigration laws and regulations. The USCIS inquiry into the applicant's moral character, consists of a review of the N-400, the interview process, fingerprint checks, and computer searches to determine if an applicant has a criminal record or a negative immigration history. Any police arrests, detentions, criminal convictions, or adverse administrative rulings (e.g.

by an immigration judge) could affect an applicant's eligibility and possibly jeopardize their residency status. Such an applicant should seek legal counsel before completing an application. Also, please note that any dishonesty during the application process shows poor moral character and can result in CIS denying an application or even revoking a grant of citizenship.

8. Belief in Principles of United States and Oath of Allegiance

All applicants for naturalization must demonstrate that they are "attached to the principles of the Constitution of the United States and well disposed to the good order and happiness of the United States." Applicants satisfy this requirement by taking an oath of allegiance when they are sworn in as United States citizens at the naturalization ceremony. The USCIS may excuse an applicant from taking the Oath of Allegiance if he or she cannot communicate an understanding of the meaning of the oath because of a physical or mental disability.

Other Important Issues Regarding Eligibility for Citizenship

Bars to Naturalization

A person with a deportation order in force at the time he or she applies for naturalization cannot become a citizen. If deportation proceedings are stopped, however, he or she can reapply for naturalization.

People who have been involved in certain political activities in the ten years before applying for naturalization are also barred from citizenship. For example, people who are affiliated with or members of a totalitarian organization cannot naturalize. Also barred from citizenship are people who are, or who have been, members of, or affiliated with, the Communist Party.

However, an applicant may still naturalize if he or she can show that such affiliation or membership is or was:

1. involuntary;

2. without awareness of the nature or the aims of the organization, and was discontinued if the applicant became aware of the nature or aims of the organization;

3. terminated prior to the attainment of age sixteen by the applicant, or more than ten years prior to the filing of the application for naturalization;

4. by operation of law; or

5. necessary for purposes of obtaining employment, food rations, or other essentials of living.

Permanent Ineligibility to Citizenship

Certain actions relating to military service can directly bar a person from becoming a United States citizen. These bars to citizenship, which occur rarely, apply to applicants who:

1. deserted from the armed forces or evaded the draft;

2. applied for and received certain exemptions from United States military service based on their alien status; or

3. failed to register for Selective Service (exceptions to this bar are discussed below).

A more common scenario, involves an indirect bar to citizenship due to violations of immigration laws or regulations. For example, any false claim to United States citizenship can effectively bar an immigrant from citizenship. Any person who falsely claims to be a United States citizen, for any purpose or benefit under any federal or state law, can be permanently barred from entry to the United States. This bar includes entry for permanent residence, which would preclude an applicant from obtaining United States citizenship. The bar to admission does not apply just to false claims made to obtain an immigration benefit, nor is it necessary for the claim to have been made to a government official. A false claim of citizenship can also be made to someone in the private sector. Most false claims occur at the border, when filing a state or federal government document, or when seeking employment. If a permanent resident made a qualifying false claim, he or she is not eligible for citizenship and could be removed from the United States by the Department of Homeland Security.

Potential applicants whose experience includes any of these situations or those in doubt about their prior immigration history should consult an attorney, or an accredited representative.

Selective Service Registration

All men between the ages of 18 and 26, living in the United States, are required to register with the Selective Service. This requirement includes all men who are United States citizens, lawful permanent residents, refugees, asylees, parolees, and undocumented immigrants. The only males between the ages of 18 and 25 not required to register are those who entered the United States as nonimmigrants (e.g. as visitors or students) and who remained in nonimmigrant status until their 26th birthday.

Men required to register may be given the chance to register before naturalization is denied. Men aged 26 and older who should have registered but did not will be denied naturalization, if the failure to register was knowing and willful.

A person who did not register with the Selective Service because he did not know about the requirement may still be eligible for naturalization. The effect of a failure to register will vary based on the applicant's age and the actions that he took after learning about the requirement. Potential applicants who have not registered for Selective Service should immediately consult an attorney, or an accredited representative, as there are remedies available.

Denied Applications for Naturalization

When the USCIS denies a naturalization application, they send the applicant a **written notice** stating the reason for the denial. If the applicant feels that the application was wrongly denied, he or she may request a hearing with an immigration officer. The applicant must file a request for a hearing within 30 days of the denial by completing and filing Form N-336 with the appropriate fee. At the hearing, the applicant can submit any new evidence or testimony to support the application.

If the USCIS upholds its earlier denial, the applicant can then file an appeal for review with the local federal district court. The applicant must file the appeal within 120 days of the USCIS's final determination. The court must make an entirely new decision on the person's application and must give the person a hearing if she or he wants one.

Instructions for N-400, Application for Naturalization

OMB No. 1615-0052; Expires 10/31/08

Department of Homeland Security
U.S. Citizenship and Immigration Services

Instructions for N-400,
Application for Naturalization

Instructions

Please read these instructions carefully to properly complete this form. If you need more space to complete an answer, use a separate sheet(s) of paper. Write your name and Alien Registration Number (A #), if any, at the top of each sheet of paper and indicate the part and number of the item to which the answer refers.

What Is the Purpose of This Form?

Form N-400 is an application for U.S. citizenship (naturalization). For more information about the naturalization process and eligibility requirements, please read *A Guide to Naturalization* (M-476). If you do not already have a copy of the *Guide*, you can get a copy from:

1. The USCIS website (**www.uscis.gov**);

2. The USCIS toll-free forms line at **1-800-870-3676**; or

3. The USCIS National Customer Service Center (NCSC) at **1-800-375-5283 (TTY:1-800-767-1833)**.

When Should I Use Form N-400?

You may apply for naturalization when you meet **all** the requirements to become a U.S. citizen. The section of the *Guide* called "Who is Eligible for Naturalization" and the Eligibility Worksheet found in the back of the *Guide* are tools to help you determine whether you are eligible to apply for naturalization. You should complete the Worksheet before filling out the Form N-400 application.

If you are applying based on five years as a Lawful Permanent Resident or based on three years as a Lawful Permanent Resident married to a U.S. citizen, you may apply for naturalization up to 90 days before you meet the "continuous residence" requirement. You must meet all other requirements at the time that you file your application with us.

Certain applicants have different English and civics testing requirements based on their age and length of lawful permanent residence **at the time of filing**. If you are over 50 years of age and have lived in the United States as a lawful permanent resident for periods totaling at least 20 years, or if you are over 55 years of age and have lived in the United States as a lawful permanent resident for periods totaling at least 15 years, you do not have to take the English test, but you have to take the civics test in the language of your choice.

If you are over 65 years of age and have lived in the United States as a lawful permanent resident for periods totaling at least 20 years, you do not have to take the English test, but you have to take a simpler version of the civics test in the language of your choice.

Who May File Form N-400?

To use this form you must be **ONE** of the following:

1. A Lawful Permanent Resident for at least five years and at least 18 years old;

2. A Lawful Permanent Resident for at least three years and at least 18 years old,

AND

You have been married to and living with the same U.S. citizen for the last three years,

AND

Your spouse has been a U.S. citizen for the last three years.

3. A member of one of several other groups eligible to apply for naturalization (for example, persons who are nationals but not citizens of the United States) and at least 18 years old. For more information about these groups, please see the *Guide*.

4. A person who has served honorably in the U.S. Armed Forces,

AND

If you are at least 18 years old, a Lawful Permanent Resident with at least one year of U.S. Armed Forces service, and you are filing your application for naturalization while still in the service or within six months after the termination of such service.

OR

You served honorably as a member of the Selected Reserve of the Ready Reserve or in active-duty status during a designated period of hostilities. You then may apply for naturalization without having been physically present in the United States for any specified period.

For more information, please go to the USCIS website at **www.uscis.gov**.

NOTE: If you are married to a U.S. citizen who is employed or deployed abroad, you may in some circumstances be eligible for expedited naturalization under section 319(b) of the Immigration and Nationality Act (INA). For further assistance, please please see the *Guide*.

Form N-400 Instructions (Rev. 10/15/07) Y

Who May Not File This Form N-400?

In certain cases, a person who was born outside of the United States to U.S. citizen parents is already a citizen and does not need to apply for naturalization. To find out more information about this type of citizenship and whether you should file a Form N-600, "Application for Certificate of Citizenship," read the *Guide*.

Other permanent residents under 18 years of age may be eligible for U.S. citizenship if their U.S. citizen parent or parents file a Form N-600 application in their behalf. For more information, see "Frequently Asked Questions" in the *Guide*.

General Instructions.

Step 1. Fill Out Form N-400

1. Type or print legibly in black ink.

2. If extra space is needed to complete any item, attach a continuation sheet, indicate the item number, and date and sign each sheet.

3. Answer all questions fully and accurately. State that an item is not applicable with "N/A." If the answer is none, write "none."

4. **Write your USCIS (or former INS) "A"- number on the top right hand corner of each page.** Use your "A"-number on your Permanent Resident Card (formerly known as the Alien Registration or "Green" Card). To locate your "A"- number, see the sample Permanent Resident Cards in the *Guide*. The "A" number on your card consists of seven to nine numbers, depending on when your record was created. If the "A"- number on your card has fewer than nine numbers, place enough zeros before the first number to make a *total of nine numbers* on the application. For example, write card number A1234567 as A001234567, but write card number A12345678 as A012345678.

5. Answer all questions fully and accurately.

Step-by-Step Instructions.

This form is divided into 14 parts. The information below will help you fill out the form.

Part 1. Your Name *(the Person Applying for Naturalization)*.

    A. Your current legal name - Your current legal name is the name on your birth certificate, unless it has been changed after birth by a legal action such as a marriage or court order.

    B. Your name exactly as it appears on your Permanent Resident Card *(if different from above)*-- Write your name exactly as it appears on your card, even if it is misspelled.

    C. Other names you have used - If you have used any other names in your life, write them in this section. If you need more space, use a separate sheet of paper.

    D. If you have **never** used a different name, write "N/A" in the space for "Family Name *(Last Name)*."

    E. Name change *(optional)* - A court can allow a change in your name when you are being naturalized. A name change does not become final until a court naturalizes you. For more information regarding a name change, see the *Guide*.

    F. If you want a court to change your name at a naturalization oath ceremony, check "Yes" and complete this section. If you do not want to change your name, check "No" and go to Part 2.

Part 2. Information About Your Eligibility.

Check the box that shows why you are eligible to apply for naturalization. If the basis for your eligibility is not described in one of the first three boxes, check "Other" and briefly write the basis for your application on the lines provided.

Part 3. Information About You.

    A. U.S. Social Security Number - Print your U.S. Social Security Number. If you do not have one, write "N/A" in the space provided.

    B. Date of birth - Always use eight numbers to show your date of birth. Write the date in this order: Month, Day, Year. For example, write May 1, 1958 as 05/01/1958.

    C. Date you became a Permanent Resident - Write the official date when your lawful permanent residence began, as shown on your Permanent Resident Card. To help locate the date on your card, see the sample Permanent Resident Cards in the *Guide*. Write the date in this order: Month, Day, Year. For example, write August 9, 1988 as 08/09/1988.

    D. Country of birth - Write the name of the country where you were born. Write the name of the country even if it no longer exists.

    E. Country of nationality - Write the name of the country (or countries) where you are currently a citizen or national.

        1. If you are stateless, write the name of the country where you were last a citizen or national.

2. If you are a citizen or national of more than one country, write the name of the foreign country that issued your last passport.

F. Citizenship of parents - Check "Yes" if either of your parents is a U.S. citizen. If you answer "Yes," you may already be a citizen. For more information, see "Frequently Asked Questions" in the *Guide.*

G. Current marital status - Check the marital status you have on the date you are filing this application. If you are currently not married, but had a prior marriage that was annulled or otherwise legally terminated, check "Other" and explain it.

H. Request for disability waiver - If you have a medical disability or impairment that you believe qualifies you for a waiver of the tests of English and/or U.S. Government and history, check "Yes" and attach a properly completed Form N-648, Medical Certification for Disability Exceptions. If you ask for this waiver, it does not guarantee that you will be excused from the testing requirements. For more information about this waiver, see the *Guide.*

I. Request for disability accommodations - We will make every reasonable effort to help applicants with disabilities complete the naturalization process. For example, if you use a wheelchair, we will make sure that you can be fingerprinted and interviewed, and can attend a naturalization ceremony at a location that is wheelchair accessible. If you are deaf or hearing impaired and need a sign language interpreter, we will make arrangements with you to have one at your interview.

If you believe you will need us to modify or change the naturalization process for you, check the box or write in the space the kind of accommodation you need. If you need more space, use a separate sheet of paper. You do not need to send us a Form N-648 to request an accommodation. You only need to send a Form N-648 to request a waiver of the test of English and/or civics.

We consider requests for accommodations on a case-by-case basis. Asking for an accommodation will not affect your eligibility for citizenship.

Part 4. Information About Contacting You.

A. Home address - Give the address where you now live. Do **not** put post office (P.O.) box numbers here.

B. Mailing address - If your mailing address is the same as your home address, write "same." If your mailing address is different from your home address, write it in this part.

C. Telephone numbers - By giving us your telephone numbers and e-mail address, we can contact you about your application more quickly. If you are hearing impaired and use a TTY telephone connection, please indicate this by writing "(TTY)" after the telephone number.

Part 5. Information for Criminal Records Search.

The Federal Bureau of Investigation (FBI) will use the information in this section, together with your fingerprints, to search for criminal records. Although the results of this search may affect your eligibility, we do **not** make naturalization decisions based on your gender, race, or physical description.

For each item, check the box or boxes that best describes you. The categories are those used by the FBI. You can select one or more.

NOTE: As part of the USCIS biometric services requirement, you must be fingerprinted after you file this application. If necessary, USCIS may also take your photograph and signature.

Part 6. Information About Your Residence and Employment.

A. Write every address where you have lived during the last five years (including in other countries).

Begin with where you live now. Include the dates you lived in those places. For example, write May 1998 to June 1999 as 05/1998 to 06/1999.

If you need separate sheets of paper to complete section A or B or any other questions on this application, be sure to follow the Instructions in **"Step 1. Fill Out the Form N-400, Number 2"** on **Page 2.**

B. List where you have worked (or, if you were a student, the schools you have attended) during the last five years. Include military service. If you worked for yourself, write "self employed." Begin with your most recent job. Also, write the dates when you worked or studied in each place.

Part 7. Time Outside the United States *(Including Trips to Canada, Mexico and the Caribbean).*

A. Write the total number of days you spent outside of the United States (including on military service) during the last five years. Count the days of every trip that lasted 24 hours or longer.

B. Write the number of trips you have taken outside the United States during the last five years. Count every trip that lasted 24 hours or longer.

C. Provide the requested information for every trip that you have taken outside the United States since you became a Lawful Permanent Resident. Begin with your most recent trip.

Part 8. Information About Your Marital History.

A. Write the number of times you have been married. Include any annulled marriages. If you were married to the same spouse more than one time, count each time as a separate marriage.

B. If you are now married, provide information about your current spouse.

C. Check the box to indicate whether your current spouse is a U.S. citizen.

D. If your spouse is a citizen through naturalization, give the date and place of naturalization. If your spouse regained U.S. citizenship, write the date and place the citizenship was regained.

E. If your spouse is not a U.S. citizen, complete this section.

F. If you were married before, give information about your former spouse or spouses. In question F.2, check the box showing the immigration status your former spouse had during your marriage. If the spouse was not a U.S. citizen or a Lawful Permanent Resident at that time, check "Other" and explain. For question F.5, if your marriage was annulled, check "Other" and explain. If you were married to the same spouse more than one time, write about each marriage separately.

G. For any prior marriages of your current spouse, follow the instructions in section F above.

NOTE: If you or your present spouse had more than one prior marriage, provide the same information required by section F and section G about every additional marriage on a separate sheet of paper.

Part 9. Information About Your Children.

A. Write the total number of sons and daughters you have had. Count **all** of your children, regardless of whether they are:

  1. Alive, missing, or dead;

  2. Born in other countries or in the United States;

  3. Under 18 years old or adults;

  4. Married or unmarried;

  5. Living with you or elsewhere;

  6. Stepsons or stepdaughters or legally adopted; or

  7. Born when you were not married.

B. Write information about all your sons and daughters. In the last column ("Location"), write:

  1. "With me" - if the son or daughter is currently living with you;

  2. The street address and state or country where the son or daughter lives - if the son or daughter is **not** currently living with you; or

  3. "Missing" or "dead" - if that son or daughter is missing or dead.

If you need space to list information about additional sons and daughters, attach a separate sheet of paper.

Part 10. Additional Questions.

Answer each question by checking "Yes" or "No." If **any** part of a question applies to you, you must answer "Yes." For example, if you were never arrested but *were* once detained by a police officer, check "Yes" to the question "Have you ever been arrested or detained by a law enforcement officer?" and attach a written explanation.

We will use this information to determine your eligibility for citizenship. Answer every question honestly and accurately. If you do not, we may deny your application for lack of good moral character. Answering "Yes" to one of these questions does not always cause an application to be denied. For more information on eligibility, please see the *Guide.*

Part 11. Your Signature.

After reading the statement in Part 11, you must sign and date it. You should sign your full name without abbreviating it or using initials. The signature must be legible. Your application may be returned to you if it is not signed.

If you cannot sign your name in English, sign in your native language. If you are unable to write in any language, sign your name with an "X."

NOTE: A designated representative may sign this section on behalf an applicant who qualifies for a waiver of the Oath of Allegiance because of a development or physical impairment (see the *Guide* for more information). In such a case the designated representative should write the name of the applicant and then sign his or her own name followed by the words "Designated Representative." The information attested to by the Designated Representative is subject to the same penalties discussed on **Page 7** of these Instructions.

**Part 12. Signature of Person Who Prepared
the Form for You.**

If someone filled out this form for you, he or she must
complete this section.

Part 13. Signature at Interview.

Do not complete this part. You will be asked to complete this
part at your interview.

Part 14. Oath of Allegiance.

Do not complete this part. You will be asked to complete this
part at your interview.

If we approve your application, you must take this Oath of
Allegiance to become a citizen. In limited cases you can take
a modified Oath. The Oath requirement cannot be waived
unless you are unable to understand its meaning because of a
physical or developmental disability or mental impairment.
For more information, see the *Guide*. Your signature on this
form only indicates that you have no objections to taking the
Oath of Allegiance. **It does not mean that you have taken
the Oath or that you are naturalized**. If USCIS approves
your application for naturalization, you must attend an oath
ceremony and take the Oath of Allegiance to the United States.

Step 2. General Requirements

All applicants must send certain documents with their
application.

For example, if you have been arrested or convicted of a
crime, you must send a certified copy of the arrest report,
court disposition, sentencing, and any other relevant
documents, including any countervailing evidence concerning
the circumstances of your arrest and/or conviction that you
would like USCIS to consider. Note that unless a traffic
incident was alcohol or drug related, you do not need to
submit documentation for traffic fines and incidents that did
not involve an actual arrest if the only penalty was a fine of
less than **$500** and/or points on your driver's license.

For more information on the documents you must send with
your application, see the Document Checklist in the *Guide.*

Translations. Any document containing foreign language
submitted to USCIS shall be accompanied by a full English
language translation which the translator has certified as
complete and accurate, and by the translator's certification that
he or she is competent to translate from the foreign language
into English.

Copies. Unless specifically required that an original
document be filed with an application or petition, an ordinary
legible photocopy may be submitted. Original documents
submitted when not required will remain a part of the record,
even if the submission was not required.

Where To File?

You must send your Form N-400 application and supporting
documents to a USCIS Service Center.

To find the Service Center address you should use, read the
section in the Guide called "Completing Your Application and
Getting Photographed" or call the NCSC at **1-800-375-5283
(TTY: 1-800-767-1833)** or visit our website at **www.uscis.gov**
and click on "Immigration Forms."

All naturalization applicants filing under the military
provisions, Section 328 or 329 of the INA, should file their
application at the Nebraska Service Center regardless of
geographic location or jurisdiction. Please send your application
to:

**Nebraska Service Center
P.O. Box 87426
Lincoln, NE 68501-7426**

What Is the Filing Fee?

The filing fee for a Form N-400 is **$595.00.**

NOTE: All naturalization applicants filing under the military
provisions, Section 328 or 329 of the INA, do not require a
filing fee.

An additional biometric fee of **$80.00** is required when filing
this Form N-400. After you submit Form N-400, USCIS will
notify you about when and where to go for biometric services.

Applicants 75 years of age or older, are exempt from
biometric services fee.

You may submit one check or money order for both the
application and biometric fees, for a total of **$675.00.**

Use the following guidelines when you prepare your check or
money order for the Form N-400 and the biometric service
fee:

1. The check or money order must be drawn on a bank or
   other financial institution located in the United States and
   must be payable in U.S. currency; and

2. Make the check or money order payable to **U.S.
   Department of Homeland Security**, unless:

   A. If you live in Guam and are filing your petition
      there, make it payable to **Treasurer, Guam** .

B. If you live in the U.S. Virgin Islands and are filing your petition there, make it payable to **Commissioner of Finance of the Virgin Islands**.

NOTE: Please spell out U.S. Department of Homeland Security; do not use the initials "USDHS" or "DHS."

Notice to Those Making Payment by Check. If you send us a check, it will be converted into an electronic funds transfer (EFT). This means we will copy your check and use the account information on it to electronically debit your account for the amount of the check. The debit from your account will usually take 24 hours, and will be shown on your regular account statement.

You will not receive your original check back. We will destroy your original check, but we will keep a copy of it. If the EFT cannot be processed for technical reasons, you authorize us to process the copy in place of your original check. If the EFT cannot be completed because of insufficient funds, we may try to make the transfer up to two times.

How to Check If the Fees Are Correct.

The form and biometric fees on this form are current as of the edition date appearing in the lower right corner of this page. However, because USCIS fees change periodically, you can verify if the fees are correct by following one of the steps below:

1. Visit our website at **www.uscis.gov**, select "Immigration Forms" and check the appropriate fee;

2. Review the Fee Schedule included in your form package, if you called us to request the form; or

3. Telephone our National Customer Service Center at **1-800-375-5283** and ask for the fee information.

NOTE: If your Form N-400 requires payment of a biometric service fee for USCIS to take your fingerprints, photograph or signature, you can use the same procedure to obtain the correct biometric fee.

Address Changes.

If you change your address and you have an application or petition pending with USCIS, you may change your address on-line at **www.uscis.gov**, click on "Change your address with USCIS" and follow the prompts. Or you may complete and mail a Form AR-11, Alien's Change of Address Card, to:

U.S. Citizenship and Immigration Services
Change of Address
P.O. Box 7134
London, KY 40742-7134

For commercial overnight or fast freight services only, mail to:

U.S. Citizenship and Immigration Services
Change of Address
1084-I South Laurel Road
London, KY 40744

Processing Information.

Any Form N-400 that is not signed or accompanied by the correct fee will be rejected with a notice that the Form N-400 is deficient. You may correct the deficiency and resubmit the Form N-400. An application or petition is not considered properly filed until accepted by USCIS.

Initial processing. Once a Form N-400 has been accepted, it will be checked for completness, including submission of the required initial evidence. If you do not completely fill out the form, or file it without required initial evidence, you will not establish a basis for eligibility and we may deny your Form N-400.

Requests for more information or interview. We may request more information or evidence, or we may request that you appear at a USCIS office for an interview. We may also request that you submit the originals of any copy. We will return these originals when they are no longer required.

Decision. The decision on a Form N-400 involves a determination of whether you have established eligiblity for the requested benefit. You will be notified of the decision in writing.

USCIS Forms and Information.

To order USCIS forms, call our toll-free number at **1-800-870-3676**. You can also get USCIS forms and information on immigration laws, regulations, and procedures by telephoning our National Customer Service Center at **1-800-375-5283** or visiting our internet website at **www.uscis.gov**.

As an altenative to waiting in line for assistance at your local USCIS office, you can now schedule an appointment through our internet-based system, **InfoPass**. To access the system, visit our website. Use the **InfoPass** appointment scheduler and follow the screen prompts to set up your appointment. **InfoPass** generates an electronic appointment notice that appears on the screen.

Form N-400 Instructions (Rev.10/15/07) Y Page 6

Penalties.

If you knowingly and willfully falsify or conceal a material fact or submit a false document with this Form N-400, we will deny the Form N-400 and may deny any other immigration benefit.

In addition, you will face severe penalties provided by law and may be subject to criminal prosecution.

Privacy Act Notice.

We ask for the information on this form, and associated evidence, to determine if you have established eligibility for the immigration benefit for which you are filing. Our legal right to ask for this information can be found in the Immigration and Nationality Act, as amended. We may provide this information to other government agencies. Failure to provide this information, and any requested evidence, may delay a final decision or result in denial of your Form N-400.

Paperwork Reduction Act.

An agency may not conduct or sponsor an information collection and a person is not required to respond to a collection of information unless it displays a currently valid OMB control number. The public reporting burden for this collection of information is estimated at 6 hour and 8 minutes per response, including the time for reviewing instructions, completing, and submitting the form. Send comments regarding this burden estimate or any other aspect of this collection of information, including suggestions for reducing this burden, to: U.S. Citizenship and Immigration Services, Regulatory Management Division, 111 Massachusetts Avenue, N.W., 3rd Floor, Suite 3008, Washington, DC 20529. OMB No. 1615-0052. **Do not mail your application to this address.**

OMB No. 1615-0052; Expires 10/31/08

Department of Homeland Security
U.S Citizenship and Immigration Services

N-400 Application
for Naturalization

Print clearly or type your answers using CAPITAL letters. Failure to print clearly may delay your application. Use black ink.

Part 1. Your Name. *(The person applying for naturalization.)*

A. Your current legal name.

Family Name *(Last Name)*

Given Name *(First Name)*   Full Middle Name *(If applicable)*

B. Your name **exactly** as it appears on your Permanent Resident Card.

Family Name *(Last Name)*

Given Name *(First Name)*   Full Middle Name *(If applicable)*

C. If you have ever used other names, provide them below.

Family Name *(Last Name)*	Given Name *(First Name)*	Middle Name

D. Name change *(optional)*

Please read the Instructions before you decide whether to change your name.

1. Would you like to legally change your name?   ☐ Yes   ☐ No

2. If "Yes," print the new name you would like to use. Do not use initials or abbreviations when writing your new name.

Family Name *(Last Name)*

Given Name *(First Name)*   Full Middle Name

Write your USCIS "A"- number here:
A

For USCIS Use Only

Bar Code	Date Stamp

Remarks

Action Block

Part 2. Information about your eligibility.   *(Check only one.)*

I am at least 18 years old **AND**

A. ☐ I have been a Lawful Permanent Resident of the United States for at least five years.

B. ☐ I have been a Lawful Permanent Resident of the United States for at least three years, **and** I have been married to and living with the same U.S. citizen for the last three years, **and** my spouse has been a U.S. citizen for the last three years.

C. ☐ I am applying on the basis of qualifying military service.

D. ☐ Other *(Please explain)* _____

| **Part 3. Information about you.** | Write your USCIS "A"- number here: |
| | A |

A. U.S. Social Security Number   **B.** Date of Birth *(mm/dd/yyyy)*   **C.** Date You Became a Permanent Resident *(mm/dd/yyyy)*

D. Country of Birth   **E.** Country of Nationality

F. Are either of your parents U.S. citizens? *(If yes, see instructions.)*   ☐ Yes   ☐ No

G. What is your current marital status?   ☐ Single, Never Married   ☐ Married   ☐ Divorced   ☐ Widowed

☐ Marriage Annulled or Other *(Explain)* _____

H. Are you requesting a waiver of the English and/or U.S. History and Government requirements based on a disability or impairment and attaching a Form N-648 with your application?   ☐ Yes   ☐ No

I. Are you requesting an accommodation to the naturalization process because of a disability or impairment? *(See Instructions for some examples of accommodations.)*   ☐ Yes   ☐ No

If you answered "Yes," check the box below that applies:

☐ I am deaf or hearing impaired and need a sign language interpreter who uses the following language: _____

☐ I use a wheelchair.

☐ I am blind or sight impaired.

☐ I will need another type of accommodation. Please explain: _____

_____

_____

| **Part 4. Addresses and telephone numbers.** |

A. Home Address - Street Number and Name *(Do **not** write a P.O. Box in this space.)*   Apartment Number

| City | County | State | ZIP Code | Country |

B. Care of   Mailing Address - Street Number and Name *(If different from home address)*   Apartment Number

| City | State | ZIP Code | Country |

C. Daytime Phone Number *(If any)*   Evening Phone Number *(If any)*   E-mail Address *(If any)*

(   )   (   )

Part 5. Information for criminal records search.	Write your USCIS "A"- number here: A

NOTE: The categories below are those required by the FBI. See Instructions for more information.

A. Gender

☐ Male ☐ Female

B. Height

Feet	Inches

C. Weight

Pounds

D. Are you Hispanic or Latino?   ☐ Yes   ☐ No

E. Race *(Select one or more.)*

☐ White   ☐ Asian   ☐ Black or African American   ☐ American Indian or Alaskan Native   ☐ Native Hawaiian or Other Pacific Islander

F. Hair color

☐ Black   ☐ Brown   ☐ Blonde   ☐ Gray   ☐ White   ☐ Red   ☐ Sandy   ☐ Bald (No Hair)

G. Eye color

☐ Brown   ☐ Blue   ☐ Green   ☐ Hazel   ☐ Gray   ☐ Black   ☐ Pink   ☐ Maroon   ☐ Other

Part 6. Information about your residence and employment.

A. Where have you lived during the last five years? Begin with where you live now and then list every place you lived for the last five years. If you need more space, use a separate sheet(s) of paper.

Street Number and Name, Apartment Number, City, State, Zip Code and Country	Dates *(mm/dd/yyyy)*	
	From	To
Current Home Address - Same as Part 4.A		Present

B. Where have you worked (or, if you were a student, what schools did you attend) during the last five years? Include military service. Begin with your current or latest employer and then list every place you have worked or studied for the last five years. If you need more space, use a separate sheet of paper.

Employer or School Name	Employer or School Address *(Street, City and State)*	Dates *(mm/dd/yyyy)*		Your Occupation
		From	To	

Part 7. Time outside the United States. *(Including Trips to Canada, Mexico and the Caribbean Islands)*	Write your USCIS "A"- number here: A

A. How many total days did you spend outside of the United States during the past five years? [ ] days

B. How many trips of 24 hours or more have you taken outside of the United States during the past five years? [ ] trips

C. List below all the trips of 24 hours or more that you have taken outside of the United States since becoming a Lawful Permanent Resident. Begin with your most recent trip. If you need more space, use a separate sheet(s) of paper.

Date You Left the United States *(mm/dd/yyyy)*	Date You Returned to the United States *(mm/dd/yyyy)*	Did Trip Last Six Months or More?	Countries to Which You Traveled	Total Days Out of the United States
		[ ] Yes [ ] No		
		[ ] Yes [ ] No		
		[ ] Yes [ ] No		
		[ ] Yes [ ] No		
		[ ] Yes [ ] No		
		[ ] Yes [ ] No		
		[ ] Yes [ ] No		
		[ ] Yes [ ] No		
		[ ] Yes [ ] No		
		[ ] Yes [ ] No		

Part 8. Information about your marital history.

A. How many times have you been married (including annulled marriages)? [ ] If you have **never** been married, go to Part 9.

B. If you are now married, give the following information about your spouse:

1. Spouse's Family Name *(Last Name)*   Given Name *(First Name)*   Full Middle Name *(If applicable)*

2. Date of Birth *(mm/dd/yyyy)*   **3.** Date of Marriage *(mm/dd/yyyy)*   **4.** Spouse's U.S. Social Security #

5. Home Address - Street Number and Name   Apartment Number

City   State   Zip Code

Part 8. Information about your marital history. *(Continued.)*	Write your USCIS "A"- number here: A

C. Is your spouse a U.S. citizen? ☐ Yes ☐ No

D. If your spouse is a U.S. citizen, give the following information:

   1. When did your spouse become a U.S. citizen? ☐ At Birth ☐ Other

      If "Other," give the following information:

   2. Date your spouse became a U.S. citizen

   3. Place your spouse became a U.S. citizen *(Please see Instructions.)*

      City and State

E. If your spouse is **not** a U.S. citizen, give the following information :

   1. Spouse's Country of Citizenship

   2. Spouse's USCIS "A"- Number *(If applicable)*   A

   3. Spouse's Immigration Status

      ☐ Lawful Permanent Resident   ☐ Other

F. If you were married before, provide the following information about your prior spouse. If you have more than one previous marriage, use a separate sheet(s) of paper to provide the information requested in Questions 1-5 below.

   1. Prior Spouse's Family Name *(Last Name)*   Given Name *(First Name)*   Full Middle Name *(If applicable)*

   2. Prior Spouse's Immigration Status

      ☐ U.S. Citizen

      ☐ Lawful Permanent Resident

      ☐ Other

   3. Date of Marriage *(mm/dd/yyyy)*

   4. Date Marriage Ended *(mm/dd/yyyy)*

   5. How Marriage Ended

      ☐ Divorce ☐ Spouse Died ☐ Other

G. How many times has your current spouse been married (including annulled marriages)? ☐

If your spouse has **ever** been married before, give the following information about **your spouse's** prior marriage. If your spouse has more than one previous marriage, use a separate sheet(s) of paper to provide the information requested in Questions 1 - 5 below.

   1. Prior Spouse's Family Name *(Last Name)*   Given Name *(First Name)*   Full Middle Name *(If applicable)*

   2. Prior Spouse's Immigration Status

      ☐ U.S. Citizen

      ☐ Lawful Permanent Resident

      ☐ Other

   3. Date of Marriage *(mm/dd/yyyy)*

   4. Date Marriage Ended *(mm/dd/yyyy)*

   5. How Marriage Ended

      ☐ Divorce ☐ Spouse Died ☐ Other

Form N-400 (Rev. 10/15/07) Y Page 5

Part 9. Information about your children.	Write your USCIS "A"- number here: A

A. How many sons and daughters have you had? For more information on which sons and daughters you should include and how to complete this section, see the Instructions.

B. Provide the following information about all of your sons and daughters. If you need more space, use a separate sheet(s) of paper.

Full Name of Son or Daughter	Date of Birth (mm/dd/yyyy)	USCIS "A"- number (if child has one)	Country of Birth	Current Address (Street, City, State and Country)
		A		
		A		
		A		
		A		
		A		
		A		
		A		
		A		

Add Children   Go to continuation page

Part 10. Additional questions.

Please answer Questions 1 through 14. If you answer "Yes" to any of these questions, include a written explanation with this form. Your written explanation should (1) explain why your answer was "Yes" and (2) provide any additional information that helps to explain your answer.

A. General Questions.

1. Have you **ever** claimed to be a U.S. citizen *(in writing or any other way)*? ☐ Yes ☐ No
2. Have you **ever** registered to vote in any Federal, state or local election in the United States? ☐ Yes ☐ No
3. Have you **ever** voted in any Federal, state or local election in the United States? ☐ Yes ☐ No
4. Since becoming a Lawful Permanent Resident, have you **ever** failed to file a required Federal state or local tax return? ☐ Yes ☐ No
5. Do you owe any Federal, state or local taxes that are overdue? ☐ Yes ☐ No
6. Do you have any title of nobility in any foreign country? ☐ Yes ☐ No
7. Have you ever been declared legally incompetent or been confined to a mental institution within the last five years? ☐ Yes ☐ No

| Part 10. Additional questions. (Continued.) | Write your USCIS "A"- number here: A |

B. Affiliations.

8. a Have you **ever** been a member of or associated with any organization, association, fund foundation, party, club, society or similar group in the United States or in any other place? ☐ Yes ☐ No

    b. If you answered "Yes," list the name of each group below. If you need more space, attach the names of the other group(s) on a separate sheet(s) of paper.

Name of Group	Name of Group
1.	**6.**
2.	**7.**
3.	**8.**
4.	**9.**
5.	**10.**

9. Have you **ever** been a member of or in any way associated *(either directly or indirectly)* with:

    a. The Communist Party? ☐ Yes ☐ No

    b. Any other totalitarian party? ☐ Yes ☐ No

    c. A terrorist organization? ☐ Yes ☐ No

10. Have you **ever** advocated *(either directly or indirectly)* the overthrow of any government by force or violence? ☐ Yes ☐ No

11. Have you **ever** persecuted *(either directly or indirectly)* any person because of race, religion, national origin, membership in a particular social group or political opinion? ☐ Yes ☐ No

12. Between March 23, 1933 and May 8, 1945, did you work for or associate in any way *(either directly or indirectly)* with:

    a. The Nazi government of Germany? ☐ Yes ☐ No

    b. Any government in any area (1) occupied by, (2) allied with, or (3) established with the help of the Nazi government of Germany? ☐ Yes ☐ No

    c. Any German, Nazi, or S.S. military unit, paramilitary unit, self-defense unit, vigilante unit, citizen unit, police unit, government agency or office, extermination camp, concentration camp, prisoner of war camp, prison, labor camp or transit camp? ☐ Yes ☐ No

C. Continuous Residence.

Since becoming a Lawful Permanent Resident of the United States:

13. Have you **ever** called yourself a "nonresident" on a Federal, state or local tax return? ☐ Yes ☐ No

14. Have you **ever** failed to file a Federal, state or local tax return because you considered yourself to be a "nonresident"? ☐ Yes ☐ No

Part 10. Additional questions. (Continued.)	Write your USCIS "A"- number here: A

D. Good Moral Character.

For the purposes of this application, you must answer "Yes" to the following questions, if applicable, even if your records were sealed or otherwise cleared or if anyone, including a judge, law enforcement officer or attorney, told you that you no longer have a record.

15. Have you **ever** committed a crime or offense for which you were **not** arrested? ☐ Yes ☐ No

16. Have you **ever** been arrested, cited or detained by any law enforcement officer (including USCIS or former INS and military officers) for any reason? ☐ Yes ☐ No

17. Have you **ever** been charged with committing any crime or offense? ☐ Yes ☐ No

18. Have you **ever** been convicted of a crime or offense? ☐ Yes ☐ No

19. Have you **ever** been placed in an alternative sentencing or a rehabilitative program (for example: diversion, deferred prosecution, withheld adjudication, deferred adjudication)? ☐ Yes ☐ No

20. Have you **ever** received a suspended sentence, been placed on probation or been paroled? ☐ Yes ☐ No

21. Have you **ever** been in jail or prison? ☐ Yes ☐ No

If you answered "Yes" to any of Questions 15 through 21, complete the following table. If you need more space, use a separate sheet (s) of paper to give the same information.

Why were you arrested, cited, detained or charged?	Date arrested, cited, detained or charged? (mm/dd/yyyy)	Where were you arrested, cited, detained or charged? (City, State, Country)	Outcome or disposition of the arrest, citation, detention or charge (No charges filed, charges dismissed, jail, probation, etc.)

Answer Questions 22 through 33. If you answer "Yes" to any of these questions, attach (1) your written explanation why your answer was "Yes" and (2) any additional information or documentation that helps explain your answer.

22. Have you **ever**:

   a. Been a habitual drunkard? ☐ Yes ☐ No

   b. Been a prostitute, or procured anyone for prostitution? ☐ Yes ☐ No

   c. Sold or smuggled controlled substances, illegal drugs or narcotics? ☐ Yes ☐ No

   d. Been married to more than one person at the same time? ☐ Yes ☐ No

   e. Helped anyone enter or try to enter the United States illegally? ☐ Yes ☐ No

   f. Gambled illegally or received income from illegal gambling? ☐ Yes ☐ No

   g. Failed to support your dependents or to pay alimony? ☐ Yes ☐ No

23. Have you **ever** given false or misleading information to any U.S. government official while applying for any immigration benefit or to prevent deportation, exclusion or removal? ☐ Yes ☐ No

24. Have you **ever** lied to any U.S. government official to gain entry or admission into the United States? ☐ Yes ☐ No

| Part 10. Additional questions. (Continued.) | Write your USCIS "A"- number here:
A |

E. Removal, Exclusion and Deportation Proceedings.

25. Are removal, exclusion, rescission, or deportation proceedings pending against you? ☐ Yes ☐ No

26. Have you **ever** been removed, excluded, or deported from the United States? ☐ Yes ☐ No

27. Have you **ever** been ordered to be removed, excluded, or deported from the United States? ☐ Yes ☐ No

28. Have you **ever** applied for any kind of relief from removal, exclusion, or deportation? ☐ Yes ☐ No

F. Military Service.

29. Have you **ever** served in the U.S. Armed Forces? ☐ Yes ☐ No

30. Have you **ever** left the United States to avoid being drafted into the U.S. Armed Forces? ☐ Yes ☐ No

31. Have you **ever** applied for any kind of exemption from military service in the U.S. Armed Forces? ☐ Yes ☐ No

32. Have you **ever** deserted from the U.S. Armed Forces? ☐ Yes ☐ No

G. Selective Service Registration.

33. Are you a male who lived in the United States at any time between your 18th and 26th birthdays in any status except as a lawful nonimmigrant? ☐ Yes ☐ No

If you answered "NO," go on to question 34.

If you answered "YES," provide the information below.

If you answered "YES," but you did not register with the Selective Service System and are still under 26 years of age, you must register before you apply for naturalization, so that you can complete the information below:

Date Registered (mm/dd/yyyy) [   ]   Selective Service Number [   ]

If you answered "YES," but you did not register with the Selective Service and you are now 26 years old or older, attach a statement explaining why you did not register.

H. Oath Requirements. *(See Part 14 for the Text of the Oath.)*

Answer Questions 34 through 39. If you answer "No" to any of these questions, attach (1) your written explanation why the answer was "No" and (2) any additional information or documentation that helps to explain your answer.

34. Do you support the Constitution and form of government of the United States? ☐ Yes ☐ No

35. Do you understand the full Oath of Allegiance to the United States? ☐ Yes ☐ No

36. Are you willing to take the full Oath of Allegiance to the United States? ☐ Yes ☐ No

37. If the law requires it, are you willing to bear arms on behalf of the United States? ☐ Yes ☐ No

38. If the law requires it, are you willing to perform noncombatant services in the U.S. Armed Forces? ☐ Yes ☐ No

39. If the law requires it, are you willing to perform work of national importance under civilian direction? ☐ Yes ☐ No

Form N-400 (Rev. 10/15/07) Y Page 9

Part 11. Your signature.

I certify, under penalty of perjury under the laws of the United States of America, that this application, and the evidence submitted with it, are all true and correct. I authorize the release of any information that the USCIS needs to determine my eligibility for naturalization.

Your Signature

Date *(mm/dd/yyyy)*

Part 12. Signature of person who prepared this application for you. (If applicable.)

I declare under penalty of perjury that I prepared this application at the request of the above person. The answers provided are based on information of which I have personal knowledge and/or were provided to me by the above named person in response to the *exact questions* contained on this form.

Preparer's Printed Name

Preparer's Signature

Date *(mm/dd/yyyy)*

Preparer's Firm or Organization Name *(If applicable)*

Preparer's Daytime Phone Number

Preparer's Address - Street Number and Name

City

State

Zip Code

NOTE: Do not complete Parts 13 and 14 until a USCIS Officer instructs you to do so.

Part 13. Signature at interview.

I swear (affirm) and certify under penalty of perjury under the laws of the United States of America that I know that the contents of this application for naturalization subscribed by me, including corrections numbered 1 through _____ and the evidence submitted by me numbered pages 1 through _____, are true and correct to the best of my knowledge and belief.

Subscribed to and sworn to (affirmed) before me

Officer's Printed Name or Stamp

Date *(mm/dd/yyyy)*

Complete Signature of Applicant

Officer's Signature

Part 14. Oath of Allegiance.

If your application is approved, you will be scheduled for a public oath ceremony at which time you will be required to take the following oath of allegiance immediately prior to becoming a naturalized citizen. By signing, you acknowledge your willingness and ability to take this oath:

I hereby declare, on oath, that I absolutely and entirely renounce and abjure all allegiance and fidelity to any foreign prince, potentate, state, or sovereignty, of whom or which I have heretofore been a subject or citizen;

that I will support and defend the Constitution and laws of the United States of America against all enemies, foreign and domestic;

that I will bear true faith and allegiance to the same;

that I will bear arms on behalf of the United States when required by the law;

that I will perform noncombatant service in the Armed Forces of the United States when required by the law;

that I will perform work of national importance under civilian direction when required by the law; and

that I take this obligation freely, without any mental reservation or purpose of evasion; so help me God.

Printed Name of Applicant

Complete Signature of Applicant

Form N-400 (Rev. 10/15/07) Y Page 10

USCIS Reading and Writing Test Vocabulary Lists

Reading Vocabulary for the
Redesigned (New) Naturalization Test

PEOPLE	HISTORY AND GOVERNMENT	PLACES	MONTHS
Abraham Lincoln George Washington	American flag Bill of Right capital citizen city Congress country Father of Our Country government President right Senators state/states White House	America U.S. United States	Presidents' Day Memorial Day Flag Day Independence Day Labor Day Columbus Day Thanksgiving

QUESTION WORDS	VERBS	OTHER (FUNCTION)	OTHER (CONTENT)
How What When Where Who Why	can come do/does elects have/has is/are/was/be meet name pay vote want	a for here in of on the to we	colors dollar bill first largest many most north one people second south

Writing Vocabulary for the
Redesigned (New) Naturalization Test

PEOPLE	HISTORY AND GOVERNMENT	PLACES	MONTHS
Adams	American Indians	Alaska	February
Lincoln	capital	California	May
Washington	citizens	Canada	June
	Civil War	Delaware	July
	Congress	Mexico	September
	Father of Our Country	New York City	October
	flag	United States	November
	free	Washington	
	freedom of speech	Washington, D.C.	
	President		
	right		
	Senators		
	state/states		
	White House		

HOLIDAYS	VERBS	OTHER (FUNCTION)	OTHER (CONTENT)
Presidents' Day	can	and	blue
Memorial Day	come	during	dollar bill
Flag Day	elect	for	fifty/50
Independence Day	have/has	here	first
Labor Day	is/was/be	in	largest
Columbus Day	meets	of	most
Thanksgiving	pay	on	north
	vote	the	one
	want	to	one hundred/100
		we	people
			red
			second
			south
			taxes
			white

United States of America Map

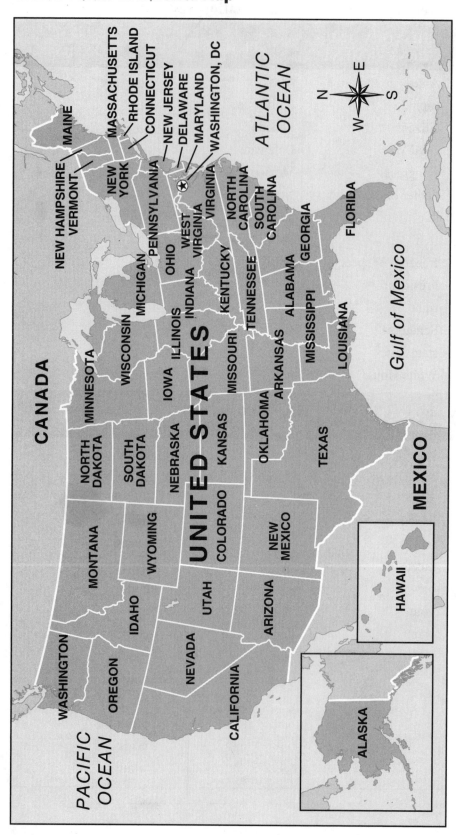